LIMERIC BANK S.

Final Cut

P: ury,
reet,

CANCELLED

D0231036

Also by Melvyn Bragg

For Want of a Nail
The Second Inheritance
The Cumbrian Trilogy:
The Hired Man
A Place in England
Kingdom Come
The Nerve
Without a City Wall
The Silken Net
Autumn Manoeuvres
Love and Glory
Josh Lawton
The Maid of Buttermore
A Christmas Child
A Time to Dance
A Time to Dance: *the screenplay*
Crystal Rooms
Credo
The Soldier's Return
A Son of War
Crossing the Lines
Remember Me

Non-fiction
Speak for England
Land of the Lakes
Laurence Olivier
Cumbria in Verse (*edited*)
Rich: *The Life of Richard Burton*
On Giant's Shoulders
The Adventure of English
12 Books that Changed the World
In Our Time

THE SOUTH ~ BANK SHOW
Final Cut

MELVYN BRAGG

HODDER &
STOUGHTON

First published in Great Britain in 2010 by Hodder & Stoughton
An Hachette UK company

1

Copyright © Melvyn Bragg 2010

A CIP catalogue record for this title is available from the British Library.

Hardback ISBN 978 1 444 70549 2
Trade Paperback ISBN 978 1 444 70552 2

Typeset in Garamond 3 by Hewer Text UK Ltd, Edinburgh
Printed and bound in the UK by Clays Ltd, St Ives plc

Hodder & Stoughton policy is to use papers that are natural, renew-
able and recyclable products and made from wood grown in sustainable
forests. The logging and manufacturing processes are expected to conform
to the environmental regulations of the country of origin.

Hodder & Stoughton Ltd
338 Euston Road
London NW1 3BH

www.hodder.co.uk

To everyone who worked on *The South Bank Show* 1977–2010.

What a great time we had!

Contents

Chapters are listed in the order of transmission. In some cases there was more than one programme on the artist, and I also draw on the interviews.

Introduction

We began to prepare the series in autumn 1977. The first programme was transmitted in January 1978. The main feature was a film on Paul McCartney. I led with McCartney because I wanted to show I was serious.

My aim on *The South Bank Show* was to include the 'popular' arts and make them an accepted part of the arts world. Advances in technology meant that popular culture could now have a future. Once it had access to posterity it could have a chance to survive and be rediscovered and reassessed like other arts. Previously that had been the province of classical music, opera, ballet, classical theatre, literature . . . Now pop songs, stand-up comedians and television plays could be part of all that. The first drama I did was a television play by Denis Potter.

Although we included the Royal Shakespeare Company, Harold Pinter, Ingmar Bergman, von Karajan, *Mayerling* and David Hockney in that first season, the point was made. There were critics who thought that by doing this we had fatally undermined any claim to be an arts programme. That, I think, has all but disappeared. It is much more of a loose and baggy monster now. Talent has many more points of entry and where there's talent there's likely to be good work.

In a sense the programme brought together two aspects of my own life. The working-class background which at that time had little access to ballet, opera, great galleries and classical concerts, and the traditional arts to which I had access later at Oxford University. The Arts establishment in 1978 had little truck with popular culture which had been much of my background and even less inclination to treasure it. That's changed substantially over the last thirty years and *The South Bank Show* has been part of that changing.

In thirty-two years I have interviewed about eight hundred artists on *The South Bank Show*. So a final cut of twenty-five? It's a start.

Here's *Pavarotti* besieged by the paparazzi who scented that the woman in his holiday home by the Adriatic was not his wife but his mistress and yet, he is in full and generous flow delivering golden insights into the 'voice' that moved millions. *David Lean*, in London and India, commanding his film crew like a dashing cavalier captain and pulling off some of the great epics of camera. *Nureyev* on his islands off Positano, regressing into the scarcely credible poverty of his Tartar childhood and talking vividly about his leap from an obscure provincial town into the great Kirov Ballet and from there to the West, to freedom, to the world stage where he revolutionised the perception of ballet.

There's *Seamus Heaney* in Dublin, deep in the rich earth of Irish poets and the landscape of his childhood in the North; and *Ian McEwan* in London, carefully picking through the theory and practice of his work as his friend *Martin Amis* does with his intense literary focus in another part of the city. *Francis Bacon* takes us on a well-fuelled journey into the bleak core of his dark genius. After a struggle, *Harold Pinter* tells us as much as he can about the unconscious and unknowable instincts behind his masterly originality. Instinct, too, is all for *Judi Dench*, whose chameleon brilliance makes her the outstanding actress of her time.

Jimmy McGovern in Liverpool digs into the murk of authority and class, lies and the establishment in *Hillsborough*, which unforgettably dramatises a swathe of life and attitudes seemingly branded into this country. His fellow Liverpudlian, *Beryl Bainbridge*, goes to the Crimea to research and think over her historical novel which takes a wholly original look at that war. And *P.D. James*, who has turned crime fiction into the finest fiction and also brings views of our society marinated in personal pain and a passionate public concern.

Victoria Wood, Britain's first woman stand-up comic, reflects on the nourishing loneliness of her childhood and then on an occupation in which she rocked our biggest theatres and huge public arenas into laughter. Now she has taken a new path.

Andrew Lloyd Webber's unique career as a composer has been supplemented by his verve as an entrepreneur – no musical theatre composer has ever enjoyed such success. We also look at his other life as a connoisseur and collector of late nineteenth-century art. Like Paganini, whose music he reworked, there is a demonic genius inside the bringer of so much pleasure to so many.

David Hockney is seen in London and Los Angeles, ceaselessly explaining and challenging the ways of art, taking photography in a new direction, playing with traditions as ancient as Chinese scrolls and British landscape painting. *Eric Clapton*, too, went back, to the blues which made his life in a London suburb at first bearable and then for ever rich, in turn enriching us with his homage to and extension of that profound cry from the American black musicians.

David Puttnam is a creative producer whose films are matched by a rare grasp of the politics of the film business and, more recently, the business of politics. His perspectives on the studio system in Hollywood and the public service dilemma in British television are fresh and incisive and a fitting complement to the directors featured here.

As for *Iggy Pop*, he seemed to me to be somewhere at the root of rock 'n' roll. Testing it, and himself, almost to destruction. It is quite difficult to think of Iggy Pop and *Francis Ford Coppola* being on the same continent, but Coppola's extreme achievement, though more public and better rewarded than that of Iggy, reflects the same nerve and urge for the new. Francis Ford Coppola, however, took on the monolith that was Hollywood and toppled it, emerging from the rubble with some of the greatest American films of the time of which at least four – *The Godfather*, *The Godfather: Part II*, *Apocalypse Now* and *The Conversation* – are classic.

Ingmar Bergman, though far from commanding the world's screens as Coppola did, yet made, in Sweden, with a small company of actors and film makers, a body of work of variety, power and elegance, whose quality is unique. We met in Germany. It was his first interview in English.

The curious pact between *Barry Humphries* and *Dame Edna* is examined by interviewing each of them individually, often using the answers of one to provoke the other. The two of them split the atom of Dame Edna's mesmerising act, a performance of such intelligent singularity that after decades it still circles the globe.

Alan Bennett is a joy to read, to watch, to interview and to be with. In this interview he spoke for the first time about a private life which had been kept private. He also talks, apparently plainly but with fine insights, about his work, which has grown in authority and lustre without losing the wit and the northern good sense which now look like a sort of destiny.

As for *Tracey Emin*, it is impossible to outsay what she has said about herself. Her determination to make her private self a public body of work, a public spectacle even, humorously, scandalously, riskily, seriously, is both in itself intriguing and a poster of our time.

On the banks of the Hudson, half an hour upriver from New York, in a severally balconied house, nesting in ancient woodland, is where I interviewed *Toni Morrison*. I went once, near the beginning of her career, for a short encounter and a few years later I went again as she was about to publish *Beloved*. In those few years she had become a matriarch of literature, her talk even more spellbinding.

Finally *Paul McCartney*, the first subject, filmed in autumn 1977 in Abbey Road Studios. One of a handful of popular song writers who proves, beyond argument, that the deceptively simple gift of melody combined with memorable lyrics of quality can and do reach greatness.

I wanted this selection to reflect the programme. Seamus Heaney *and* Barry Humphries, both of the highest calibre in their respective fields;

Toni Morrison *and* Victoria Wood, two women who occupy, with distinction, territory once the monopoly of men; Eric Clapton *and* Ian McEwan – and so on.

The process of selection was often little more than a stab in the dark. There are three Nobel Prizewinners here; seven others absent. But it goes across a broad waterfront. There are insights into the instincts, thoughts and craft of artists of immense and perhaps enduring talent, even, in a few cases, I believe touching genius. These are spots in a time of their lives, like painted portraits – a few sittings. The honesty and the seriousness with which they talk about their work is, I think, impressive, often exhilarating.

Though far from all *South Bank* programmes were interview-based, many were. I think that a good way to discover what artists are up to is to ask them. A 'talking head' can be the best of television. If there's trust and if the preparation and research have been good, the results can reveal truths. What matters is not the personality of the interviewer nor the questions, much, but the quality of the reply. There are many ways to interview people but for the sort of programmes our team set out to do, collaboration was the key. Invariably those we decided to concentrate on were artists we admired. Now and then they were nervous. The objective was to help make the meeting a place where they felt they could talk to the best of themselves and say something new, or at least fresh.

I began in television as a researcher, then a director, and I thought then and now that in any portrait of an artist the interviewer's job is to help gather material. This would sit alongside readings, performance, dramatisation, archive, the comments of others, contextualising film . . .

I did not want to be a critic. There are plenty of those in print. Our job was to put together a portrait. I would be part of it, but, as far as possible, outside it. My conviction was and is that the viewers can make up their own minds about the subject. Our job is to provide the fullest evidence we can in the time available for them to come to their decision. It is a different enterprise from that of a critic . . .

I am immensely indebted to ITV over so many years. They backed the programme with good will and enthusiasm until near the end. I have hopped between 'I' and 'we'. All these programmes were made by small teams of people. *The South Bank Show* has been very lucky to have attracted so many good directors, researchers, camera crews, film editors and production teams. Making the programmes is often fraught – problems with budgets, deadlines, copyright . . . But making these programmes is often privileged work. All of us thought that. And to lead such talented and dedicated teams was as good as work gets. Curious to think that working on the final cut of all the films over the years in a cutting room, a cramped, invariably windowless, space together with the director, researcher and film editor provided the most enjoyable stretches of my work in glamorous television.

Finally, thanks to all the artists themselves. It has been good to put them on that most democratic forum – television – and let them have their time to shine alongside the soaps and the sports and the news and the entertainment. Part of the landscape of all our common lives, as artists, there to be counted.

Paul McCartney

It became something of an obsession: to get Paul McCartney to agree to be the first artist profiled on *The South Bank Show*. I suppose 'obsession' means Dostoevsky and Beethoven and monomania and it was not in that league. But I had picked up a scent that I felt I had to follow: the manifesto I wrote about in the introduction had to be seen to mean something. To start with McCartney and not the Royal Shakespeare Company or von Karajan who were in the wings would show that I was serious.

When I met him he had already written more than 200 songs – 'Yesterday', 'Paperback Writer', 'Penny Lane', 'Hey Jude', 'Hello Goodbye', 'Silly Love Songs' – and since then there have been several hundred more.

McCartney has always been wary of the media and rationed himself carefully. This was a new programme; unseen. It was to be the opening show and could expect to attract publicity. I was not a music critic nor a musician. Why should he do it?

What I had in my favour was one of the programmes I had been making at the BBC called *Read All About It*. It was a book programme which I'd put into a panel show format and invited writers – Gore Vidal, Martin Amis, Antonia Fraser, Clive James – to mix in with readers who might be footballers or popular entertainers. The writers were always in the majority. It dealt exclusively in affordable paperbacks and moved at a clip. The signature tune was 'Paperback Writer' by Paul McCartney, and when I met him he said, 'I was dead chuffed you picked that for your signature tune.' That mattered, I think. So I waited for 'the moment'. As with others in that pop or even serious success stratosphere, the mood, the moment, the timing was sacred.

We set up cameras in Abbey Road Studios. It was while he was recording 'Mull of Kintyre', unloved by many critics but to prove the biggest selling single in the UK of all time. An instant traditional ballad which took its place with 'Over the sea to Skye'. Abbey Road Studios, October 1977, hired by Paul, just around the corner from his London house, a place for him to shuffle to in slippers at whatever time of day or night the impulse took him. The mood on him.

I had no idea of the vagabond nature of stars and turned up with the crew on time, prepared to go, ready for action.

It was not unpleasant to wait for a few hours in a fabled recording studio. You learn a lot. I had a book to read. Linda came ahead and took photographs, with profligacy, like someone burning fivers. She was intense, best American – polite, democratic: a good sport.

I had seen the Beatles perform and brushed against McCartney once or twice, yet, more importantly, the public presence and the private pursuit of the Beatles had been intense and there was that sort of 'knowing' by proxy. I thought their songs would outlast most of the work of their contemporaries in classical music and that in a hundred years' time the songs of Paul McCartney would still be around. He was a proof that quality in the arts was no slave of traditional forms: it appeared wherever it found talent.

He slipped in, open-necked shirt, open waistcoat, and blue jeans: of course. He's not only a handsome man but also a bonny lad. He has a face that responds immediately to the sense he is expressing. It acts out his thoughts or illustrates them vividly. The cherubic can become sly, suppressed, wicked, amused, angry, entertained, thoughtful – on it goes – plain to see, a picture show, an accompanying drama, his face. Most constant, though, when I've seen him interviewed since, is the watchfulness. And there was that here at first.

He had been the Villain in the Epic End of the Beatles. He had been savaged by John. All the Lennon wannabes who generally held the critical arena had piled into him, showered his contribution with dismissive scorn, and severally dumped on him for being him. Linda faced even worse – she was the terrible temptress, the lure, the . . . on it went. McCartney had taken the sensible course and retreated. For some time.

This interview, his manager Brian Brolly said, was his 'get him out again'. He was just as defensive with me as with anyone. But perhaps because I carried no 'insider' luggage; perhaps because of that signature tune and the programme he'd 'followed', as he said . . . anyway. He was open. He warmed to the encounter. I interviewed him a few years later and he was nothing like as open – nothing impolite, no 'cooling' – just that he had moved on and the veil which is so often over him had come down once more, the distance he so wants to maintain in public was back; and the self-consciousness which is as plain as his clothes was a shut door.

So maybe I was just lucky, late at night in Abbey Road, maybe . . .

There's 'generational kinship' as was the case with several of the artists I talked to over the years. It helped people from similar backgrounds, of a similar age, whose lives follow a relatively similar pattern, can know each other well without meeting. The social context, country and history are the defining factors. I had enough in common with McCartney – class, geography, the religious background, the cultural surround, radio, films, pop music, comedy – there was enough to feel easy, to know what his references meant to him and without having to say anything, to know that he knew we both knew. Whatever it was, we got on, and got on with it. It was a conversation, a chat, his style simple-seeming but lined with insights, I thought. He sat sideways on at the piano, I sat a few feet away. Most of the programme was the interview, interrupted now and then by flashes to a big hit or work on 'Mull of Kintyre'. As the interview went on, it became more of a monologue with not so much questions from me but nudges or nods as he tentatively and then enthusiastically rolled out his story in his measured Liverpool-lite honeyed accent.

'So how did it begin?'

'There's a few musical people in my family . . . My dad was a pianist by ear. He was a trumpet player until he got false teeth. He was a good pianist but he would never teach me because he thought I should learn "properly".' (His hands did the inverted commas.) 'A bit of a drag, actually, because I never did learn "properly" and he could've taught me. He did, actually, "by ear". People say I do chords like he used to so I suppose I picked it up over the years.'

'Picked it up over the years' is a key to McCartney. He can seem to be someting of a medium. He trusts his instincts strongly and absolutely. He watches and listens and from what he sees and hears the vaults are filled. He is the polar opposite of the reading, researching, in any way academic autodidactic artist. He sees the world go by and relies on the flow of it to give him what he will need for the work.

'What sort of music were you listening to before "Long Tall Sally"?'

'*Billy Cotton's Band Show* on a Sunday. Everything really. Except classical, which we used to turn off. Certain tunes in classical I liked. I never sat down and listened to it properly. The nearest I came was piano lessons.' (He plays air piano.) 'But by then I'd written little songs of my own.' He leaned across, played and sang. 'It was just one chord plonking away but I didn't like to have to come back to the discipline, the hard discipline of "making me a great pianist". I just wanted something to plonk along with.'

'And you started on the trumpet?'

'Yes, because me dad had been a trumpet player and at that time it was *Look Back in Anger* but I couldn't sing and play a trumpet. I swapped for a guitar which was right-handed. I couldn't work out why I couldn't play it 'cos I'm left-handed. I thought, I'm never gonna make it. You've got to use the hand you're good at to vamp with because the rhythm's there. So I got home and worked it out. And turned all the strings round. Ah. I was off. Then I wrote a little song on that guitar, the first song I wrote, called "I Lost My Little Girl". It was three chords.' He leaned over to the piano:

> I woke up late this morning
> My head was in a whirl
> And only then I realised
> I'd lost my little girl.
> Ooh – aa – huh, huh, huh.

A Presley voice, a shoulder shrug, all in a moment.

'It's all right, actually. I'd better rehearse it. Just the three chords – G, G7 and C.'

'Did you want to be a singer?'

'My dad was a big influence. He'd play piano and stuff and he'd teach us things like harmony – not officially – he'd just say, "When I'm singing *that*, if you sing *that* while I *keep* singing *that* – that little noise is called harmony." '

'How old were you when you began to write songs regularly?'

'About fourteen. The main thing was I knew this thing . . .' – plays a few chords – 'went against this . . .' – more chords – 'then a little harmony thing I'd got. Then I worked that into a song and put a few words in. Rock 'n' roll was coming up then. There was just that electric atmosphere, wasn't there? You knew that. The kids know about things the grown-ups don't and that gives it a totally magic air. And I'd friends who had blues records and Liverpool being a port we got stuff from America – Chuck Berry, Ray Charles . . .'

'And Elvis?'

'Of course. Yeah! I loved Elvis. He was my boy. He was the lad. And Little Richard.'

'Did you feel that to like them was rebellious?'

'It never felt rebellious to me. Me dad didn't particularly like it but he told stories about how *his* dad didn't like his music because he was playing things like . . .' – he sings – 'Chi-ca-go, Chi-ca-go . . . and *his* dad was saying, "Tin can music, son," 'cos his dad was a brass band player. It goes back, the music line. He used to play an E-flat bass. So my dad was tolerant of all that . . . When I wrote "She Loves You, Yeah, Yeah, Yeah", he would say, "Son, there's enough of those Americanisms around. Couldn't you say, 'Yes, Yes, Yes'? Just for once." ' McCartney acted out this little scene with evident delight in his dad's point of view. 'I would say, "You don't understand, Dad. It can't be 'yes, yes, yes'. It wouldn't work . . ." But . . . you know . . . that's dads. Can you sing "yes, yes, yes"?' The recollection made him look extraordinarily happy.

'When did you make up your mind you would try to be a singer and song writer?'

'When I started to write my tunes I got together with John – we used to bag off school together and go back to my home where there wasn't anybody in in the afternoon. We'd smoke Twinings Tea in one of Dad's pipes – it didn't taste bad at all, actually – and we'd have a little bang on the piano and we had guitars. Mainly Buddy Holly stuff because he had the least chords and we wrote about a hundred tunes before getting to "Love Me Do". I've got a little old book of them somewhere. It's good actually. It's got things like "Ooo-aaa" and "Angel Voices".'

'How many of those did you record?'

'I don't think any of them. It was just an apprenticeship. Oh yeah – "Love Me Do" – that was the only one that came out of it. It sounded the most likely to do with the group. I put a harmonica on it.'

Film of them playing 'Love Me Do' shows four well-groomed, uniformed, unblemished young men drilled to stage order, almost rigid, still well stuck in the older regimentation of popular music. Antique in appearance. But the music had moved on.

'We were the only people playing that song. That's what started us doing stuff you made up yourself. You could do rhythm and blues, but Gerry and the Pacemakers would be doing them. Hippy hippy shake – the Blue Jeans would be doing it. You couldn't stop them . . . so we thought that if we wrote a couple of tunes maybe somebody would notice us a bit more and we could write' – he mimes – 'Dear sir – we – have – a rock – and – roll group. The average age is . . .'

'Did you write those letters?'

'Just a few. And you'd be able to say, "And by the way, we've written a few ORIGINAL COMPOSITIONS." And that was the little extra plus.'

'So you started off with that?'

'And we were with George Martin and he says, "If you want a really *big* hit – I mean, 'Love Me Do' is all right, lads, but if you want a really *big* hit – you should do something like 'How Do You Do It?'." We said, "But we don't like it." Then we got the heavy word from Brian Epstein. "It doesn't matter if you don't like it. *Do it*." '

'And then?'

'We made a demo. It still exists. But we still didn't like it. We didn't want to be like everybody else.'

'So you stuck out for that?'

'Not doing "How Do You Do It?" we ended up doing our own song "Please, Please Me". A Big Hit.'

'That seemed to trigger what became a phenomenal run of success. Seventeen hits. Worldwide . . .'

'Yeah. Mind you. We were *trying* for all those public levels. Like, literary. John was writing his own book, trying to be a literary person. We were trying to impress people at *The Times* – your upper crust. There was a bit poetry and a bit artistic and a bit new. We were *trying* to be big. For instance, you'd had a lorra groups who'd gone over to America and played fifth or twenty-fifth on the bill. So we said we'd only go when we had a Number One. That's the way to do it. 'Cos when we got there we were *huge*.'

And the film cut to the four of them, tiny figures, still neatly mop-topped and uniformed, going out to a stage in the middle of Shea Stadium, welcomed hysterically by tens of thousands of screaming, weeping, applauding fans in a mass orgy of adoration. The next two years were Beatlemania: touring, the music scarcely heard above the noise of the crowds, pressured, invaded, photographed, lionised, subject to learned articles and public debate, iconic, every new song and then every new album an examined event in the lives of hundreds of thousands of fans and addicts.

Yet McCartney kept a steady head. There was 'Eleanor Rigby' for instance.

'I had that song . . .' – he played the opening on the piano – '. . . I just sat down and got the first line. It came out of the blue. But I didn't have a name. I think it was "Daisy McKenzie picks up the rice in a church where the wedding had been". So then I had to think, What's it about? "Picks up the rice" – oh, she's a lonely old lady type and continue from there. I remember walking round Bristol one night looking for a name because I wanted a really nice name, that didn't sound wrong, sounded like somebody's name but different, wasn't just "Valerie Higgins" . . . was a little bit more "*evocative*".' He sent up that word. 'Then I saw a shop. Rigby. Normal, but just that little bit extra thing to it. Then I got Eleanor. And it just flowed from there.'

'What's the longest you've worked on a song?'

'I'm a fan of old-fashioned writing – Sammy Cahn, Cole Porter, I like all that *when* it comes off – there's great little things in their writing – I always try to put that kind of thing in . . . it's . . .

'It's nothing you can really explain. It's funny trying to talk about music. If you could really talk about it, it wouldn't be music. I mean you don't sit around like you imagine poets do with millions of manuscripts and say "the boiler?" *No.* "The oven?" I've never done that. I can't explain it. I've never been able to explain it.

'It comes out of the blue – it comes *at you*. I'm sure the funnel it comes through has a lot to do with it – the *Billy Cotton Band Show* here, Cole Porter there, millions of influences through to Chuck Berry and I'll filter out a lot of stuff I don't like . . . But I've always felt it was not *me* doing it, really . . . Not "Beethoven's calling me, I want some new sonatas, he's contacted me . . ." but Paul is fluent but in this passage he hesitated, paused, was clearly digging deep '. . . just that it sort of just comes . . .

'I mean, all the best little bits of melody . . . I just fell out of bed one morning and had the tune "Yesterday". I don't know how I got that. I just got it. And I thought, I like that one. That's a nice one. I didn't have any words so for weeks it was "scrambled eggs . . . oh how I love your legs . . .". "Michelle" was a joke French tune when I was at a party.' He put on a cod French accent and picked out the tune. 'That's all it was and you thought, That's quite a good tune. I'll put some words to that. "When I'm 64" – I had that when I was sixteen. I never did anything with it till I was twenty-four. It's kind of magic. You're just plonking along . . .' – he plays air guitar – '. . . and you decide to reach out and see what you can pull down. You can do it any time. It'll probably be crummy but . . .'

He turned to the piano and sang: 'Melvyn Bragg . . . was in the parlour . . . and he said he was going to have some tea . . .

'Now that's not very good but you could work on that.' He repeated it and added, 'Come and have some tea with me, Melvyn Bragg.

'It's the name. That's the problem.'

'You'll have to go round Bristol again.'

'Now Melvyn *Rigby* . . . that's not good' . . . he is referring to the way in which he began that composition. 'I shouldn't have dared to do that . . . I'm showing what a lousy writer I can be but that's what it all comes out of. It'll be bad three times but the fourth time a little bit of inspiration will come and that one little thing will make it good. You try another chord. It's pulling it all in. I think it's great if you can get a good song. You're feeling lousy and you hear a good song and it lights you up. You put on an Elvis 78 "Don't Be Cruel" . . .' – he throws his hands in the air – '. . . you're right up there again. Cures any blues.'

'And that's why you enjoy your songs coming out of the jukebox?'

'Or the milkman whistling them. That's a big thrill. Actually I heard a bird whistle one of my tunes. Yes, folks, he had gone crackers. I did. One morning. At dawn. It goes . . .' He whistles 'From Me to You . . .'

'After the Beatles broke up you took a lot of stick. Did it bother you?'

'Yeah . . . Did it *bother* me? *Yeah* . . . When the Beatles broke up John did a big thing about me saying "it's all muzack", "it's all rubbish", "you couldn't rock if you tried" – which was all rubbish itself but it did put me off for a while . . . I'm a bit gullible like that . . . and I listened to him for a few years and thought . . .' – he shook his head – 'Can't write any more of those soppy love songs I keep writing . . . I've got to get hard and rocking . . . But in the end I've just got to be myself, really. If I like all that I've just got to do it. No need to be ashamed of it. Bolder to say, what the hell, I like it . . .'

'You couldn't have made it much harder for yourself. You decided to form another band. You brought in Linda.'

'It was the only thing I could think to do and that's the craziest thing – bring in your wife who hasn't any previous musical experience!'

'Why stack the odds so highly against yourself?'

'I didn't think I was. I thought I was just doing what I knew how to do. Just to get back on the road with anything.'

'Why was it so necessary to go out and perform?'

'I dunno . . . I dunno . . . I thought that the longer I waited with another day of no work, another day of nothing to do, the more I was just getting stagnated. I just had to do something. I thought – the man who sings every day is going to have a better voice because he's practising every day. It's got to be good for you.

'So I hit on the idea – a bunch of people, and me – big time, small time – just play – Linda there on keyboards, first time – terrified and she was getting picked on something silly. People couldn't accept we just wanted to go back to square one and be one of those little skiffle groups again. A van up and down the motorway. At least you got out of the empty room . . .'

'Do you read much? Go to plays?'

'I'm a telly person. A lot of people are snobby about telly. I watch it a lot. I get a lot of education off telly. I read bits and pieces – not much. A bit of science fiction. There was a time in my life, I would take a pipe on to the top deck of a bus and feel like Dylan Thomas reading Beckett or Tennessee . . . Ernie Williams. I used to fancy that.'

'Do you think what you do resists analysis?'

'Rock 'n' roll and pop? I don't think it should be analysed. It's not that precious . . . I don't like, say . . . the opera critic of the *New York Times* is now the rock critic. He judges rock 'n' roll by opera. Well . . . it's like why I haven't learned to write music . . . there's a vague suspicion it'd change if I knew too much . . . There are things you're not supposed to do, there's a time when you mustn't do double harmonies – but when I want I do them. Then you get the expert view. Experts are only good for a few years. The world was flat once. That was the expert view.'

'You really enjoy making a lot of people happy.'

'Yeah . . . I like all that . . . Yeah . . .' Then, perhaps remembering his dad, he added, emphatically, 'Yes.'

I'm sure there are other faces of Paul McCartney, but that encounter carries, I think, a substantial truth about him. His performance and the words and the music make up a whole which stands for itself. Just as somewhere on screen Nureyev is forever dancing and Pavarotti singing, so Paul McCartney's songs peal out the music of his age.

Harold Pinter

It seemed that 1978 was a good time to do a programme on Harold Pinter. *The Homecoming*, which some consider to be his best play, was about to be revived for the first time. *Night School* was coming on to television, as was *No Man's Land*. He had just finished a play unlike any other he had written, *Betrayal*. A selection of his poems and prose was to be published. And he had done a screenplay of Proust's *Remembrance of Things Past*. He had not given a television interview for ten years.

Harold Pinter began writing as a teenager in the East End of London where, he has said, his preoccupations were 'cricket, girls and literature'. He went to drama school, became an actor, trudged round England in touring companies, wrote his first play, *The Room*, when he was twenty-seven, then *The Birthday Party*, then the play that made his reputation, *The Caretaker*.

He was lumped in with John Osborne, Arnold Wesker, John Arden and a few others as an 'Angry Young Man' and although the anger was to grow as he aged, he was never part of that cluster. His work, from the beginning, was too private, rather mysterious, opaque, to be summoned for service in any journalistic regiment. He had no easy early ride as a playwright. Noël Coward immediately recognised him as an original and a superb craftsman . . . others said the mystery only covered a lack of substance.

I had met him years before, in the early 1960s when I was a director on the BBC arts programme *Monitor*. We had worked on a programme in which he was briefly interviewed by Huw Wheldon. We also met through a close friend of his, the director David Jones, who cottoned on to Pinter's talent from the very beginning and who was to go on to direct several of his plays and the film of *Betrayal*.

David, like everyone else who knew Harold, was forever talking about him. Not only did he early on give the language 'Pinteresque', he also gave his friends enough instances of ferocious outbursts, bold confrontations, and wholly unexpected turns of phrase emphatically delivered to furnish them with a larder of anecdotes. In my experience he was far and away the most talked about writer in London by those who talked about writers. He soon became a dominating figure in the metropolitan literary and especially theatrical landscape, dressed in black, a cigarette, a drink and, for most of the time I knew him, accompanied by Lady Antonia Fraser, the historian, whom he had married after a divorce from his first wife, the actress Vivien Merchant.

Harold and Antonia became a princely couple in London intellectual life, a movable salon, with communities of equal weight in New York, Hollywood and Eastern Europe. Their initial courtship had triggered headlines of Burton-Taylor proportions. It would have rocked most people. It made them inseparable: and, as I found, increasingly as we saw each other more regularly over the years, it made them a couple whose company was like no other. At times, the thunder of Harold's cannons, turned on the foreign policy and the iniquity of America, the UK and Israel, could ricochet across the room and rip a tear in the evening murmur of the West End restaurant. Especially as, when he got older, the expletives, and the politics, both absent in 1978, grew more common. It could take a little time to complete the meal.

His voice was markedly actorly. I presume it had been set like that in his late teens and he had honed his own new tongue. Many did who came up to London from the outer darknesses. The East End of London, though in the greater city of London, was every bit as outer darkness as my own cradle 300 miles north in Cumberland. If you end up in London media-class land – theatre, television, publishing, galleries – you tend to see your vowels lose their local association and rub into conformity with your peers, with the going talk. To stand against that can be a constant sign of integrity – or it can be too much trouble. Actors especially, I think, who have to find a new voice for every part, must be more tempted than most to find a median actor's voice to fill in the gaps between parts. Anyway, Harold's voice was 'actorly', it had an old upper-class tinge, his pitch deep, his delivery considered with . . . yes . . . the pauses, but quite clearly for further thought and not for cheap effect. His talk corrects itself, persistently as it goes along, embraces repetitions, digresses, yet always comes back to the line, not unlike the work.

We met in the morning in his and Antonia's grand town house in Campden Hill Square, west London. We set up in a large drawing room, marble fireplace, books, rugs, two easy chairs floral-patterned. I had a sheaf of notes and a pile of his books. Harold had the first of what would be about a dozen Black Sobranie cigarettes (gold-tipped) and, later on, a tumbler of whisky. I was just into my first season of *The South Bank Show*, largely panned by the critics, and so I had decided to go for broke: *Mayerling*, Hockney, Ingmar Bergman, Harold Pinter.

Harold wore heavy black-rimmed spectacles which, eventually, he removed. The ten-year gap had not been accidental. There had been a lot of bruising after his move to Antonia.

'When you were a boy in Hackney, in the East End of London where you grew up, it was a place heavily bombed – you were evacuated for a while – but when you came back there was still political violence in the East End. Did that affect you directly?'

'Yes. Yes indeed . . . I'm Jewish, of course. And I used to go to a Jewish Boys' Club. Boys and girls in fact. In Hackney. On the way to Bethnal Green. It was a very strange situation. I am talking about 1946, when the war had just ended and we'd on the face of it been fighting fascists. But in fact immediately after the war, in Dalston Junction, fascist groups used to meet to . . .' – he paused; his hands mimed a shape as they were to do several times in the interview, as if drawing a thought before expressing it – 'and . . . have their discussions isn't the right word – make speeches . . . very provocative speeches. A number of Jews in the area of course.

'And we used to leave the Boys' Club and pass under a very dark arch which led to the main road. It was quite common to be surrounded by people with broken milk bottles. I remember they used to smash them' – a violent slam of his arm – 'as we approached, on the walls. And the only way of really dealing with it – because broken milk bottles were no joke, we were only sixteen . . . seemed to fall out in this kind of manner . . .' (Here, and I'll stop stage directions soon, he did what he was often to do when telling a story – he looked about him, never at the camera, almost acting it, intent on recollecting it dramatically.)

'You would say, "You all right?" And there's something, the native courtesy of the English gentleman, he'd be bound to respond saying, "Yes, I'm aa' right. How about you then?" "Are you sure you're all right?" I would say, and then, "Well, that's all right, then," and all the time keep walking to the lights on the main road and we did this and then made a dash when we got to the main road.

'And on one occasion we did this and suddenly realised that one of our number wasn't on the bus, he'd gone, we'd lost him. And when I got home, I had a very big stick at that time and I remember feeling quite coldly angry and I got hold of this very heavy stick and went all the way back expecting to find him dead and of course he'd just gone across some fields and got home safely, but my anger I *do* remember clearly. To this day.'

'You came from a Jewish household which traditionally has a respect for scholarship and learning – was that there in your household?'

'Oh very, very much so, yes . . . my father cared a great deal for, as you say, learning and . . . civilised behaviour really . . . and understanding. And they encouraged me when I became an actor of *all* things . . . they were slightly worried about that but they encouraged me. But they were even more worried that I became a conscientious objector when I was eighteen but they stuck by me wonderfully then, too.'

The Black Sobranies came ceaselessly. On the final cut – about fifty minutes out of a two-hour interview – it looks as if Harold is chain-smoking, which is not far from the case. And why did I not follow up the 'conscientious objector'? Perhaps I should have done. But it was not news. And this is not a potted biography. He had taken the decision, post-war. Later he said that he might have fought in the Second World War had he been of age.

'What set you on acting?'

'It was the only way I could possibly earn a living.'

'What were you in?'

'I was pretty formidable in *Ten Little Niggers* I remember. There were these tours. Between tours I used to do odd jobs. I was actually a chucker-out at the Astoria Ballroom. It was in its prime then, of course.'

'Hard work?'

'No. It was tea-dancing. I was once – can I tell you a little anecdote? Maybe you won't use it but it's true. I was once – you see a chucker-out does various things, one of which was tearing the tickets at the door, a very exacting task, and one day a chap came in and gave me his ticket and pressed a £5 note into my hand. Whereupon I looked at him and he looked at me and I looked at the note and he passed into the ballroom . . . I was mystified of course. However I put the note in my pocket and it was a *lot* of money. And the next day the police arrived with a photo of this man and asked everyone whether they'd seen this man the afternoon before . . . and they were coming to *me* and I had no idea whether I should say "yes" or "no" . . . and I made a last-minute split-second decision to say – logically it must be "yes" otherwise he wouldn't have reminded me of his presence so – whereupon I said to the police, "Oh yes, absolutely, he was here yesterday afternoon. I saw him." "How long did he stay?" "All the time. He was there till six o'clock. The afternoon dance." They didn't like that at all, but there it was. A sweaty experience.'

Harold looked absolutely delighted.

'They wanted him to be somewhere else.'

'Of course!' And his delight swelled up even more. 'He obviously *was* somewhere else. He came in and went straight out the back!'

'You talked about your friends in the Jewish Boys' – and Girls' – Club. Were any of them doing what you were doing?'

'No. They weren't doing similar things. None of them was an actor at the time. Henry Woolf who was one of them and still is one of them – he's now an actor of course. But he wasn't then. They were all doing National Service. Half of them. But we did keep very close together and in fact, now, two of them, or rather, three, remain as close as they were then.'

'Wasn't it Henry Woolf who not so much commissioned as demanded your first play?'

'Yes. He did. He did.'

'You'd said you'd write a play some time . . .'

I was struggling here. There were subjects, I guessed, that Harold had pre-censored himself on. This was to be a problem but there was nothing to do but plough on. Let's say a cooler air began to circulate in that opulently comfortable drawing room.

'Well. I was actually acting at Chichester at the time. About 1956. And a woman in the company invited me to a party in London, you see . . .'

There's a pause. I say nothing.

'. . . on a Sunday evening. And I went to the party at a house in Chelsea. Big house . . . And during the course of it, she said to me, "There's someone I'd like you to meet. He lives upstairs. I think you'd be interested to meet him." So I said, "Fine," and off we went up the stairs and she knocked on the door and the door was opened by a little man with the most extraordinary coloured hair, bare feet, and extremely fluid clothes. That's all I can remember . . . He was absolutely charming, never stopped talking, welcomed us and gave us a cup of tea, discussed philosophy, metaphysics, literature, the weather, fabrics, you know, unceasingly.

'All the while at a table sat an *enormous* man with a cap on, reading a comic, and the chap, the little man, was dancing about, cutting bread and butter and making bacon and eggs for the enormous man who remained quite silent throughout the whole encounter.

'And rather dazed we left after about half an hour and I asked this woman what this chap's name was and she said it was Quentin Crisp.

It was a very bizarre encounter and a very remarkable man he was and remains so as you know. But in fact the image of the man sitting at the table, silent, and the other man dancing about, bread and butter . . .' – Pinter's hands were like glove puppets – '. . . remained with me for some weeks and I told Henry that I might write a play from that image. And he was at Bristol University Drama Department at the time and he said, "Fine, when you write it, I'll put it on." I said, "OK, but . . . it's going to take me some time."

'A couple of weeks later he phoned and said, "Well, where's the play?" I said, "Don't be ridiculous, it's going to take me six months to write . . ." He said, "It can't take six months for you to write because I have a niche for it next week, at the end of the week, and I could actually do it for four performances." And I said, "It's out of the question."

'By that time I was in Torquay and, as I remember, I suddenly sat down and – I think I was acting in *Separate Tables* – I remember that – and we were rehearsing another play in the morning, of course – but in the afternoon and at night I wrote *The Room*. In four days and sent it to Henry. It just *came*.' His right hand swept through the air. 'Just like that. And he put it on.'

By that time, Pinter's knowledge of how a play worked, from a practical point of view, must have been, given his instincts and intelligence, very well developed. He was always and remained a poet who waited for the poem to come, not a writer who set himself the daily task of trawling the waterfront. Writing at speed is more common than readers or theatre-goers would like to believe. Noël Coward, who admired Pinter, wrote the brilliantly constructed *Private Lives* in three days. Golding wrote the first – long – draft of *Lord of the Flies* in four or five weeks. I think that out of this experience, the habit of waiting for the play to come to him, like a poem, and then moving very fast became Pinter's usual method.

'Can you tell us how it differed from the encounter with Quentin Crisp and the enormous man?'

'Totally different. Quentin Crisp, the man, became a woman for a start . . . And the woman was rather glum which Quentin Crisp certainly isn't and the whole thing developed in its own way.'

This was shot in tight close-up. Ingmar Bergman praised the strength of the face on screen, the intensity of it. Pinter was now beginning to dig into himself and we could see it as well as hear it.

'It had nothing to do with Quentin Crisp or the house I was in. As you know from the play, there was a mysterious person in this basement and a mysterious . . . the whole thing was a lot of mysterious goings-on, really. And I didn't know what was happening. It just took its own form.'

We saw an extract. The big man sat at the table shovelling in food while he read his propped-up comic. His wife meandered around him, attending to him, talking, rather flatly, but talking incessantly. Of course it was different. But it is no diminution of the piece to say that its links with what Harold had seen in the room in Chelsea were resonant, at least that.

'I wrote that play totally without calculation. In other words I also wrote it consequentially. I started at the top – I try to do that anyway – but perhaps not quite so fully as I did with my early writing – in other words I started at the top and at a certain point there was a knock on the door and someone came and I had honestly no idea who he was, what he might be, what he might say, and let it run, let it happen, and found he *did* have a voice. That was the landlord in fact. Then two visitors arrived and I didn't know what they were on about really, what they wanted. But they were just part of the whole atmosphere.'

'When you *didn't* know who the person was who came into the room, did that bother you or did you seek to discover it?'

'Oh, I sought to discover it, of course. It didn't *bother* me.' (A long pause here.) 'I mean, suddenly to have a blank page. It remains one of the . . . it remains the central joy of writing, I think. You have a blank page. One moment there's nothing on it and the next moment' – he clicked his fingers – 'there's *something* on it. Now if you *know* what the subject's going to *be*, fully and comprehensively before you get to it, I don't quite see where the spring of, as you say, discovery, how it can exist. The discovery exists in the act of discovering.'

'After you saw *The Room*, your first play, performed – it had four performances, you said you were terribly excited and stirred by it. Did you think – this is the life for me?'

'Well. I must admit I became very excited with the way an image could be clearly expressed on the stage in theatrical form – it hadn't occurred to me before and I immediately started to write *The Birthday Party*. It was an interesting existence because I was acting all the time, you see, and I suddenly remember again. I don't know whether you remember the interrogation scene in *The Birthday Party*? I wrote it in the interval of playing *Doctor in the House* in Leicester. I was playing the consultant but I wrote the interrogation in the dressing room.'

'Where they interrogate Stanley?'

'Yes . . . so it was a varied . . . existence.'

'Was *The Birthday Party* itself related to or based on any particular event?'

'Yes it was. I was on tour in fact. I was on tour with a play called *A Horse, A Horse* in Eastbourne. I had to do the ears' – mimes – 'of the horse, you see. It wasn't a real horse. I had to make it *seem* like a real horse. I failed dismally. It wasn't a happy experience.

'But I was looking for digs and one rainy day I found them after a long sweat through the good counsels of a rather strange laconic man I met in a pub. He said, "I could take you to some digs but I wouldn't recommend them." I'd nowhere else to go and I said, "I don't care what they're like." And I went to these digs and there was' – arms outstretched – 'a *big* woman, the landlady, and a little man, the land-*lord*, and this chap. There was no one else there. And the digs were really quite filthy in this house, quite filthy. And I slept in the attic with this man, shared the attic, and there was a sofa over my head, propped up, from which hairs and stuff fell continuously. And the man – I said to him one day, "What are you doing here?" And he said, "Well, I used to be, I am a pianist, I used to play for a concert party here. But I gave that up." I said, "Did you use to play elsewhere?" He said, "Oh, I used to play in London. But I gave that up." I said, "Well, how long are you going to stay? *Why* are you staying?" The *woman*, the landlady, was really a quite voracious character. Always tousled his hair and tickled him, goosed him, couldn't leave him alone. And he said, "There's nowhere else to go . . ." That remained with me and a couple of years later the image was still there and the idea came about two men coming down to "get" him.'

We showed the interrogation scene. It is fierce bullying, two skilled and tough operators attacking, in the end, the sanity of Stanley, bespectacled, bewildered, accused of everything under the sun and allowed no chance to speak for himself. It was cruel.

'The play was put on and every critic but *one* panned it.' I said.

'Oh, there's never been a panning *like* it. I mean I've experienced quite a few, in my own experience and others, other writers, I've seen pannings done but I think *The Birthday Party* takes the cake.'

'It was your second play.'

'My first play professionally done, in fact. At the Lyric, Hammersmith. It was quite a shock, yes, quite a shock . . .' And he did, you can see, even now, look shocked, and, bewildered. Then he began to pull out of it. 'I still have the box office returns for that week.' It only ran a week. 'Eight performances, £260; £140 was the first performance. So the other seven performances took £120 between them, including the Thursday matinee which I had the misfortune to pop in to see how it was going.

'I remember going into the Thursday matinee and I said, "I'm going up to the circle," and the usherette said, "You can't go up there." I said, "Why not?" She said, "Because we've closed it." So I *then* said who I *was* – young at the time! – "I am the author." "Oh," she said' – (and Pinter raised his eyes to heaven, remembered imitation of her unimpressedness) – ' "*are* you?" So I went into the circle alone, and looked over the edge and saw six people in the audience. The takings that afternoon were two pounds and six shillings.'

'Did you feel like giving up?'

'Yes. I did. I was really bewildered. I thought, The hell with it. I won't go on writing plays. But the feeling only lasted about forty-eight hours as I remember.'

'It was *The Caretaker* that gave you your head of steam?'

'Yes. *The Caretaker* was very warmly received and ran for a year in London.'

'Did the critics who had panned *The Birthday Party* refer back to it, revise their opinion, or just erase it?'

'I once said, some years ago, when I was talking to some students, I said, "I've written two full-length plays. The first ran a week and the second ran a year. In the first I employed *dashes* between phrases – as it were – 'Look, dash, you, dash, can't, dash, do this, dash.' In the second I employed dots between the phrases. It would be, 'Look, dot dot dot, you, dot dot dot, can't, dot dot dot, do this, dot dot dot.' " I said, "Clearly dots are more popular with critics than dashes. You can't fool a critic for long. They can tell a dot from a dash. That's about all I've got to say about critics." '

He took his glasses off here – his glasses off? A mask off? A layer more likely – and in the next shot had, in his Sobranie-free hand, a tumbler of whisky.

'When people watch your plays they see that things are not traditionally explained.'

'Well, there is a tendency, there is a traditional tendency, as you know, for playwrights to really discuss their characters on the stage and see that the audience in fact has all the information it could possibly want which is a way of looking at it, a way of doing it, I suppose. But I've tried to maintain a presence, an attitude towards my characters, I think, of knowing as much about them as they would allow me to do and *not* to impose on them either my own judgements or arbitrary information.

'You see I do think we do know very little about each other. We bump into each other as I bump into my characters. My characters are not my closest friends or my family or whatever. They're strangers to me. I get to *know* them in a certain way but they remain, finally, strangers and you don't know very much about strangers. You don't know very much about other people . . .'

'*The Homecoming* is being revived. It was highly acclaimed, here and in America, on its first outing.'

'Mixed. Mixed.'

'Mixed reviews?'

'I've always received mixed reviews. Very much so.'

We then saw an extract from *The Homecoming* in which the father humiliates his brother, rather taunts his three stone-silent sons and addresses to the wife of one of his sons almost all his monologue which oscillates between sentimentality about his past, as a butcher, his wife, his family, to excoriation of them.

It was at this point that the interview became sticky. Both of us felt it immediately. Harold did not want me to pursue this line of questioning. His reluctance was understandable and his business. But there was a little antagonism. In some interviews you take it on the chin if you think it will reveal more about the subject. This was an example. Perhaps Harold was enjoying the tension a little too much for my liking and so I decided to keep going.

More than once, over the years, as we got to know each other well and warmly, he would say, 'I stepped over the mark there,' or 'I feel bad about that.' In a way he need not have said that. It seems, from today's point of view, an enjoyable joust. And despite the fact that it looked as if I was being a bit too intrusive and he a bit bullying, it revealed, I think, important aspects of his thinking and his work. It began very simply.

'What would you say *The Homecoming* was about?'

'*Oh!* What's it *about*?' He took his time and whetted his wit. 'Well, it's about a family.' (Each word given equal emphasis as in talking to the stupid.) 'Three brothers, and one brother brings his wife back to the family after an absence of six years and it's about *that*. About the arrival, the homecoming, of the older brother. And his wife . . .'

'Who stays on with the family when he goes away, possibly to America.'

'Hmm. It's about *that*, too . . . It's about how that develops in other words. It's not *about* anything else at all. It's just *about* what takes place.'

'It's a play that seems to me' – I was faltering here – 'to have a lot to do with sex.'

'It's a relevant factor, yes.'

'A relevant factor . . .?'

'I always think sex is a relevant factor.'

'Because it's rather . . . the brother arrives with his wife and the wife is taken on by the other brothers and the father as a prostitute to earn money to keep them and keep herself. It's a dramatic turn of events.'

'Yes.'

'I'm getting nowhere with this, Harold.' I laughed, I write, but I laughed at the time. I think it was funny. 'I thought I wouldn't get anywhere talking to you about themes, but I wanted to have a go at it.'

'It's tough, you know.'

So I went on.

'Seeing your plays there's a great deal to do with menace, a great deal to do with teasing and taunting and joshing and a great deal to do with sex. And an enormous amount to do with domination' – which felt locally relevant at that moment – 'who's winning this, who's losing. Are you saying, "Good, but I don't want to, and in a way I'm not able to, talk about themes"? If so, I'll move on.'

'Yes. That's what I'm saying because (a) I don't know what themes . . . they are . . . you have in front of you all these books. I have them on my shelf. I've written about sixteen or so plays. They sit on my shelf. And *very* occasionally I take one of them down and look at it with some curiosity as if I'm looking at something which is *quite* outside myself, nothing to do with me whatsoever. And in a certain way that's what I do think – that the stuff is what it is and it's separated, although there *is* an umbilical cord, you can't actually *feel* it. I'm not actually distancing myself from the plays. What I'm saying is that they have an existence of their own and if I attempt to discuss them and talk about *them* specifically I know I'll only talk a load of guff, even more guff than anyone else.'

That, I thought, was bull's-eye for him. Then I think he rather misunderstood the next question.

'Some people have said that what comes across in your work is a strong feeling of despair.'

'Well, I've said I can't say anything about my work, as it were, but I'm prepared to make a tentative definitive statement here and that is, you seem to be implying that my work is despairing . . .'

Not true. '*Some* people have said'. But more would come by saying nothing, I hoped. And besides, he had a right to be testy.

'I don't feel that to be the case . . . I feel that really there's a . . . there's a body of feeling in it that, it is true, certainly escapes some people – a feeling *for* others, in the stuff. In other words, I don't consider myself to be a bleak playwright, though there are bleak elements I'm sure.' He took a drink of whisky.

'In *Old Times, one* of your themes – I know you're not going to address your themes but I'm going to drag them up willy-nilly' – now that was wholly unnecessary – 'is memory. Did that play come from a particular remembered incident in your own life?'

'No!' Delighted again – the mood changed again. 'I was actually lying on a sofa, thinking of absolutely nothing at all – the next moment I found myself rushing up the stairs to my study to make some notes and a bit of dialogue. I've no clue where it came from.' Triumphant. 'At *all*!'

'You acted in that yourself. What was that like?'

'I was only concerned about getting the lines right. I found them very difficult to learn. I didn't have to think about what I was *doing* because I knew what the character was *supposed* to be feeling and expressing.'

'What was that?'

'Oh, I can't put it into words. I just *felt* and *knew* what *he* was doing at the time. He's in a corner there. Trying to fight his way out of it. That's about as far as I'll go.'

'An odd life, being a writer.'

'Not a bad life.'

'The advantages?'

'Freedom. One can dictate one's own . . . to a certain extent . . . and I hope this doesn't sound too complacent . . . because I'm not that . . . but to a certain extent one can dictate one's own destiny. The ball is in your court if you see what I mean. I'm not dependent on . . . others

– generally speaking, although I'm totally dependent on others in the course of an actual production. But that's more interdependence because I can make myself heard.'

'And the disadvantages?'

'The disadvantage is when you can't write. I started – I was quite prolific in a way – when I was young – and now the gaps are four or five years between plays.'

'Nothing you can do about that?'

'Hopeless.'

'What do you do instead?'

'I write poetry of course and I write films, which I enjoy, and it keeps the old wheels oiled to a certain extent, but it is not the same thing.'

He had just finished an adaptation of Proust's *Remembrance of Things Past* – a monumentally long novel. 'I read it every day for three months – and in the end I thought it was totally impossible. Then Joe Losey – the director – said one day, "Go home now and *start*." "Start what? In what way?" "Put pen to paper. Just *start*." And I did.'

'And there's a new play, the first for years. Are you pleased with it?'

'Yes. It came out of the blue, really. I can't say much about it. It will be done by Peter Hall at the National Theatre. It's very different from anything I've written before, which interests me.'

This was *Betrayal*. Different in many ways. Its structure, which started at the end of the 'affair' that was its subject and tracked back through the play to the beginning which was the end of the play. And the content, known to a few at the time and to an increasing number ever since and now to everyone who has read Joan Bakewell's memoirs, drew directly and autobiographically on a seven-year affair she had with Harold while both of them were married. *Betrayal* took him from the opaque to the totally transparent.

And that was more or less where we wound up, that morning in west London. There were drinks and then we pushed off for something to eat. We talked about what we'd talked about and thought it had worked or could be made to work in the cutting room. I now think of it as one of the most truthful interviews with a writer I've done. In defending his rightful privacy and the real mystery of his art, Harold told us a great deal about it.

I did two more programmes with him, over the next thirty years. In one of them he whipped out a poem he'd just written – 'just like that' – while he was sat on a bench in the National Gallery, and he asked if he could read it. It was 'about' a walk with his old schoolteacher across Hackney Marshes. More plays and poems, campaigns and speeches against Blair and Bush and all others implicated. The Nobel Prize.

We met more often, Harold and Antonia, and it was always an event. There was always drink involved and laughter – despite the hand grenades he would hurl now and then and the rants he would rail now and then – or maybe because of that. Sometimes the language was so extreme and disproportionate and violent I thought it might be part of his slow-gathering illness. The energy of Harold Pinter seemed to grow angry, railing more tenacious as he beat off that long and painful illness which finally took him. And a great light went out.

Ingmar Bergman

Ingmar Bergman took control. That is what he does when he makes a film. As near total control as any director has ever achieved. And though this was not his film, and though we were a small crew in a small room somewhere in the labyrinth of the film studios in Munich, he could not break the practice of a lifetime. He came into the room and within moments, with charm, with authority and with the consent of all of us, he took control.

The chairs had to be closer together for the interview to be more intimate. The chairs were pushed closer, but not too close, back a bit, perfect. The lighting had to be arranged so that the eyes were the centre of focus. The lighting was delicately rearranged. The one feature of this bare room was a second door. To be just half open: just – *so*! For these few minutes our television crew was his film crew, and very pleased to be.

Then he sat down. Waited until the clapper boards were snapped and exclaimed, in a loud voice, 'HA!' To which, fortunately I think, I had the instinct to return a quiet 'ha!'

And we were on. He was in someone else's film now and he was as willing, open and uncontrolling a subject as any I have known before or since. There is about some people on screen an unmistakable and unfakeable quality: you can 'see' them thinking. In my view, just as the camera can be a lie detector, so it can be a diviner of truths. Bergman, now secure on 'his' set, was prepared to give himself up to the quest to find out truths about his work, truths that would confirm and illustrate my view that he was the finest film author-director there has ever been.

His vision, his world, his sensibility bred in a small Scandinavian country, transmitted largely in black and white and in a language spoken by very few, imprinted itself on the eyes and minds of cinema-goers the world over in the second half of the twentieth century. It remains a body of work equalled only by the finest dramatists and novelists. 'Bergmanesque' was an adjective. I had loved what he did since the first few minutes of the first film of his I saw, twenty years before this encounter.

I had been to Munich a few weeks previously to talk to him about the interview. He had never given an interview in English or on British television. He was in exile in Munich following a fracas about his taxes in Stockholm. At the time I was in a hole. I had no confidence that *The South Bank Show* would last beyond its first season. I decided to go for broke. Get Israel Merchant and James Ivory to do a film on Indian miniatures; take on the difficult Harold Pinter; do a ninety-minute film on the ballet *Mayerling*, and, while I had the chance, try to make a film about Ingmar Bergman.

We met in his flat for lunch. The flat was small and bare. The lunch was a sort of weak porridge. His wife served silently. Bergman asked me about his films. Though it had the tone and pattern of a conversation, it was an examination. I was glad of it. Making small talk with Mr and Mrs Bergman would have been a nightmare: I was too nervous. What did I know? What did I know of what he knew? But to talk about his films! I had done that for years.

He is a tall, rather gangly figure, slightly built, thinning hair strictly parted and brushed down, rather rosy cheeks, hands almost constantly involved in semaphore, nothing much out of the ordinary: except that sitting down, across the table, crouched forward, eyes cowled, you were compelled to take on the intensity and often the lightness of the expression in his eyes. It was unnerving and unpromising but it was OK. I had come to see him without great expectations of getting a film: at least I could tell him how he had changed my life.

In 1958, I was homesick, lovesick and stuck in Oxford University, a place of splendour and significance but in those first weeks alien. Walking is always a way through. I went round and round the spectred city, ancient golden colleges, bicycle flocks, young men all apparently confident, settled men, at home. Mine was 300 miles to the north in what seemed by contrast a wild, even uncivilised, land, but much warmer, I thought, much richer in what mattered and above all it was where my girlfriend lived.

I saw the poster for a film called *Summer with Monika*. The girl on the poster was near twin to the girl I'd left behind.

It was the first time I had seen or heard a film in a foreign language. Had it not been for Harriet Andersson I might have walked out. But I think not. It took only a few minutes. It was like reading the first few pages of a novel or a poem you know will be a friend for life, or listening to that song or sound you will always remember. I was Bergmanised and my three years at Oxford were transformed. I became addicted to Bergman and through him to Fellini, Antonioni, Truffaut, Renoir . . . to European cinema, my New Found Land. With a friend, Gavin Millar, I helped make a film and became the film critic of Cherwell the university newspaper.

It is inevitable to have heroes: in childhood, sportsmen usually; in adolescence, authors. At twenty-one, Ingmar Bergman became a hero, his work to be aspired to, his example as an artist gold standard. So I had encountered Mr Bergman twenty years before the thin porridge in the flat in Munich and seen, I think, all his films; some of them, in those pre-video, pre-DVD days, more than once.

I had seen many films in the local cinema back home in Wigton, Cumberland. An average of two a week between the ages of five and eighteen; that would be about 1,300 films. They had been 'the pictures' or when American set in 'the movies', and I went to see the actors. After Bergman I went for the directors. And of course the pendulum swung too far. But I had not consciously known what contribution a director made until I saw *Summer with Monika*. Perhaps because it was in a foreign language. Although, blessedly, the subtitles were clear – I had to work harder. Or perhaps there were so many resonances, difficult to articulate on that first visit but growing through time which in sum added up to the recognition of an author I wanted to know more and more about. Not just the landscape of his stories but the landscape of his mind. I saw Bergman alongside the novelists I had fed on in a book-wormed adolescence; I could think of no greater compliment.

So that was my first encounter. In Oxford. At times, seeing his films, there was the almost unbearable sense of another being.

The second was our dry lunch – at which, it belatedly occurs to me, Bergman might also have been testing out both his English and mine – he leaves nothing to chance.

And now 'HA!' The Third encounter we were in a small room in Germany, filming.

At the time I interviewed him, he had made thirty-six films in thirty years and directed more than sixty plays at the National Theatre in Stockholm. He was sixty. He was much fresher in the face than when he had cross-examined me. Unhooded. Eager to engage.

'I saw my first picture at six years old,' he said when I asked, inevitably because it is for me the necessary first step, how he thought it had all begun. 'I was completely lost. All I wanted was a projector of my own. And at Christmas, when I was nine, there was' – he made the shape of a mound: a heap? – 'Yes. A heap of presents for us and one was in a brown package and I knew it was a projector. I couldn't eat. I couldn't sleep.'

It has been said that genius lies in the heightened, even freakish, facility to revisit, reconstruct, relive childhood. Like all generalisations, it is only true for some people. But Bergman fits into that category. Some writers climb above and beyond their childhood experiences although it must be the case that those experiences initially enabled them to climb above and beyond. But afterwards they seem to have pulled up the ladder.

For others, though, it seems true enough as in Bergman's case. He was captured by films aged six and never sought to be free of them. Again there will be those who came later to what proved to be their work, even their vocation. But Bergman seems to have been on the trajectory of his life, clearly assured, from a very early age which means in my view, that he was forever 'years ahead' of his contemporaries and there has always been something of the prodigy about him. He still carries that boyish dazzle evident in the interview.

'The projector was for my brother,' he said, and he can laugh about it now. 'But we had both been given tin soldiers. I had already many soldiers. A few days after Christmas, I gave my brother my whole army for the projector.'

His 'whole army'.

I noticed, watching this interview on DVD several times for this piece, that his eyes reminded me of someone. Pause. Rewind. Play. Stop. It was one of the portraits of Rembrandt in the National Gallery. In that, there is one of the painter's eyes which looks as dead as the other looks alive. The more you 'see' it the more striking it becomes. It is the same – though not as marked – with Bergman. The left eye is more closed, less giving, much harder to read. The right calls you in. His hands, given full play away from the dining room table, also addressed the questions in a language of their own.

Summer Interlude was the first film in which, he said, 'I managed the whole machine for the first time.' It is a film that still matters to him. 'Some films are close to my heart, some I don't care about.' Not even a little? No. And even *'Summer Interlude* – I think now it's a very bad picture – but I like it.' It is a story told around the tragedy of a ballet dancer who has lost her lover when she was young. 'It had to do with me,' he said, 'it was very personal in a way. But,' he went on immediately to repeat, 'I think it's a very, very bad picture today . . . It would be much better if pictures were like theatre performances. Once and then just disappear. But I like it.'

Bergman's personal life has been one of many marriages and mistresses and bolt-lightning anger and literally bed-ridden, hospitalised illnesses when tormented, usually over a script. There was a willingness to let this life out. It's not something I look for in an interview. For most of the time I stick to the work rather than trawl the life. The work is the

reason we are there. And I think it pays better dividends in talk. Yet
sometimes, when the autobiography of the artist is not only core to the
work but plain in the work, it comes through.

We talked about *Sawdust and Tinsel*, which is a story of jealousy,
sexual humiliation and the brutal growl of military men on manoeuvres, distracted and aroused by the sight of a woman bathing naked, and
willing to sport with some of them until it gets nasty. Her husband, a
circus clown, comes, in his costume, to seek out and rescue her.

'I think the whole thing is about jealousy,' he said. 'I am a very
jealous man.' Involved with some of the most beautiful and talented
actresses of the time there would be a large scope. 'So I had to find a
solution. I wrote it as a very brutal fairy tale . . . It was a tremendous
fiasco . . . I thought I would never be allowed to make another film. I
thought this would be my last project.'

The key scene shows a gaudily glamorous woman who, it emerges,
is part of a circus troupe. She is walking to the sea through scores of
soldiers on summer manoeuvres, cannons pounding their shells out to
the ocean, men half-heartedly following orders. She disrupts them with
her open sauciness and a few of them dare her to strip off and bathe with
them while the mass of others look on and cheer and jeer. Her husband,
Frost the Clown, in his clown costume and his clown make-up, comes
looking for her. He is mocked and pursued by the soldiers. When he
sees Alma, his wife, in the sea, he takes off his shoes, goes into the sea
and carries her out. Their clothes have been stolen and hidden by an
odious boy soldier and Frost has to carry her, naked, his bare feet bleed-
ing on the stony ground, through the gawping merciless mob.

The love and jealousy of Frost is unbearable. 'It was originally a
translated dream, a nightmare. In my dream light is very important.
Here I wanted very intense light so I made experiments with prints
over and over.'

In one short scene there is the clearest proof of Bergman's superlative
technical skills and artistic gifts. What dominates is the music, a sort of
hurdy-gurdy circus music; and the sound of the cannons which become
slow, dragged drumbeats as Frost staggers back with the burden of his

faithless wife. Sometimes when the men are jeering we hear them, at other times their cries are mouthed but not heard as in a silent film. When Frost cries out, 'Alma! Alma!' we see the shape of the word but it is silent. Bergman's range of talents in this brief moment is formidable: even the odious boy whose nasty little action of which he is so proud takes just a few seconds. It is cast and played to such a perfection that you have time to dissect and loathe his fawning character. As often with Bergman, it can seem straightforward and naturalistic – and it is. But the essential dynamic is achieved through stylisation and artifice to a meticulous degree. The dream becomes a filmed nightmare.

And did this relieve him of the pressure of jealousy? 'Sometimes, yes.' Without pause, rocking slightly in the hard chair he had requested and still in his mind back on the stony beach with Frost the Clown carrying his naked wife whose experience had stood in for mass rape which was the trigger for the rage against the film, he said, 'I am very afraid of most things that exist in the world, especially the death.' And after *The Seventh Seal*? 'Death was not an obsession any more. That picture was good medicine.'

The Seventh Seal is his most famous film. 'Death is present the whole time in that film.' Based on paintings in a medieval church, the film chronicles the return of a knight and his squire from the Crusades. He meets Death but delays his own by challenging Death to a game of chess which, if he wins, will spare his life. The story then follows the knight on his homeward journey through plague and flagellation and witch-burning stalked by Death.

Death is played by an actor in flowing black robe, white make-up, almost a clown, with a priestly demeanour. 'If you take a chair and you say, "This is the most fantastic, expensive chair in the world, no chair is like it," and put it on a stage – everybody will believe it. Everybody will handle it in that way. So if Death comes as an actor and says, "I am Death," you believe it. It is that incredible magic of film-making and theatre-making.'

The Seventh Seal hit a nerve. The tightness of the storytelling, the grimness, the bold assumption that the Middle Ages were our own time. There is the power of the ensemble acting and within it one of the several examples of Bergman working through his and more particularly his father, the Lutheran minister's religious conviction and bigotry. Like many others, I was and remain devoted to Bergman's relentless seriousness in films like *The Seventh Seal*. The timeless, and childhood questions of the meaning or meaninglessness of existence are confronted and the pilgrim's progress of a life examined.

All the more extraordinary, then, that *The Seventh Seal*, which had been turned down by every studio, was made because of the success of one of Bergman's happiest soufflés, a flawless light comedy, *Smiles of a Summer Night*, which won the Grand Jury Prize at Cannes. Called in from Stockholm, Bergman arrived clutching the script of *The Seventh Seal*. 'Now is my chance, I thought' – and in the euphoria got it commissioned, 'provided we could make it in thirty days. We did. Thirty-two.'

This is the best Bergman example of one man's vision being so intense that though at odds with fashion and expectation and worldly financial backing, it bit into the imagination of people the world over, many of whom had very little purchase on the rooted medieval torments and faith of the darkest times in medieval history. Its 'authenticity' is astounding. You are taken into the forests of centuries past. It is without any taint of glamour. The cast appear to have been wearing their costumes for unwashed years.

Save for the opening sequences, shot in four days on the shore in southern Sweden, the film was made on the back lot of old studios outside Stockholm. The forest is a few trees through which, if you look keenly, you can see the glint from the windows of neighbouring flats. The stream comes from a hosepipe in the back yard. The climactic 'Dance of Death' was grabbed on the way back from the south when Bergman saw an encroaching sunset behind a hill on which the characters in the film would be silhouetted.

The magic is in the idea and the bold realisation of the idea on meagre resources. Perhaps meagre resources can help. The speed of storytelling in *The Seventh Seal* – like one painted panel after another – might come from lack of money but it has helped lead to a plot that drives hard.

The religious lining of Bergman's mind is often present. Although he rebelled against his father and literally struck him to the ground and left the family home to live alone in another part of the city, he carries the Church and the faith with him. *Winter Light* is close to his own belief, I think. In that, a priest cries out against his own belief, pours doubt and despair on it, destroys it. All this in the presence of a man at the end of his tether who has come to seek help and comfort and some sort of faith. The man is later found dead, self-murder, helped neither by God nor priest.

The priest is faced with only one person in the congregation and the temptation is to cancel the service. 'But the only important thing is to go on,' says Bergman. And the service is held. The suicide and the empty church which is yet filled with music and the 'words of God' seem to be near Bergman's belief and lack of belief. There is desperation here as in other films.

He has said that he thought of each film as his last. I asked him if he meant that. 'Yes. I always have that feeling. I cannot think otherwise or I am thinking, How can I please *this* one or *that* one or to do it so I can finance another film. The only thing to be loyal to is the picture and the people making the picture. Everything else is of no importance.'

As a theatre director, Bergman had access to the best actors in Sweden, a company which he took on to the screen: Max von Sydow, Gunnar Björnstrand, Harriet Andersson, Bibi Andersson, Liv Ullman Erland Josephson, Ingrid Thulin. The cameraman, Sven Nykvist, and the editors are part of the film. They come back again and again, old friends, a repertory company on celluloid, showing us their range and demonstrating as an ensemble, remarkable control. But then control of his art and his artists is an absolute.

Yet, in the interview, he is so very open, responding not steering. After we have taken a break and reloaded the cameras, I talk about this company of his and he said, 'Sometimes there is a miracle happening in front of the camera. If you are very close as a group there is an atmosphere of confidence . . . confidence . . . real confidence. Suddenly something happens in front of the camera. To hope for it, to wait for it is the best thing in the world. You can't calculate or rehearse. I see you don't believe me.'

'I find it strange. Don't you?'

'I can give you an example. In *Cries and Whispers* there were problems in the death scene. Technically it was very difficult because I had the idea that when she was about to die the sun would come into the room. We took it two or three times. It was very exhausting for Harriet.' (She is violent in her death spasms.) 'But then, she looks into the eyes of Anna and she disappears in a very strange way. Something disappears out of her. Perhaps it is something close to me. A little bit of me.'

As he speaks he seems to see it once again and we cut the death scene into our film. As if shaking off a mood like a wet dog shakes off water, he said, 'Even the most tragical scenes must have some joy, some lust; if they are not present, the picture is just boring. If it is boring it is dead. You can go home and kill yourself.'

Again and again I was drawn back to his insistence on full control. To make a film is to employ many different artists and craftsmen, each one independent and banked up with their own skills. To get a film under way needs financial persuasiveness and a persistence which can stretch over years. To see the end film as you imagined it and wrote it before a shot was taken is something of a miracle but this is what Ingmar Bergman did time and time again.

'It is like a virus. It is all in me. When I shoot the film I already plan to edit it. I work with an editor of high standards and good nerves. To work with me in the cutting room is not always pleasant. I am furious in the cutting room. The cutter has to be *extremely* precise. She must know where every frame is immediately when I say, "Can we make that frame longer?" I am a pedant. Sometimes it is torture for my collaborators.

'But if you want to create a little universe – now I am talking a little romantically, I hope you forgive me – this universe is not the reality. Reality always sabotages your dreams. So your details out of reality have to be perfect.'

He was in his private unassailable but not entirely comprehensible thought system: one which was essential to him and, perhaps deliberately, rather obscure to others.

He sat a few feet away from me, a composed, elegant man, an artist who had found his own voice early and the world had listened, relaxed, hesitant in the best way – that is to say, not glib, not responding with the many times repeated answer – and yet again and again it was his fears which claimed centre stage. But he maintains he is moving on.

'When I was younger and was scared I made excuses,' he said, 'and I built a wall around me to protect myself. But now I am sixty and almost everything has happened to me and I have taken these walls away. In my life – but not in the studio!'

Examples of obsession are not rare in art, in gardening, in sport, in sensuality, in life. Bergman's obsession is more intriguing than most because of the quality of the art, the greatness of it. And for that obsession is the handmaiden, not, I think, the hand.

The film which gets closest to him, I think, is *Wild Strawberries*. It originated in a visit he paid to his grandmother's flat in the city of Uppsala. He arrived there at four in the morning. 'It was already daylight. The streets were empty. The birds were singing, obsessed with the spring.' His grandmother and her flat had been his sanctuary as a boy. Here he was totally secure. 'It was much more difficult at the home of my mother and father.' He went into the flat, up the back stairs, the clock in the great church striking four, and 'then I thought that if I opened the door to the kitchen, everything would be as it had been when I was seven years old.'

In *Wild Strawberries* the old pedantic professor, played by Victor Sjöström, a silent-film actor who had taken up the young Bergman, repeats the journey to Uppsala, enters into his past, the large family around the table, on the shore, all dressed in white, a dream of purity and perfection. Victor is taken back into it.

'Sometimes I love my childhood. Just before falling asleep I can go through the rooms at my grandmother's almost photographically. Whenever I am unhappy or unsure, it is some sort of technique, I go back to my grandmother's.'

This is practically word for word what is spoken by the old pedantic professor as he reaches out for sleep in *Wild Strawberries*.

'Outside,' he said, 'I'm grown up. It's a mask. Inside I'm still a child, I'm playing games. I can look at myself now from outside. It is only Ingmar, playing a game.'

Somehow Bergman builds to artistic perfection the bridge between the deepest inwardness of himself and the real world as he finds it. Through his own passion and the orchestration of many skills in music, photography, sound effects and cutting, and with the help of actors and collaborators chosen like select disciples, he puts together pictures and films which reach into the heart of things, often through close-ups: 'the human face is the most cinematographic thing that exists.'

Three hours have gone by. I have enough material for at least two films and some years later, more confident, I will undertake two-part profiles of David Lean and Laurence Olivier. I still wish I had done that with Bergman. But we have more than enough now and sadly I call it to a halt by saying, 'Thank you.' He nods, and then it registers.

'It's all over!'

'Hey!'

'Good heavens!' And he leans forward to give the exultant embrace which must make those he works with feel 'mission completed'.

He goes back to his bare flat inside the studio complex. Unmasked? Or to take off the mask? We, the crew, in a race to the airport and the cutting room.

I think we admire people partly because they show us what we could become. We are attracted to them in the first place because of a bond, often hidden for years, an affinity which becomes a most unlikely relationship. On the one side the distinguished artist: on the other side, the admirer willing to be an acolyte, nose pressed against the glass, an outsider but able to see and feel what the artist has to offer.

Bergman offered me access to his imagination and to his education. He was deeply read and, through his work in the theatre he was, experienced in great plays and operas, the best of the European tradition. He could call up a religious background, now rigorous, now authoritarian, even tyrannical, but still a world with a God. And he was part of a metropolitan arts community in Stockholm which freewheeled him into passions and complexities and fed his work.

I had found some of that on first encountering the plays of Ibsen – read not seen – and in Chekhov and Strindberg; more had come through novels, especially French and Russian novels. The cinema for me, the picture house, the 'flicks', had been for entertainment and thrills. It was a place dominated by stars, built on suspense and adventure and sometimes taken over by dancing and singing that sent you out spinning down the street. It was just 'the pictures' like the light bulb in the kitchen. Culture was a chandelier and in another house.

Bergman, I came to realise, brought the two together. He used the common tongue of films to express what the classical authors had written in theatrical drama, in novels, in poetry. He harnessed these two cultures and added to both.

I found him at just the right time for me. Real heroes never die. I wrote a book about *The Seventh Seal* and Bergman's films are referred to and discussed in my novel *Remember Me* which opens in Oxford at the time when *Summer with Monika* took me into the Scala Cinema and into a new world. It's odd to contemplate that but for an aimless walk in Oxford I might so easily have missed it and never got interested in films and never got into television and so never gone to Munich to film with Ingmar Bergman.

Andrew Lloyd Webber

When I made the first *South Bank Show* on Andrew Lloyd Webber, he was thirty-eight. He was already the most successful composer British musical theatre had ever known. He had written seven major hit musicals and was the only composer ever to have had three shows running simultaneously in the West End and on Broadway. I interviewed him in the first stages of preparing *The Phantom of the Opera* with Hal Prince in New York, then in a London recording studio, but mostly in his house in Berkshire which he had bought from his share of the £1.4 billion netted by *Cats* (£600 million more than the *Titanic* at the time and both still rising).

Phantom was to soar over the £2 billion mark. 'Memory' was to be covered by more than 150 artists and sell over 2 million copies. His anthems were sung on football terraces, his 'Pie Jesu' in cathedrals; re-casting for his first professional musical, *Joseph and the Amazing Technicolor Dreamcoat*, became a television smash hit . . . awards . . . and of course brickbats . . . acclaim . . . and of course critical curses . . . he is a phenomenon with, in my view, a streak of genius.

I first met him at the beginning of the seventies when I was working as a screenwriter and took up the challenge to do a screenplay for *Jesus Christ Superstar*. I think I was the third writer to have a crack. I had not seen the stage show but I'd heard the record, liked it, and worked from that. My idea was very simple: shoot in Israel but not in the (over-crowded, overrun) obvious 'holy' places; write no dialogue, pretend I was doing a 'silent' film; and build it around a group of young kids who had taken the story back to where it started from. In the course of this I met Andrew and Tim Rice. Andrew was mercurial, incredibly fast in conversation; as if about to burst with the tension of being himself.

Several years later, when I was looking for title music for *The South Bank Show*, Andrew's *Variations* were just about to be released. The key variation was perfect. Classical and rock, cello and the heavy beat of rock drums climaxing on a visual of the ceiling of the Sistine Chapel where a bolt of creative lightning was introduced to fill the gap between the outstretched fingers of God and Adam. They are the only titles in television history to have won a Prix Italia.

Over the years I'd got to know him better. He can be wildly funny, and also serious company, erudite, frighteningly obsessive, wholly unexpected, devilish, with a command of expertise from Roy Orbison to Rossetti, Wells Cathedral to the Everly Brothers, forever hatching up a new project or arriving with a new 'wheeze'. He has a second major preoccupation as a world-class art collector with one of the great private collections; and a third, now, as a judge on television programmes which search for new stars in musicals. Our films were made before that last development and at a time when, though famous, he still retained a shyness when appearing in public. The first shots of our film showed him at the piano in New York, playing the score of *Phantom* to Hal and talking him through the action. His concentration, the angle of his body over the piano, the way his head was dipped down to the notes, all this was exactly like the photographs of him at the piano, aged six, already precocious.

'He was a very difficult baby,' said his mother Jean, a rather stern, handsome woman, who could easily be thought of as an academic. 'He never needed any sleep *at all* . . . the only way to keep him quiet was to get up oneself and put on Edmundo Ros – very softly. And then he was perfectly happy. He jumped about in time to the music for hours, literally hours on end.'

We played Ros's 'Blame It on the Bossa Nova'.

His brother Julian the distinguished cellist, said, 'It was the noisiest household. My father would always be practising – he had a piano fitted out with pedals because he was an organist; he would be playing away in one room; I'd be scratching the cello in another; Andrew would be banging something out on the piano. It was bedlam in that flat. I'm surprised we weren't all thrown out.' Photographs of the two of them show two very happily smiling boys.

'I had a toy theatre,' Andrew said, 'which I built at the house. I used to bore the family by staging musicals.'

'There were trains and rush hours,' said Julian. 'It was great. It was real theatre.'

'My father kindly arranged for a man who had a magazine to come and watch one of these terrible performances. The net result was the publication of a piece of music of mine, "The Toy Theatre", published when I was nine . . . My father was a director of composition at the Royal College of Music and then appointed to the London College of Music as the Director. He wasn't really an academic man – although he had that. He was a composer, underestimated in his own lifetime. There's a piece of his music called "Aurora" coming out for the first time and it's burgeoning with melody.'

'His father had this tremendous sense of melody,' said Jean. 'Andrew inherited that from Bill. I'm sure of it.'

In 1965 Andrew decided to leave Magdalen College Oxford after only one term, to devote himself to writing musicals. For many this would have been a step taken with grave apprehension or a flamboyant sense of boldness. Andrew was breezy about it. Oxford wasn't considered to be a good enough environment for the writing of musicals. An association with Tim Rice, whom he'd just met, seemed a much more likely possibility. Tim thought the same.

'I remember the first time I met him, going to his flat and he sat down at the piano and said, "I've written eight musicals in my schooldays," and he played excerpts from various scores and I remember thinking, This guy's gonna make it. This is a red-hot certainty.'

'I remember the first time I met Tim. He was very, very tall and, I hope he won't mind my saying' – shy laugh – 'very pretty. He was always very good-looking and he was always the one who got the girls – still is. But

Timothy had this extraordinary way with words. It was like something I'd never heard before in any of my studies of musicals. He would write a song in a way that anyone else would say, "How dare you?" '

They worked on a musical about Dr Barnardo's for two years with no success. Then in 1968 they wrote a twenty-minute piece, *Joseph and the Amazing Technicolor Dreamcoat*, for an end-of-term junior school concert. In the audience was Derek Jewell, the music critic of the *Sunday Times*, who took it up.

'What we hit on, I think,' said Andrew, 'was a way of being able to tell a story in a straight line through music and words without dialogue.' Small acorns. *Joseph* soon 'emerged as an album. It got a lot of attention but it didn't do well. It didn't make the charts or anything like that. It was a great calling card.'

One of the first to pick up the card was David Land.

'I thought it was brilliant. It was melodic. There was nothing like it around at the time.'

'David Land,' said Tim, 'is an agent-entrepreneur – one of whose claims to fame is the Dagenham Girl Pipers whom he took around the world with enormous success. They played Vegas.'

Andrew smiled affectionately throughout all references to David.

'David has been a support, friend and godfather over the years. He's the one who comes up with, "My boys have just made 30 million quid off this!" He's the origin of most of those sort of quotes. He may deny it, but he *is*!'

'You can't stand over a composer and a writer with a stick,' David said. 'I remember to this day. I said I'd give £3,000 to each of them for three years – £18,000. Andrew said, "Do you realise we've just signed a contract for £18,000 and we needn't write a note of music!" '

Within twelve months they came up with *Jesus Christ Superstar*.

'I wrote the basic theme in a restaurant in Fulham. I rushed in and put it down on a table napkin.' (He played it – he was at his piano for this part of the interview.) 'Gosh it's simple. But that thing of taking it on' – he did so – 'and the grandeur of it is what I think makes it happen.'

'For years I'd wanted to write something about Judas Iscariot,' said Tim. 'I thought he was a very interesting character. The artistic success of *Joseph* encouraged us to go by that route. Nobody – not even David Land – thought it was a good idea *commercially*. "Religion – forget it! The kids aren't interested and adults won't go to a rock version of Jesus Christ." '

'You don't know the opposition we had,' said a converted David Land after the event. 'I play cards with Lew Grade. "Mucking around with a subject of that description – you want your bloody brains tested!" '

'It was turned down all over London,' said Andrew. 'So we went the *Joseph* route and wrote it as an oratorio and got it recorded that way. It got quite good reviews and quite good sales in England. But when the Americans discovered it, it went through the roof. Number 1 in the charts.'

They had a hit score without a show. They decided to do the show on Broadway first because of the American demand. The show on Broadway wasn't very good whereas in London it took off and in the UK the show then sold the album.

'It's easy to spot with hindsight why it went so big in the States,' said Andrew. 'There was the Jesus revolution, records like "Spirit in the Sky", people talking about religion and peace and love, and we told the story in a new way.'

Rock 'n' roll and the Greatest Story Ever Told but it was told by the villain. It was Tim Rice who turned Judas into a modern-day questing soul.

As well as the Anthem, it has some fine melodies – 'Gethsemane', 'I Don't Know How to Love Him', 'Everything's All Right'.

And then enter Paganini, who in his day some thought demonically gifted, a dark elemental force of energy: there are similarities with Andrew.

Yet again, Andrew comes at it from an angle you would not expect. This was not an attempt to ingratiate himself with the classical music world or to up the brow of his profile – he has been totally open about his passion for pop music. He wanted to write something that his brother Julian and six or seven musicians could take on the road and perform.

'It's the best piece for cello since Benjamin Britten,' said Julian. 'It's a gift to the cellist. Nobody writes these tunes for the cello any more. He also used the cello in a more percussive way.' We filmed it for *The South Bank Show*. It sold massively. It became our signature tune. Wayne Sleep danced to it to rapturous audiences.

This was in a double bill with another of Andrew's unexpected ventures – *Tell Me on a Sunday*, a woman singing/performing about her life in New York. He described how he had added a phrase near the end of the title song in order to 'take the roof off the building'. 'I'd never got the reaction I wanted. Then I realised why.' He played them and added the bars which suddenly put the song on to an operatic scale of emotion. 'That did it.'

Like *Joseph*, like *Variations* it was a hit from left field. Then on to *By Jeeves*, with Alan Ayckbourn. Two high quality hitters. Three counting Wodehouse – and a flop. 'I couldn't get across the affection I feel for it. Maybe I'm not capable of writing that sort of thing.'

'What's the difference between a string of good songs and a musical?'

'A musical is not a series of songs in isolation. If you take *Sergeant Pepper* – that was turned into a musical and it was a complete disaster. You can see the difference immediately. There's been a great change since the forties and fifties. Musicals were still making the charts. But once Elvis and the Beatles got going, young people thought – let's not do musicals any more because it's not the way to become successful songwriters – write pop. Very, very few writers decided to concentrate on musical theatre.'

It was all the more evidence of his determination and obsession that Andrew did and that he persuaded Tim, who loved playing with his own rock band, to join him.

'I just heard a radio programme on Eva Peron by chance and I thought it was a great story' said Tim. 'The more I researched it, the more fascinated by Eva Peron I became.'

'It was an idea Tim was very passionate about. It did seem to me it had one wonderful theatrical moment – which was something I saw – which is that you could take one piece of music that became your anthem – *your* theme tune – and twist it round completely. I saw that happen to Judy Garland when she did a performance at Talk of the Town. This wrecked lady trying to do "Over the Rainbow", having been so late for an audience that was, as it were, throwing cash at her. It was an extraordinary, devastating, theatrical sight. And she said "I'm sorry" and that was it – and so I thought, of Evita, there's a notion here. One could use it. Something that would become an anthem for the woman throughout the evening and then somehow turn it against her in the end.'

Harold Prince, the best director of musicals in the USA, took it on. Elaine Paige got her first starring lead in the West End.

'It was fun to do,' said Andrew. 'Lots of drum rhythms when the army and aristocracy were both marching across the stage, just avoiding each other. I think *Evita* paved the way for a lot more things than were realised at the time. It was tackling a subject that up to that time you would not think you could *in any way* do as a musical. It was using an operatic form.'

Andrew's success has provoked some vicious criticism. His music, his almost unimaginable success in creating musicals that ringed the world and still do as no others have done and his wealth all make him a big target. One of the charges is plagiarism. When I asked him what he had to say about that he took the question on the chin.

'What can you say? I know it's nonsense. I know where I work from and it does tend to be here.' In a diffident and unusual show of personal emotion, he briefly tapped his heart. 'There are going to be similarities, whatever you do. There are only so many notes on a piano – gosh – there was a whole campaign in America about Stephen Sondheim doing that . . . anybody can do that.'

'Have you ever consciously borrowed a tune from someone else?'

'I have definitely come up with one that I wish I hadn't. But I didn't consciously do it.'

'What was that?'

'I'm not going to tell you!' And equilibrium, laughter and his normal expression, between eagerness and amusement, were resumed.

Later, talking about *Cats*, Andrew played the 'Memory' song.

'When I first wrote 'Memory', I realised it was very Pucciniesque. To be honest about it, it was written previously for a notion I had for a musical about the writing of *La Bohème*. I remember when I first came up with it I thought, What do I do? I went and played it to two or three people, the last of whom was my father, and I said, "Does that sound like anything to you?" He said, "Yes. It sounds like 5 million dollars." ' *Cats* was based on poems by T.S. Eliot, one of the most intellectual and revered poets of the twentieth century. It was perhaps the most extraordinary idea for musical theatre and it succeeded. Andrew rather gleefully listed the negative comments racing around London at the time.

'It had an unknown producer, Cameron Mackintosh. It was my first venture without Robert Stigwood' (best known for managing the Bee Gees). 'An unknown and untried director of musicals, Trevor Nunn. A whole lot of poems.'

'And dance. You'd never written for dance before.'

'It was an important part of why I came to write the piece – it was just after the "dance explosion" in England. I was intrigued by it. Oh yes – and it was in the New London Theatre, considered to be *the* no-go disaster theatre of all time. There was a lot of tutting about "poor Andrew – he's off his head".'

Cats was and continues to be a worldwide success on a scale never before seen in musical theatre. It had at least two unexpected consequences. The first was to enrich and possibly guarantee the long-term independence of Faber & Faber, the publisher of the poetry of T.S. Eliot and Ted Hughes and Seamus Heaney and many other poets, novelists and scholars. The second was to unleash Andrew on to the international art market and allow him to realise a lifelong collecting ambition which culminated in the rare occurrence of the Royal Academy in Piccadilly, London, giving its entire space for a public exhibition of his collection. Norman Rosenthal, the then director, believes 'he writes music in order to collect paintings. This is *not* an academic collection. It comes out of one man's passion. It is quite extraordinary. We can fill the largest gallery of the Royal Academy with his collection of Burne-Jones alone.'

It's a passion that parallels that for the musical theatre. It began with 'my love of architecture and churches as a boy. The churches were open and free and that changed my life. I used to get very depressed at school and I would take days off to see an old musical in the cinema or to look at buildings.'

We made a film about his collection and the first place he rushed us off to was All Saints Margaret Street – just a few minutes from Oxford Circus but largely unknown. 'One of the three greatest churches in London, alongside St Paul's – actually I think it's better than St Paul's – and Westminster Abbey. This is where the Gothic Revival became magnificent.'

As always with Andrew, high art and pop go, in this case literally, to the altar, hand in hand. 'I brought Madonna here for communion. We were recording *Evita* nearby. She brought her dog.'

His brother Julian: 'We would spend two and a half hours driving to some place when he was nine or ten. And there would be no castle or turrets – just a small pile of bricks. And he would make these notes.' And, at that age, make them up into books, bound by himself, still in his library, several of them, *Ancient Monuments in England and Wales* by Andrew Lloyd Webber. They are every bit as remarkable as the piece of music he had published at that age. And his knowledge of medieval architecture and history is extensive.

Equally as extensive is his knowledge of Victorian paintings, which he could buy very early on (a Burne-Jones drawing for £15) partly because they were unfashionable and cheap. He collected from his teens but *Cats* 'changed my life completely. It made me a lot of money and tax changes meant that a person who continued to live in England could keep a lot more of it. I'd never done sensible things with money. I'd always bought pictures. This gave me the firepower to compete with foreign collectors.'

And he has. In our film he delivered a series of lectures in front of paintings – mainly Victorian and Pre-Raphaelite but they included

Picasso, Canaletto and Stanley Spencer, which were another aspect of Andrew. He was wholly unselfconscious, teeming with information and unrestrained in his enthusiasm to get it across to the audience.

'Your tastes were not only formed but dug in very young?'

'Yes. Music, especially musical theatre. Things visual – especially the Pre-Raphaelites. A sense of history – especially architecture. And rock 'n' roll – which is another form of theatre.' We played Roy Orbison over one of Andrew's paintings by Rossetti.

He's in the big frame now, the international auctions, the secret meetings to locate and then try to buy rare works in private hands. He is advised by the dealer David Mason.

'The first time I met David we went to an auction and he wouldn't stop talking to me. Talking, talking. The pictures I'd gone for just went. It was a disaster. I got rather upset.' (Andrew has moments of getting 'rather upset' now and then, and his often scarcely controllable will to get his own way, to have the thing done exactly as he believes it should be done, is part of his character, his power and his legend.) 'I said, "David, this is not a promising start." We went back to his office. And there were the pictures!'

'I told him that I'd got a surrogate bidder and told him that as long as I was talking to Andrew he could bid.' Which neatly solved the problem of Andrew and David's mere presence in a saleroom resulting in a price inflation.

'When I was at school' (Westminster, next to the Abbey, opposite Parliament, along from the Tate Britain Gallery) 'I used to go to the Tate. My art master would tell me that the Pre-Raphaelites and the Victorians were rubbish. But when I went there – so many galleries were empty – but the Victorians and Pre-Raphaelites were heaving!' His collection is now worth – who knows? – £200, £300 million. He intends to leave it, and the house in Berkshire where most of the collection is hung, to the nation. He already has plans for where the car park should be located.

After *Cats* he wrote a musical – *Starlight Express* – based on a race between two railway engines and sung and acted by a young cast on roller skates. It was a Las Vegas production. 'It's my rock 'n' roll side. I thought, Let's do a fun thing and who cares whether it gets good or bad reviews. It was just too expensively produced for my taste.'

He has taken on board some very savage reviews, especially in New York where such reviews have killed many a show. Not his. He goes to the theatre the morning after the opening night, reads them aloud to the cast, laughs, encourages the cast and sticks with the show which in at least two crucial cases goes on to run for many years and eventually wins many awards. I put some of these criticisms to him and, in the film, so did the influential critic Frank Rich. Andrew weighed them up and calmly fought back. I would guess there is bound to be private anger and hurt and a sense of 'Unfair! Unfair!' But it doesn't stop him.

'I find material for ideas in a lot of things. I have five ideas at the moment that could be made into musicals. Whether they can be or not depends on the crucial ingredient – collaborators.'

'What are they?'

'Let me give you two – the most ridiculously opposite ones. There's *Aspects of Love* by David Garnett – a latter-day Bloomsbury book about a delicate area of English, slightly literary life. The other – a musical about an American game show! Both are wonderfully theatrical ideas.'

'One of the great things about Andrew,' David Land says, 'is that he always has "a good little wheeze" about something. He's a Master of Marketing with an enormous flair for publicity. His work is great. His marketing is wonderful.'

We cut to royal openings, wheezes with steam engines for *Starlight* and then, the Archbishop of Canterbury with a red-cassocked choir-boy, Sarah Brightman and her husband Andrew Lloyd Webber. The archbishop was clutching a platinum copy of 'Pie Jesu'. 'It must be unusual,' he said, 'if not unique for Latin to get into the charts. But I believe the profound sentiments of a requiem come through in any language.'

It is a fine piece of work and, sung by a soprano and a chorister treble in a cathedral with full orchestra and choir, rouses the congregation as much as any West End audience.

'Was the *Requiem* a bid to be taken seriously?'

'I don't think any composer sits down to say, "I'm deliberately going to do this because it looks good." But what did happen to me was what most composers never get the luck to do. *Cats* changed my life. Up to then I'd done fine out of my music but not as well as everybody thought. *Cats* had this extraordinary success one would probably never be able to repeat.' (Later, *Phantom of the Opera* did.) 'And I thought, Hey! – I can take sixteen months off now and write something that nobody will ever perform.' And I did. I submitted it to two conductors who turned it down and finally to Lorin Maazel who said he'd like to give it a whirl.' (He plays some of it on the piano.) 'I mean, to put those chords together, it's just lovely. I'd love to hear the Everly Brothers do "Pie Jesu" one of these days . . . one can live in hope.'

Another factor might have been the crystal soprano voice of his second wife – who had been a dancer in *Cats* – Sarah Brightman. In *Phantom of the Opera* too, there was a part, the lead, which could appear to be written for her voice.

'It's funny – you get a subject offered you that you *don't* think is a very good idea and then somebody persuades you and you look again. I was offered *The Phantom* as something to produce and I thought of it as one of those slightly campy stories and I thought maybe it would be quite fun. I never thought it would be a subject for me to tackle as a composer. Then we went to see the man who was going to direct it and he said, "You are crazy. You should do it. Don't you realise it's one of the greatest love stories of all time?" I thought, No way!

'Then as happens, luck, I saw the book in New York for 25 cents and I thought I might as well have a copy of the old thing and read it to see if it's different to what I know. And it's *very* different. It's one of those wonderful opportunities for a composer because it's *not* a masterpiece. It's got some terrific things in it but I think I've been able to fashion it into something very different to anything that's been based on that subject before.

'The piece really is about someone who, through a physical deformity that he was born with, is unable to expose himself and could never expose himself particularly to a young girl singer whom he's tremendously in love with and who he writes music for.'

The score is sumptuous. Some of it is much darker than he usually does. He drove it through, the chandelier crashed down on cue. The audience rose to applaud at the end, the show's success and Andrew's superlative business acumen (another accomplishment taken to extremes of effectiveness) took it into billions ... and, as has happened again and again, millions of people enjoyed it hugely, bought the records and the CDs, hummed the tunes and had a great time at the theatre.

'I don't really know what I am going to do next. I want to take stock of a lot of things at the moment. There are no suites of *Evita* or *Cats* or *Superstar* – I'd quite like to do them myself and get back to doing orchestrations again ... I know something will emerge soon.'

There are many ways in which this man who, as the New York critic Frank Rich says, 'has a huge talent for anticipating public taste' is rather from the past. A time of an unashamed upper-class accent and uncommonly good manners, a time of 'wheezes' and other Wodehousian frolics. In his friendships he is matey, in his manner he can seem rather grand, even patrician. The man who remained bright-faced and boyish way beyond youth and early manhood now has the air of a landed gentleman, which indeed he is; and of the titled owner of a castle and other grand houses, which indeed he is. With his wife Madeleine, an outstanding horsewoman, he has made a dramatic entry into the sport of kings with a stud already in the top bracket in England. He will come from a rehearsal of his re-launch of the pop song 'She Wore an Itsy Bitsy, Teeny Weeny, Yellow Polka Dot Bikini' to make a strong speech in the House of Lords on, say, the state of the West End theatres, some of which he owns, or the English countryside, some of which he owns. There's no boxing him in, there's no putting him in one category. He is some sort of Renaissance Man, with his many well-worked gifts, the opulence of his houses, the collections and the huge circle of influential acquaintances and well-weathered old 'mates' who gather around for flights of talk, fantasy projects, always breaking down in laughter. They help him drink some of the wines of which, over the years, he has inevitably made a connoisseur's collection. And somewhere, quietly, in a faraway room, Edmundo Ros plays on.

Francis Ford Coppola

I met Francis Ford Coppola in San Francisco in 1979 when he was flying. He had directed *The Conversation*, a brilliantly original film on the new technology of surveillance. As well as a superlative performance by Gene Hackman, the film foreshadowed much of the imminent surveillance society. He had written and directed *The Godfather* and *The Godfather: Part II*, he had just finished *Apocalypse Now* and he was still a young man. He was as black-bearded as a Russian revolutionary thinker, as can-do, did-do-anything as any American could ever be, and he was Italian.

He was hours late for the interview we had set up in his office in a handsome period slice of Cheddar cheese building at an intersection near the city centre. Messages kept us informed of his progress. We were well supplied with coffee. His lateness was legitimate, not a diva display. We began the interview at about 9.30 p.m. after he had showered and changed and put on what looked like an unaccustomed tie. His office was deep in vast old leather sofas and the decorative clutter of a man with good taste. He must have been tired but he was insistent that he was not pressed and we talked until about midnight.

We were to start our documentary on him with part of the helicopter attack sequence in *Apocalypse Now* and I had looked at it again as I waited. With Wagner in my ears and San Francisco several floors below in excited preparation for a lavish gay ball, we began.

He was the first pupil out of the new film school in Los Angeles to get into the business. Like several others of his generation, he had been given a break by Roger Corman who did rapid turn-around cheap horror films: Coppola's film was called *Dementia 13*. Bravura hustling got him work on *Finian's Rainbow* and *You're a Big Boy Now*; his screen-writing talent got him *Patton*, for which he won an Oscar. Meanwhile he had built up what would prove to be one of the most successful and influential group of film makers in the history of movies.

'I'd worked in the theatre and I enjoyed a group; group effect. So I moved to San Francisco and other young film makers came and hung around the office. There was George Lucas, who was one of my students, Steven Spielberg, Martin Scorsese, John Milius. We wanted out of LA, to be independent and away from the unions, to be more liberal in our thinking, to edit our own films. I wanted a bohemian group. Instead of that, in no time we outgrossed Hollywood – and the success split up the group.'

Apocalypse Now came out of the group when it was working at its best. 'George Lucas and John Milius were full of these stories about the Vietnam War. They were so extraordinary. They were beyond every-thing I could imagine about war. A colonel would bomb out a village so that people could surf there. They would ride in helicopters dressed like the US Cavalry on horses. There was dope, there was LSD. I did what I always do. Got all the books I could find and researched it.'

A key decision was to use Joseph Conrad's novel *Heart of Darkness* sometimes as a spine, sometimes as a sounding board, sometimes as a guru. He got on with the script.

'I had two sides of how I felt. First, America has always done what other great powers have done – push weaker powers around. But America has always said they did it to help someone. In *Heart of Darkness* Conrad writes: "I have always loathed the stench of a lie." When Genghis Khan took Persia it was honest. In Vietnam America carries the stench of a lie. They say they are protecting Vietnam. They are destroying it.'

As we addressed *Apocalypse Now* we intercut scenes from that film: in one of which is surely one of the most memorable lines in all cinema. Lieutenant-colonel Kilgore, bare-chested, on the field of battle as the bombers sweep in behind the helicopters, squats on his haunches and tells his young squaddies (the 'grunts') about the preparation of napalm which is making a bonfire, a lurid wash across the sky above the trees behind him: he says, 'I love the smell of napalm in the morning.'

'There is a feeling that the American political life has been destroyed as much as Vietnam. You don't deal with that.'

'I chose to deal with a very specific area. I wanted to put the audience through an experience so that they *knew* it. Not to hear those idiots who are still around, talking about it, making money. They have nothing interesting to say. We know what happened in Vietnam. I wanted to give the audience an experience which they could digest for themselves.'

He did. And he went out on a limb. The film cost $30 million and he put up half himself from the profits made in the *Godfather* films.

Despite its wild, spontaneous, psychedelic appearance, the film holds tightly to story and character and is lashed to authenticity.

'If you see a beer, it's the right beer for that time even though we had to remake the labels.'

'Are the three key elements still casting, casting and casting?'

'Talent casting. A director finds real talent in other people. I interviewed Vietnam veterans and some Vietnamese people and cross-compared stories without cheating. Every detail in that film is correct. The helicopters, the troops landing – you can ask any Viet-veteran: it's correct.'

'Film inevitably glamorises, doesn't it?'

'I can't believe anyone seeing *Apocalypse Now* would want to participate in a war.'

'I don't know. A seventeen-, eighteen-year-old, those helicopters, that music!'

'That's a six-minute sequence. I wanted to show how people could be thrilled in a helicopter spraying people with bullets. There's so much hypocrisy.'

'Robert Duvall. The Colonel. Dressed up in a yellow scarf, the John Wayne costume?'

'They were kids, seventeen, eighteen. They found a John Wayne figure very comforting. Some of them [the officers] found that by being that sort of figure they would be followed into battle.'

'You'd been there before to some extent when you wrote *Patton*.'

'With his pearl-handled revolvers.'

'Ivory-handled. Your script.'

'When they asked me to write *Patton* I thought he was a cruel war general. I had a problem. My producer was a general. So if I wrote Patton as a killer and a sadist I'd get fired. If I made him a hero, all my friends would turn against me. I made him a sort of Don Quixote figure. A great general, but a monster.'

We cut to a speech Patton makes to the troops. He is standing in front of a gigantic American flag. He wears leather riding boots, jodhpurs, his medals . . . His message is emphatic. 'Americans love to fight. As kids, they like the fastest runner, the toughest boxer . . . I wouldn't give a hoot in hell for a man who lost and laughed . . . All real Americans love the story of battle . . . that's why Americans never have and never will lose a war . . . The army is a team. All that individuality stuff is crap. The bilious bastards who wrote that stuff about individuality don't know any more about real battle than they do about fornicating . . .'

There's a gusto in that speech which is surely part of the truth of things as Coppola sees it. There is a pleasure and excitement in making war, the speech says, and solely to wring our hands is to fail to understand all that.

We turned to *The Godfather* and I asked him about working with actors, Marlon Brando in particular.

'Marlon has heard everything before. He has distaste for people who try to "handle" him. I deal with actors in a sensual way, a quiet rehearsal situation, like the theatre, comfortable chairs, a lot of tables, with hundreds of props on them – a cigarette lighter, glasses, bottles, books, an actor can take what he wants. Actors are frightened. And along the way I set up improvisational rehearsals. That was the biggest success I had when we were rehearsing *The Godfather* – to set up an Italian dinner.

'Marlon was at the head of the table. My sister – who was in the film – served the food – they were playing at being the family. Al Pacino was silent to try to attract Marlon's attention, Jimmy Caan cracked jokes, Robert Duvall looked a bit out of it. And it worked. Because they all loved Marlon, he was so important to them, just as they loved the Godfather.

'Once an actor has found his track, the director is merely the actor's eyes. He sees the product and tells him what he saw.'

We showed the scene in which Brando turned down the offer of a deal with another Mafia gang who ran drugs. In a few minutes we see the apparatus of a formal heads-of-state encounter; made serious by Brando's grave and courteous demeanour. There is the silent but decisive rebuke by Brando to a son – Jimmy Caan – who interrupts him and begins to talk about the family's business. This is done without humiliating the son but without any room for doubt. At the conclusion of the meeting, the non-deal, Brando says no to drugs and explains why it would be bad for his business, congratulates the man on his business success, shakes his hand, and we see the exit of the delegation. Then Brando quietly calls back the errant son and, transformed into frightening authority, tells him never to talk in public about the family again and dismisses him. It is a quiet tour de force, beautifully written, directed and acted, a masterpiece in itself inside a film of great style.

But, I said, 'despite Brando's immense qualities which bring compassion and sympathy to the part, he still runs a Mafia outfit. People get destroyed.'

'I've seen movies about Francis Drake. They were killers. On the level of genre movie there are the good bad guys and the bad bad guys. When people talk like that – most of the films they like are like that.'

'Why do people talk on that level, then?'

'Because the Mafia's frightening and still something real. I was hired as a quasi-bankrupt film maker to make the book.' By Mario Puzo. 'Look at Bond and Eastwood movies. They're killers, right through the movie. *The Godfather* had real performances. It had pedigree. James Bond. Nine films. He's a murderer.'

'But the idea is he's defending great freedoms. And he's a good bad guy.'

'So the moral question is which side wins.'

We would get nowhere.

The keyword, he was right, was genre; and it is true that there are good bad guys and bad bad guys and a pursuit of counter-opinion would not add to what had been said.

Back to *Apocalypse Now* and the actual filming of it.

'You can't photograph something without glamorising it. Then again I believe it's good to see the glamour of war. Everybody says they would not have any part of this. So who are the people shooting all the people? Have you ever walked down a street with a loaded gun in your pocket? You feel powerful. We feel powerful with a loaded gun. We all want to feel important and powerful. There's a tremendous pleasure in war. Unless we talk about it in all its aspects, we'll not know it.'

Then he threw in a grenade.

'I am seriously believing there will never be another war. I believe that. It's the most ludicrous notion to think that it's possible.'

It was a full stop.

'Is there a tendency, when there's so much technology involved, that the characters tend to get flattened?'

'There are different ways to treat character. In Noh theatre, in Kabuki, in Shakespeare. I'm very capable, as you see in my other films, of creating "characters" who cry and such. But here I wanted some prototype characters – the good black guy, the kid from the Bronx – but I think the performances are as good as in *The Godfather*. They're just not pushed in your face. It's hard to give a subtle performance. Martin Sheen in *Apocalypse*, Pacino in *Godfather: Part II* – they created a character to suit the drama. I'm proud of them. You can have any style you like as long as it's naturalistic. You have a little crippled boy in a chair. And his father says, "Walk." And the little boy tries. "Walk!" And he *does* walk. And everybody cries and says it's great acting. And I don't want to make naturalistic films any more! There's fantasy and psychology.' He stretched out his arms. 'There's all of this!' Then he pulled them together until the hands almost touched. 'And all we use is this.'

In *Apocalypse Now* Marlon Brando plays Kurtz, the man at the end of the quest up the river, which becomes more like Conrad's novel. Kurtz is a figure of great power, thought to exercise it for evil ends.

'Of all actors Brando is the one who has the most mystery. And I knew him from *The Godfather* and the two of us together again would help with the financing.'

It was not made easy.

'We were on the last section but we were waiting for Marlon to arrive in the Philippines to get an indication of how he would play it. I worked on different endings. By that time, *Apocalypse* had seized itself and said, "I will not be the movie you want me to be." '

It was late, we had been talking for some time, Coppola had come from an exhaustingly busy day and though neither his courtesy nor that pulse of driving energy had slackened, there had been tensions – as when we discussed the morality of the Mafia. Now he seemed to think himself back into the last days of filming *Apocalypse* in almost mystical terms.

'Marlon was big. So I wrote Kurtz as a lustful man, letting himself go, a Gauguin figure with a girl and food but Marlon didn't like that. So there was a dialogue. I asked Conrad for his guidance. Francis doesn't want to make it your average blow-up-the-bridge-at-the-end-of-the-movie film. Marlon is big. What do we do? Conrad said, "Don't be afraid to push it into myth." '

'How far did the myths of that part of the world enter into it? I asked. One of Kurtz's well-thumbed books is Frazer's *The Golden Bough* and one of the stories/myths is the idea of killing the old bull. The Old King has to be killed in order for life to go forward.'

'Yes. People were outraged that I'd lifted that from *The Golden Bough*. You can lift whatever you want. That's why it's there. It's the oldest story there is. The most true. The old must die so that the new can be born. I'm giving the audience an experience of war in a new way, an experience they've never had before which will enable them to get out of it. Maybe America could kill the old and turn into a new America. This country is sick. The Vietnam War and 150 years of various colonial adjustments . . . It's a strange movie. But the audiences are *enormous*. People come out talking about what the ending means. About morality. A couple of years ago they were talking about sharks.

'I did what I intended to do and now I'm ready to go on to the next movie.'

We stay a while as the cameras were packed away. His manners were strikingly fine. He was the instant Godfather to this English delegation. Go to the Gay ball, he urged and phoned up to arrange tickets. San Francisco was past midnight, humid, and the searchlights from the ball stroked the sky. As we left he gave us advice on making money. 'Buy film,' he said solemnly, 'any footage. Francis says buy film. Soon the world will want all the film it can get.'

Coppola went on to make other fine movies but his name, his legend was already in place when we met in San Francisco. I could feel – and you can see on screen – the sense of strain under the composed courteous manner, and in his attack on the subject, any subject. Everything at that time was food for the hunger of Coppola to wolf it down and store it for future films.

Coppola was the personification of Modern Movies. He was an expert on their history, their content, the actors, the cameramen, the writers, directors: they had consumed his life and he had added to the fire.

When I first saw *The Godfathers* I had worries about the 'Family'. But the worries were more likely about my reaction. Where were the broken knees and cigarette-burned arms of the 'little guys' who did not pay up on time? Where was the bullying and intimidation in the outside world: not between gangs but between the predator gang and the prey?

I still think that is legitimate. But after the interview I saw the film again and partly due to what Coppola had said I saw that these, together with *The Conversation* and *Apocalypse Now* were of such a high order of film-making that they earned the right to deal with the subject as they pleased. Homer's warriors were brutal but heroes they remain. What legitimates his films as art is the telling, the making of them, which puts them in a box umbilically joined to but sufficiently independent of 'real' life which they also portray. Coppola has class: he was, he is, a contender.

Toni Morrison

I'd read Toni Morrison's novel *Song of Solomon* and thought there was a new voice in the land. *The Bluest Eye* and *Sula* confirmed it for me and in 1981 *The South Bank Show* went to America to interview her.

It's fair to say that at that time she was little known in the UK. Those who knew her work were passionate about it. I remember being urged on by Nikos Stangos, the poet and editor at Thames & Hudson. His passion for her work certainly strengthened my decision to make the trip. We often did short films in those days and this was one of three films in the programme. But there was, I thought, after that first interview, so much more to be said. Six years later I went back and did a second, full programme on *Beloved*.

Toni Morrison has a magnificent house on the pebbled shore of the Hudson River an hour from New York. The house, at the water's edge, is three-tiered, balconies all the way up, light, spacious, framed by huge trees. Although it was once the servants' quarters for a great estate, it seems, now, to *be* the estate. It was there we went to film the interview.

The Song of Solomon had won prizes: Toni Morrison had a parallel career as a senior editor at the publisher Random House. She was also already a star lecturer. She is a very handsome woman, relaxed about the film crew in her home; however careful they are, they can seem invasive.

There's not a long backlist of black writers of American fiction – Richard Wright, Ralph Ellison, James Baldwin. The ranks grew exponentially as the twentieth century swung on but Toni Morrison,

70

in 1981, was still quite rare. She was also different. From her novels it appeared she was not interested in confrontation between black and white people – there's only one white character in those first three novels. She concentrated on the black 'tribe', as she calls it, and much of what she did was based on her own upbringing in a small town in Ohio.

Her speaking voice is sonorous and lulling, soft but emphatic, always steady.

'There are writers I admire – James Baldwin I *love* – but their address was to someone just over my shoulder. They were not enlightening *me*. There are some things I wished I had read which I didn't read because the books weren't there. My books address the people in the book, in that village, in that life. They are the ones who tell me it's authentic. That's the life I want to recollect with metaphor as well as plot.'

'Baldwin was explaining blacks to whites. You were talking to the blacks about themselves.'

'That's exactly what it is. There was no literature saying to black people – let me tell you what we *have*. Let me tell you who we *are*.'

'The music?'

'The music had kept us alive. But it may not any more. It's all out there. It doesn't have the made-up soul sense quality it used to have. It's very slick now. Everybody knows how to do it. Before, it was *ours*. People used to sing in the streets.'

'Can you talk about the place you were brought up?'

'Everybody reared us. All the women reared us. We were accountable to everybody. They could stop us, they'd praise us, they could punish us. Everybody knew everything about one another. When we grow up we think of that as meddling. The churches – such as the one my mother and our family went to – they were places you could go to and have a fit, and cry and shout, and say, 'Why me?' in the company of people you trusted and then come out and go to work the next day. Where can you do that now? People took care of each other. It was a *duty* to take care of the sick. There were no orphanages. You never *needed* the institutions. What agencies do now, black people did. And of course the language and the legends were there.'

'Legends?'

'I thought they were local. I've discovered they were *everywhere*. One, that before black people came to this country as slaves, they were able to fly and some of them still had the gift. Somebody went round the States and asked, "Know anyone who could fly?" Everybody said, "Yes." *Everybody* knew about it. I used that in *Song of Solomon*.

'Your family?'

'My mother was a fiery intelligent woman. *Her* mother more so. And then *her* mother came, my *great*-grandmother, and I saw my grand-mother sit on the edge of a table and swing her legs like a girl – it was just unbelievable – because my great-grandmother was God's God. A woman who could not read *anything*.

'People came to her from all over. She was a midwife. She was a coun-sellor. She was a really *brilliant* woman. There were lots of women like that. I had an aunt, 104, never read, owned property all over.

'These women had had life-threatening lives. My great-grandmother left Greenville, Alabama, in the middle of the night. Her husband was away, playing the violin. Sending money back. The daughters were reaching puberty. This is Alabama 1907 – dangerous. White men would round up black girls who reached puberty and she was fright-ened to stay there without a man. She had to leave at night because she was hugely in debt. Share-cropping *is* debt. They caught the train, all seven of them. She wrote to her husband: 'I'll be on the train. If you want to see us again, you'd better join up on that train.' He joined them. She had no idea where they were going. I thought: If they can do *that*, maybe I can do *this*.'

'Does your anger break through when you think about it?'

'I'm not *able* to think about that. Just as I can't read books about South Africa or about the Native Indians in this country. I don't have the discipline. It gets quite out of hand with me . . .'

So far she had sat back, relaxed but wholly alert, not a nuance un-noticed, watchful, careful. Now she leaned forward. Threw her hands in the air and said, 'I'll tell you what! I'll tell you the truth. How about that?'

72

I waited. Her voice dropped and when I was watching the tape for this piece I had to play it three times to catch the words, so quietly were they spoken.

'I always felt superior to white people. I think it's because I was the only black child in my first-grade class and the only one who could read. I was always smarter than they were. There were *some* who were as smart as I was but I always felt superior as my mother and father always thought we could do *anything, really*. Then I went to a black college, then to a white graduate school and I felt quite comfortable there. I never was in *awe* of white people, never. And it was a long time before I could figure out why black people had it. There are lots who have it. Awe and fear.'

By now we were back in her original mode.

'I have great respect for many white people I know – but not fear and awe. I don't think they have much knowledge of the range and impact of black culture in this country. It is *enormous*. As a matter of fact, it *is* American culture. There isn't any other except a response to the Old World. American music *is* black music. There's nothing else that's American. That's what jazz is, that's blues and gospel – that's *ours*. That's a gift to the country.'

The work at the publisher Random House?

'My presence in Random House – I *love* the work – I am there to make certain Third World literature gets its full attention.'

It was to be a short film and the interview was coming to an end. We were in one of the rooms overlooking a broad span of the Hudson, the water slapping over the pebbly beach, New York an hour and a century away.

'This house is *mine*. When I came down the stairs the first time I saw it, my father was there, and he's been dead a long time now, so I knew it was my place. Right here, by the river, in these servants' quarters. Which is what it was. I wish it weren't in a place quite so ritzy but I can't help that! I've got friends. About eight close friends that make up a family.'

'Are they all black?'

'Yes.'

'Is that a bit sad?'

She paused.

'Oh no. I have my white friends. But when the trucks come down the road and some go to that side and some to *that*, I have to know who I can trust.'

We packed up and went down the road for lunch. As often happens, off camera had elements which can rarely if ever be caught on camera and Toni Morrison was in high form, stories, an ebullient anecdote about meeting Muhammad Ali – 'It's my time to shine,' she said, and the lunch lasted until late afternoon.

On the way out we stood apart and talked a little and she said, 'Tell me. Do you have any close *black* friends among *your eight*?'

'No.'

'Is that a bit sad?'

I thought we made a good film but I wanted another chapter and so we returned to her house in 1987, just before her novel *Beloved* was published in the UK. With *Beloved* her reputation, already high, soared: the book was made into a film, and when Toni Morrison won the Nobel Prize six years later, it was *Beloved* that placed the result in no doubt.

It begins in Cincinnati in 1973. A black woman, Sethe, has escaped from slavery. The house in which she lives with her teenage daughter is haunted by her dead baby whom she murdered when the slave catchers tried to take her back into slavery. In the course of the novel, the dead child returns, reincarnated as Beloved, a young woman. And tragedy starts to repeat itself. Around this situation, the novel moves back and forth in time, explaining the devastating physical, spiritual and psychological effects of slavery on her characters.

Toni Morrison began, in the same room as six years before, by talking about the true story behind the novel.

'There was a black slave woman, Margaret Garner, who escaped from Kentucky in 1855. She got to Cincinnati with her four children and lived with her mother-in-law who was a teacher and was caught by slave catchers. When she saw them she ran out to a shed behind her house and succeeded in killing one but tried to kill all four. She hit the boys on the head with a shovel, cut one of the girls' throats and was about to slam the baby's head against the wall. She was made much of by the abolitionists of the time who said, you see, how terrible it is. Because when she was interviewed – she was a young woman in her twenties, and the pictures of her, she's so serene, she was not crazy, she was not frothing at the mouth, she simply said, "They *can't* live like that. I will not permit them to live the way I lived."

'For me that was the ultimate gesture of the loving mother. Also the outrageous claim of a slave. The last thing a slave woman owns are her children. As an expression of her pain, it is extreme, but on the other hand, when you think of the way that mothers and fathers relate to their children, you say to a child you, of all things, cannot be sullied. Because that is the best part of you, that's the immortality, that's the best thing you've ever done. So you move that whole collection of emotions into this desperate circumstance and you say, "I prefer to kill my children. It's preferable to have them die." '

We illustrated the first part of this interview with graphic period drawings and photographs. These were the constant accompaniment to Toni Morrison's background descriptions which outlined the brutality of the transport to and history of slavery in the New World. There was the Middle Passage – the horrific, often fatal journey from Africa to America where the surviving slaves were separated from their families and mostly from others in their tribe. They were sold to the highest bidder and put to work, permanently at the risk of beatings, torture and lynchings. We illustrated the last point with a photograph of four black men strung up from a tree, crudely hanged in a clumsy way guaranteed to take time to send them to death. This oppression lasted for hundreds of years and millions of slaves were involved. We showed men and women in iron neck collars, chained, strung between poles like a horse in front of a cart. Toni Morrison did not confront this horror head-on but, mostly, used it as the background to the book.

'Other slave books leaned heavily on the horror of the institution, the physical brutality, in a sort of abstract way in which a group of black people were being forced to do something because they were being brutalised. What I wanted to do was to put the locus, the heart of the story, within the minds of the slaves themselves and have the white people drift away, be the background so that I could concentrate on the slaves.'

She writes how slaves got 'rented out, bought out, bought back, stored up, mortgaged, stolen or seized, beaten, tricked and, of course, raped, so that Baby's eight children had six fathers.'

In this interview, Toni Morrison was both more controlled and also, I thought, under control, much more angry than I'd seen her before.

'Was there a sense in which you were drawn to slavery or the post-slavery condition of people in America as part of the start of the book?'

'Quite the opposite. I was always frightened. It would never occur to me to go into that area. I never thought I had the essential resources to deal with slavery. In fact I thought it was a very contemporary story I wanted to write about self-murder – the reasons we can sabotage ourselves with the best of all possible intentions. Then the story occurred to me of Margaret Garner who had indeed killed a child when she was a slave, so I was sort of pulled into slavery by this other idea. But since it was such a classic example of what I wanted to write about, I had to do it. And I thought – I never liked books about slavery, they were always so big and flat and you could never get close to them. So I thought if I did something narrow and deep it would be successful. Slavery. It's like having World War Two for 200 years. It's exactly like that.'

From now on, until the interview turned to the appearance of *Beloved*, it was accompanied, almost stalked, by terrible images, the more effective for being crudely drawn – but always full of terror and pity. There's a slave child being burned and a group of white men looking on – there's a slave being branded on the back. There are slaves being thrown out of ships to lighten the load in a storm. And more hangings.

'Two things were clear. I had done the same thing that *most* Afro-Americans had done. That is, not remember. Because you can't if you want to get up and go to work the next day. The other thing was to absorb a little but not the totality because it's paralysing and that became the question when I came to research the book. I found there wasn't a great deal of information.

'Now that may sound surprising because there's a lot of history and songs and folklore. But there was something untold, unsaid, that never came down, some deliberate, calculated, survivalist intent to forget certain things.

'There were almost no references. No songs. I knew no songs about it. I knew no stories about it, about the trauma of that voyage' (across the Atlantic) 'and the deaths that took place on it. They don't exist. One has to go to the white slave ship captains and owners for that information because frequently when they were about to die they wrote their life stories as a sort of confession, but almost nothing came down to *my* generation.'

Beloved. 'There will never be a time when I am not crouching and watching others crouching too.'
'If we had more to drink we could make tears.'
'Somebody is trembling . . . he is trying to leave his body.'

'The other things that were forgotten were the collection of tools that remind you of the Inquisition. Over and over again one can find in the diaries of a very prominent slave family in Virginia, "He would say, 'Put the bit on her today.' " In one passage alone there are eight references to "having the bit put on her". So what I was trying to do was to find out what do they mean by "a bit"? Like a horse? And the restraining things. Like the masks they wore.' We saw drawings of three women in iron masks which covered their heads, leaving only holes to breathe through. 'Presumably to keep them from eating the cane they cut. When they took them off, the skin would come right off. There was a real industrial age invention about some of those things. Hooks, collars, mouthpieces. They did for me. First of all they surprised me – although I *sort of* knew it – but as a writer it was something I could attach myself to.'

'You've talked about this late medieval apparatus. You mentioned "the bit" – the horse's bit – which you use with tremendous power in the novel.'

'It had important meanings for me. First, there's the thing itself. The obscenity of having this instrument go in your mouth. As it turns out, it's not at all like a horse's bit. It's a tongue, a metal tongue that goes into your mouth with a circle around it like the tongue of a shoe, and you can tighten it and bring it in. It's acutely painful. It's also inhuman. They thought slaves were animals.

'The next thing is they stop you from talking. As a human being you do not speak and having no language is the final devastation. And that kind of restraint little by little by little, atom by atom by atom, *should* destroy you, certainly spiritually, and all your human qualities would evaporate. So it had, for me, in essence, what the whole institution was about. People not being put in a hole or a cell, but to *work* this way, to cook, to nurse, to change the linen, to plough the fields with these instruments attached to them. It was very successful in a way. But what is always striking is when it wasn't.'

So the victims become the heroes. Some of the slaves master their condition and set the great example, the tongue-clamped speak.

'I am just repeatedly overwhelmed by the heroism of these *ordinary* people. When I was a little girl, it was taught to me that slaves in this country managed to be free because there were some very serious, well-meaning white people who thought it was a good thing to do. It never occurred to me that there were these active, original, serious, risk-taking black people who developed other lives and their principal life was to help escaped slaves.'

'Resistance to slavery wasn't only physical,' I said. 'Baby, in the north, in the novel, gives a sermon about spiritual survival in the face of the brutality.'

'The past, the heritage of black people and under-educated people is oral and we tend to diminish that knowledge because it is not in print. It has something to do also with the distinction made between those who read and those who do not. But the ability to remember is the ability to say it, to repeat it, as a metaphor. What she's saying there is quite different from anything you would have in a grand church. It's a very clear picture of how the *soul* can survive under the circumstances. *They* don't love it. *You* have to love it.'

From the novel: 'Love it. Love it hard. They don't love your flesh, they despise it. They don't love your eyes, they do not love the skin on your back, they flay it. And o my people, they do not love your hands . . .' [and on the passage goes] – 'through the body, the mouth, the neck, the liver, the heart . . .'

Toni Morrison took it up. ' "They will not hear anything coming from your mouth so love it. They will break your neck, so stroke it and anything you *imagine* you can have. There is no grace but you can imagine it." This would come from that tradition of sermonising. It would come from that feeling black people always have for language. It surfaces in our culture in a lot of ways – when one listens to the speeches of Martin Luther King, Jesse Jackson, people say, "They're extraordinary speakers." But that's the way all those people talk because of the whole idea of styling the message in biblical terms, parables and what have you. They do not expect you to listen silently as in the Western tradition. Something visceral is supposed to happen. You're supposed to tap your feet, or say Amen or jump up or dance. There is the connection between the orator and the listener.'

'Is there any sense in which you want to idealise or mythologise these people?'

'I don't, you see. My grandfather was born a slave. And my great-grandmother. It's extraordinary what they did to get through sixty years of existence. So I thought, I'll cut them down to size and make them digestible but I couldn't. So when I've been accused, and a lot of the time I *have* been, of making characters larger than life, I realised that what I had in fact done was simply describe characters who were as large as life. Life *is* that large.'

When Beloved comes into the story it is both seamless and, simultaneously, a whole different tone. The locus becomes the house. The character of the house holds all the tension, all the love all the problems.

'And it is the domain of women.'

'Oh yes. Because it's important in a slave society that there be no connection. Otherwise there would be marriage ceremonies and you can't have marriage where you're not allowed to have legal children. Slavery reproduced its own product that was also for sale. Everything was done to make sure that these men were not at all feeling responsible for women and children.

'And I wanted to use my language. To write very simply which is what I do but the elaborateness, the ornate, the rich quality of my work that some people have called it, really comes from simple sentences in which the reader is invited in with his own emotions. You can't use fiery language to describe a fire. You have to use quiet language so the fire can be seen.

'There's another stage in the novel where the three women – the mother, the daughter and the "resurrected" Beloved – trade, exchange, invest in each other's personalities. Sethe is talking and then Denver, her daughter, is talking and the woman she believes to be her resurrected daughter is talking and they begin to take *into* each other, taking on each other's personality, each other's feelings and language.

'These are unspeakable thoughts unspoken, done as soliloquies – interior language shaped by what they could not say to each other directly, but certainly everyone understands. They all need each other *so much*, individually and collectively, that they form this triad of desperate need to love the other and to have their love also. Ultimately I wanted the language to be spoken in such a way that each sentence, when they are all talking at the same time and clearly it's a sentence by one or the other, but they become like a threnody, a song of desire.'

From the novel: 'Beloved you are my sister.

You are my daughter.

You are my face.

You are me. I have found you.

You've come back to me.

You are my Beloved.

You are mine.

You are mine.

You are mine.

You are mine.

You are me.'

'The child comes back as a real woman, Beloved. It's a resurrection. Can you talk about that?'

'The idea of resurrection is not alien or foreign in the black culture. The notion of a child reappearing in the guise of a cousin or a friend is not at all unusual. The resurgence of spirits and the ability to be possessed by another spirit, to actually exist in other things, human beings as well as non-human beings, is not outrageous. It's not foreign. So it seemed to me in the milieu with a slave population in 1853 through to post-civil war 1873, it was very much in the realm of possibility. So you have a mother who hasn't seen her child since she was two and all she would need would be the *signs*. So she appears and all the *signs* are there.'

From the novel: 'Beloved could not take her eyes off Sethe. Sethe was licked, tested and eaten by Beloved's eyes . . . She is everywhere for Sethe. At her going out . . . and her coming in . . . Sethe would not have welcomed this from a daughter . . . This attention pleased her as a zealot pleases his teacher.'

'And then you use the ancestors of the characters in the book. They're there. They're spoken to. What value does this have for you as a fiction writer?'

'It's part of my feeling that what is really infinite is the past. The future always appears to me to be finite. The past is *infinite*. There's so much back there to mine from and part of black culture has to do with the intimacy between the self and the ancestors. The ancestor fills a place no parent can. It's benevolent, but with no pressure, that's always accessible.'

'From Margaret Garner to *Beloved* was a long journey?'

'It rocked me in a way no other work I've done has done. There was so much more to remember and to describe for purposes of exorcism and of the rites of passage, some fixing ceremony must be made, some memorial, some altar somewhere where those things can be realised, thought and felt. There are certain things that *only* artists can deal with. It's our job.'

If the democracy of American literature would allow for a grande dame then Toni Morrison is now one of those. She has turned the tables on one of the basic stories of the founding of the States. She is listened to, and rightly, respected, and rightly. Her place in the aristocracy of letters has been well earned. And as we talked, just those few years on from the rather bouncy, even at times rather edgy, first encounter, there was a serenity about her, as from one whose work has been realised and whose message, whose history has been signed, and sealed.

Afterwards we had tea, on one of the balconies overlooking the Hudson. Behind us were the rich woods where Native Americans had lived well until they were wiped out by the settlers from the Old World.

Alan Bennett

'You only feel a writer, it seems to me, when you're actually *doing it*,' said Alan Bennett, in his study in Camden Town. 'But between *being* it and *doing* it, though, the writer sometimes has no choice. Philip Larkin was someone who, on his own admission, ceased to be able to do it for the last ten years of his life, in the process becoming more famous for not doing it than he had been for doing it. And this happened to E.M. Forster. But any writer will tell you that though the sales and the plaudits come not with doing it but having done it, the best medal to have would be, as it were' – he looked at his typewriter – 'won in the field of battle. In recognition of yet another fruitless morning spent at the typewriter. Or after a week' – he looked up to the window – 'or even months spent staring out of the window.' (And the camera rested on Alan staring through the half-closed venetian blinds which enabled him to see out but no one to see in.)

After an opening sequence of Alan, rather unaccountably wheeling his basket-fronted bicycle in Primrose Hill in North London, a few hundred yards from where he then lived, we had got into the study, not pausing to linger on the fine art collection, straight to the lair. The table is modest, easily dominated by the heavy upright typewriter. A cup of tea; a couple of biscuits; a couple of personal items; neither minimalist nor extravagant: just right. There was no paper in the typewriter.

That opening piece was delivered as a performance. He wore one of his fifties' ties, this time, as often, blue with the inevitable blue shirt. His clothes are generally stuck in the intellectual fifties, his haircut in the rational forties, his accent in the pre-war Yorkshire droll. It is an accent resurrected, he once told me. It was Leeds-Yorkshire as a boy, Oxford-purged as a young man, but Yorkshire Dales-restored when he hit his London stride. Perhaps that too is part of what can appear a perfect public invention: himself.

He is certainly happier in a performance than in an interview which is one reason he gave them so rarely. He has been intensely private until recently. Yet he appears so easy to read because of the open undenying public face, the defender of public libraries, the champion of cyclists, the mocker of politicians, a man whose stance and bons mots have gathered devotees who relish quoting him. His sentences gather like smooth pebbles in their pockets and when they take them out they find he speaks for them. The phrase 'A National Treasure' irritates him, and any study of his work would demonstrate the stratum of subversion and a darkness. But he has become a fixed and admired and then loved figure in the national landscape.

Before we leave that opening statement it might be worth noting how much of Alan is in it. The wit, the sentence turning, the easy references to and association with Larkin and Forster, the melancholy, the kick of hyperbole at the end which is faintly self-mocking, the willingness to perform and feel free in that mode.

Unlike the interview. We met in the morning in the upstairs of a pub near his house. It was a restaurant, empty at that hour, laid out for lunch, white tablecloths, expectant, the location for an Alan Bennett encounter. Enter the man himself, tall, newly cut hair, the daffodil-yellow tie tightly knotted just popping up over the rim of the dark pullover. He does not feel at home in interviews, he is wary and, unexpectedly, sometimes at something of a loss.

All the more tricky, in a way, because the man I have met, not frequently but a steady now and then over the years, generally with his friends, often mutual – Russell Harty, Tristram Powell, Gavin Millar, Jonathan Miller, Patrick Garland – has been unbuttoned. When you meet him privately he is as cheerful as can be. In company he is a rich giver, in constant pursuit of laughter. He is a first-class giggler.

Serious, diffidently erudite, trenchant, strong opinions in full working order, now and then curmudgeonly northern, as you would expect, but above all, someone who lights up the scene. To adapt from T.S. Eliot on Ralph Hodgson: 'How delightful to meet Mr Bennett. Everyone wants to know *him*.'

'You seem, in your notes and diaries and plays to be able to write about the most sensitive of things but you've already told me you find yourself very reluctant to do an interview. What's going on?'

'I don't talk very well.' He looks away. It takes some time before he looks anywhere near the camera. 'I mean writing, you've got time to get it right, whereas talking' – he shrugs – 'it's off the top of your head.' (It need not be, I think, but don't say – Francis Bacon? Ingmar Bergman? Denis Potter? Martin Amis? Norman Mailer?) 'Also I find that the more I talk the less I write and if I didn't write you wouldn't want to hear me talk anyway. You know, you say to me, "You dislike being interviewed," but' – he waves his hands expansively – 'here I am. Being interviewed. Graham Greene – there used to be an interview with him practically every week and he was supposed to be famously reclusive. I do readings. I do question and answer. *People* are more respectful of your privacy, I think, than journalists are, really.'

And yet in his new volume *Untold Stories* he has opened up his private life as never before. There had been a discussion about that before we did the film. There were things in the book he did not want to talk about. My opinion was that it was as if television were being regarded as a less adult medium than print. Alan of all people, whose television work – just *Talking Heads*, for instance – had explored and celebrated the medium as successfully as any contemporary playwright, ought to be challenged on that. Was the suggestion that we should do an interview but for certain episodes refer the viewer to the book? It was not quite formulated like that, but unmistakably, given his serious conviction that only in writing could he describe exactly what he meant and in the precise way he meant it, there was an impression that certain territory was too personal for a television interview. So that was one of the challenges.

'We're in Primrose Hill, in Camden Town. You've been here for thirty-five years or so.' Dug in. Especially into the street in which he lived, Gloucester Crescent, which became a nesting place for a generation of influential intellectuals. Michael Frayn, with whom Alan had done revues while on National Service; Claire Tomalin, the literary editor and eminent biographer; Mary-Kay Wilmers, editor of the *London Review of Books* in which Alan wrote his personal diary. And Jonathan Miller, who had been one of the Famous Four in *Beyond the Fringe*. With Alan, Peter Cook and Dudley Moore it had conquered the West End and Broadway. It had landed the superlatively talented quartet in massive and what Laurence Olivier once called 'the right sort of fame' and, one presumes, a sufficient and secure fortune. Since our interview Alan has moved house, after many many years, six hundred yards away.

'But you also have a place in Yorkshire near Leeds, where you were born and educated. Is there a north-south divide in your work?'

'Some stuff I write is metropolitan and hasn't really got a lot to do with the north. What I like about the north and what you don't find in London, certainly not in Camden Town, is the pleasure in language they still have.' And he segues comfortably into performance as the story comes out. 'I went into a supermarket in Settle to get some Parmesan. Parmesan I think is a relatively recent arrival in Settle . . . But anyway I went to the cheese counter and said, "Have you any Parmesan?" and he said, "Oh yes." Then he reeled off a list of Parmesan and finally he said, "And this is the Reggiani, the Rolls-Royce of Parmesans!" ' Alan is still delighted with the story, as am I, in the telling as much as the tale. 'Now you'd never get anybody in Camden Town saying that! "The Rolls-Royce of Parmesans"! My father never said, "I'll find out", he said, "I'll ascertain", and it's a slightly piss-taking way of talking, but it's got a lot of flavour still that language down here doesn't have.'

I doubt if the last sentence could have been improved had it been written and not spoken.

We went north with Alan and filmed him on the train and on the same theme, and once again he went into the comfort of performance: a much loved anecdote.

'Despite being called Customer Operations Leader and other such absurdities, the conductor still retains a degree of individuality. The train was coming into Leeds Station and the conductor announced, "We are now arriving at Leeds Station, may God go with you, if you'll only allow Him to." '

There are in that passage two of the characteristics of Alan's stance, as it were. As well as the wit, there's the dismissal of the new techno-jargon, empty-pomp, and a powerful nostalgia for an individuality, threatened, becoming an extinct species.

On the train again, this time going south.

'Going south always represented an escape for my parents until they actually tried it for themselves. It ended disastrously. But for writers or actors who've made this jump, the going south has always had a place in their mythology. Eric Portman got out of a Bradford Gents' Outfitters – my auntie claimed she had been served by him – J.B. Priestley got out, John Braine followed in his footsteps. So far as my mother knew the Brontë sisters never managed to. She'd never read the books but she'd seen the films. There was always a sense in which success for my mother and father was described by a one-way ticket to King's Cross.' At which the train docked; less than fifteen minutes from Camden Town.

Back in the upstairs of the pub.

'There was a lot of music in my childhood. My father was an amateur violinist and so we heard a lot of music at home. I've never thought much of the violin on its own. Thin stuff.'

'That's because you were no good at it, isn't it?'

When Alan laughs, he throws back his head and directs the sound at the ceiling.

'My father tried to teach me but it was hopeless. He seldom lost his temper but he did then. He took up the double bass as a way to augment his income as a butcher. He would work nights in a jazz band. His "Geraldo phase" my mother called it. No one was surprised when he never got far with the bass, quite literally, as they wouldn't let him put it on the trams.'

One of his father's customers was Leslie Whitemore, the leading violinist in the Yorkshire Symphony Orchestra in Leeds. 'He gave my parents complimentary tickets, so every week I used to go to concerts in Leeds Town Hall.' That priceless education is mentioned in *Untold Stories*. He also found a secondary association in discovering that Delius and Butterworth were from Yorkshire and therefore as real and touchable as core members of the orchestra, some of whom he travelled with in the bus on the way home. 'I saw that the men who'd made this ecstatic music were just ordinary people, tired, in mackintoshes.'

That connection between the sublime and the commonplace, which is a source for some of his best strokes of wit, might have been seeded on a late-night bus in Leeds sat beside a tired trombonist.

We took Alan to churches. Not that he needed encouragement. 'I've always liked looking in churches, though I'm not quite one of those who in Philip Larkin's words "tap and jot and know what rood lofts are" – though I do know what rood lofts are.' Anglican hymns from Hymns Ancient and Modern supplied the soundtrack. 'I've never found it easy to belong. So much about England repels. But in a church . . .' In one of his pieces he writes about learning hymns 'at a state school where we sang them every morning in assembly' and the diminishing band who now know them and can be picked out at weddings and funerals as those who sing the hymns without needing to look at the words.

I've 'followed' Alan's work since *Beyond the Fringe*. I've seen much of his work and from the revue sketches to the first plays to the monologues to the late plays I've enjoyed and admired his skill, his invention, his wit and his ability to encapsulate a moment in history as well as a story and drama in its own time. The previous film we made about him, twenty years before, was at the time of the filming of *A Private Function*. I don't think he did another television interview in the intervening years. This time we were in the frame of the publication of *Untold Stories* and the filming of *The History Boys* which, in a strong field, is for me his strongest play and the best new play I saw by a living writer in the year it was first performed.

Maybe here it's worth saying that the value of making a programme with an artist when they have work coming out is threefold: they usually have the time to spare and a useful overspill of anticipation – anxiety, excitement – which gives them the adrenalin for it; the public is alerted through the publicity given the new work in magazines and newspapers; and it gives the programme some journalistic edge.

The History Boys, which shows a number of state school sixth-form boys in the fifties being drilled through examinations to get to Oxford, is firmly based on Bennett's own experience.

'I went to a state school in the fifties and some went to university but very seldom to Oxford or Cambridge. In 1951 the headmaster pushed some of his boys towards the older universities. Snobbery was part of it; we switched from soccer to rugger at the same time. That had little impact on me. However about eight of us went up for examinations and all of us managed to get in, some with scholarships.'

Bennett had not had an untroubled school time. He was short for the first span of his teenage years until he suddenly 'shot up', over six feet. More cruelly, given an all-boys school, 'my voice did not break until I was sixteen and a half – I was a boy in a class of men which made me unhappy at school.'

There are two teachers in *The History Boys*: Hector the romantic and also the toucher-up of boys who is an inspired teacher of literature, interested in learning more than in exams; and Irwin, a supply teacher, who has analysed what Oxford examiners will be impressed by and trains the boys to beat the system.

'Irwin proceeds by strategies. That was based on me. That's how I operated and got the scholarship and also in my Finals at Oxford I did it in the same way.'

'You sound as if you disapproved of yourself.'

'It's a bit of a swizz, that's all.'

'Hector, in the play, is much loved – by the audience and by the boys. He seems the ideal teacher.'

'Indeed. In the sense that everybody would like to have learned reams of poetry at school. Nobody would have wanted Hector to educate their children, not because he touches them up on the back of his motorbike but because his kind of teaching wouldn't get them through any examinations at all.'

'But *you* would like that sort of Hector as a teacher?'

'There is a sentimental longing for that sort of thing. But it *is* sentimental. I just like the character. In a sense I'm not a good person to write about a school. I've no children. I haven't had to educate anyone. So I'm totally without responsibility. In that sense I can write what I want without thinking of the consequences and I – and I . . .' (pause) '. . . er . . .' (flaps his hands at the camera) 'so I can't . . . er . . . this is why I don't do interviews, Melvyn . . . agony . . .'

We cut to the playing fields of a Victorian school in Watford which was standing in for Alan's old school now demolished. The actors in uniform white shirts, black trousers and, when necessary, blazers, are in their early twenties 'but when they're together they act like fifteen-year-olds'. He says, 'I always feel a bit spare on a film,' but it's clear the cast love having him there and he is strolling along very contentedly.

They tease him because he won't join in their football and suggest he's got the legs for synchronised swimming. 'All right, all right,' he mutters and paddles away. 'They don't treat me with any respect which I find very refreshing. The fact that you're not invisible to them is a compliment in itself, because you usually find you're invisible to young people. They take the piss out of me – another compliment.

'Actors are very good company because of the relationship of their work in a play and *play*, so you've no need to feel your age. I'm seventy-one but I've no need to stand on my dignity. I can be silly and I like that. There's not enough silliness in life. I think that's what's wrong with politics. Too little silliness in Downing Street.'

He talked about working with Maggie Smith and Patricia Routledge and Thora Hird. 'I like working with the same actors because I know what they can do. Actors don't always find that welcome. They want you to see them in a new light and give them new things to do.'

One of the actresses he used often and tested most was Thora Hird, whose sense of humour is very like Alan's. When I interviewed her she made me laugh as much as anybody I've ever met, and all through the way she told true stories from her life. It's a gift, I think. Eric Sykes has it. It's storytelling, character, plot, cliffhangers, sudden twists and all encapsulated in, for example, some poor soul being persuaded to go into a shop to buy twelve frogs' feet for frogs' nest soup. Thora, who began as a glamorous film star, became a remarkable character actress, never better than when in one of Alan's monologues. 'Thora could play old people because she still had her marbles, almost right up to the finish.'

Alan's method of writing varies. When he writes about Anthony Blunt and the Queen, or George III's madness or, I presume, the still distant play on W.H. Auden and Benjamin Britten which is to go into the National Theatre, there is a state of preparation which differs from the observational method which so indelibly characterises his diaries, his monologues and some of his plays.

'I like looking out into the street,' he said, 'there's always something going on. You see things which are interesting and sometimes I put them in my diary and then go back to what I'm writing.'

At the time of this interview he was in the process of thinking about or beginning to (it was not wholly clear) move house and it bothered him a lot. Would the same conditions obtain? Would the view be as perfectly modulated? Might he thereby lose the knack? 'The knack?' I asked. 'Why that word?' 'Because it's the *right* word!'

Like all writers he watches his reputation although by any standards he has little to worry about. He picked up a copy of the Waterstone's Birthday Diary and read out a few of the entries. His was not among them. He gave the camera a neutral look. Henry Kissinger, of all people, once said that the reason writers care so much about rewards is because they are so small. Untrue. The stakes are as high as they come, the bet is a double – the present and the future. But the present could be a fashionable blip, and the future is frustratingly unknowable.

When Dr Johnson wrote that no man but a blockhead ever wrote for anything but money at least he was grounding the activity.

The Lady in the Van illustrates the observational Bennett.

He writes for the *London Review of Books* and *The Lady* first appeared there. Miss Shepherd had her broken-down van pushed into his front garden to stay for three weeks until it was sorted out. 'Miss Shepherd stayed for fifteen years. I could see her there, in the corner of my eye, she was a kind of diary. When I came to the play it was easy to write up, I had all the material. She died in 1989 but I could not write the play until ten years later.

'It took so long because I could tell *her* story, I couldn't tell my *own* story. And then I saw that the person who was writing the story was different from the person who was occasionally having to go out and interact as they say nowadays with Miss Shepherd. The observing Alan Bennett was different from the person who was having it all to do and once I saw you could write it for two people it became much more fun to write for a start. She wasn't in any sense a funny character. I don't think I ever saw a smile in the whole of her life. But funny things happened. Once when she was not too well I went out and asked, "Do you want a cup of coffee?" "No, I don't want you to go to all that trouble . . . I'll just have half." Then the other Alan Bennett inside writes that down but the Alan Bennett who gets the coffee is cursing like billy-oh.'

'Miss Shepherd could be seen as a counterpoint to your mother's later world?'

'My mother suffered from depression before my father died but after he died she was really seldom out of a depression for twenty years. It was only when she began to lose her memory that it lifted but by then it was too late. She just wasn't there any more.'

'You've written about it in this new book.'

'With difficulty. In the book it's part of a longer story. When my mother became depressed in 1966, it was very sudden, over a few weeks, apprehensive, lost all her sense of humour, frightened. It was an utterly mystifying condition that I'd never seen and neither had my father.'

She was admitted to the Mental Hospital in Lancaster which Alan described as Hogarthian. Used to the respectful hush of a normal hospital, the Mental Hospital was a place of wild dementia, scream- ing howling women, his mother literally unrecognisable, his father movingly answering her accusations by taking her hand and saying, 'Nay, lass.'

Alan has written about the visits made to Lancaster with his father. Although his older brother took the burden of it, his own attendance was regular and he seems to have got much from these fearful journeys with his father across the bleak spine of England.

It was at this stage where the memory of a No Entry sign loomed up, but by that time we were well into it. Even so . . .

'Is there any aspect of your life you didn't want to write about in your diaries or would write about but not talk about?'

There was not much of a pause, and perhaps a momentary steeling.

'I now live with my partner as I have done for fourteen years.'

I think this was the first time he had said that in a public place. Subsequently he spoke more easily about it and more often in public interviews.

Alan Bennett's sexuality had rightly remained Alan Bennett's business. There were, there always are, 'those in the know' but there was no wildfire comment, nor did he court it by in the remotest way 'flaunting it' or 'asking for it' as the tabloids might say to excuse themselves. I think it was in good part down to the respect in which he was held that the pack held off at a time when to be 'outed' could still be, or at least be seen as in one of several ways, damaging.

But now he had not only written about it but described a terrible attack made on Rupert and himself by some men on a beach in Italy one evening. The mistaken assumption was that they had been 'cruising': the 'law' concluded they were not only homosexuals but by being so disparate in age, doubly to be damned for that. The verdict more or less defends the actual battery to Alan's skull as a deed which satisfied the honour of Italian manhood.

I asked why he had published the most recent and open notebooks. Again, as in the previous question, he knew I knew the answer and that was OK privately but in public? But it *was* written. When you freeze frame, you see a hard look.

But he threw back his head, just as he does when he laughs, but this time he was forcing himself to a public revelation. First he addressed the ceiling. 'It's because . . . I suppose . . . a few years ago I had cancer . . . I'm in remission now and I'm fine. But the prognosis wasn't good and the prospect of death is a great diuretic – out it all comes – and I wanted to write it down because nobody else could tell the story but I thought it would all be posthumous. I didn't think I would live to see the book published. But then I survived and I'm well and I've got the book. I'm afraid I didn't have the moral strength to sit on it,' and he thawed into a warm, self-deprecating smile. 'So I published it.'

'Are you concerned what people say about what you write?'

'I used to be bothered. I'm not bothered now. No. That's a lesson of my parents' life. They were bothered all through their lives by what people might say about them. And it was terrible. They could have had so much a better time if they'd cared less about what people thought. They aspired all their lives to be like everybody else, to be ordinary people, but they weren't ordinary people. They would have been so much better recognising that.

'I live in Yorkshire some of the time in a little village and we go there and I think, there's thirty years' difference between Rupert, my partner, and me and what do they think? But I don't care what they think really. And that, at least, my parents have taught me. Not to care.'

It was over. 'Thanks.'

'All right, love.' He got up. 'It probably comes from those first experiences of being interviewed with Jonathan, in the shadow of Jonathan! With his perfect periods and ideas and so on, and me never being able to do it. No matter.'

The last shot's of him with his bicycle, still pushing it on the crowded pavements of Camden Town in the direction of Primrose Hill.

Francis Bacon

There's bound to be a truth in clichés some of the time or they wouldn't be. *In vino veritas* is less spouted now that there is less Latin about but still the notion persists that people when drunk tell the truth. That they also tell lies, come out with rubbish, destructive abuse, venom, hysterical hyperbole and all manner of degrading speech has not entirely impaired its claim. When Francis Bacon and myself appeared on *The South Bank Show* and for a few minutes were caught in a state of naked inebriation it provided, I think, a true insight into Francis as a man and as a painter. So I left it in the film.

We were at Mario's in Kensington after a long lunch, alone save for a film crew which dissolved before our blurry eyes as bottle succeeded bottle. Michelangelo, Francis proclaimed, had made the greatest drawings of nude flesh that existed. 'I have a different attitude to you,' Francis had just said, 'I like men. Male flesh is very interesting. It always attracts me in men. The brain and the quality of the flesh. Michelangelo gave the greatest male voluptuousness to the body.' The way he expressed the word 'voluptuous' warmed by much strong red Italian wine was vintage.

'It's a great word,' I said, through the haze, 'voluptuousness – we ought to live in a state of voluptuousness.'

'Yes,' said Francis, and repeated the word once more and then I suggested he was not interested in fantasy.

To be fair – but is *vino veritas* fair? – we had made a gradual but quite stately descent into this twilit zone. 'Fantasy? No, I'm not interested.

I'm interested in reality.' He glared at me, his face afire. 'There *you* are,' he said, 'Melvyn Bragg. Real. How do you render that in another art?'

'Why do you want to?' Off-camera, my voice seemed to call up from an open tomb.

'I want to be able' – each word perfectly clear despite the alcoholic breath on it – 'to make in another medium the reality of an image that excites me.'

Once more from afar, my voice. 'But why do you *want* to, Francis, why do you want to?'

At which he got to his feet, a redoubtable effort, picked up the bottle and steadily filled my glass once again. 'Because I want to. 'Cos I happen to be a painter. That's all.' The wine almost reached the brim. 'Cheerio,' he said and did not waste a drop.

I had first met Francis in the mid-sixties.

The house was in Knightsbridge. It was the most luxurious and by far the grandest town house I had ever visited. I was taken there by a fellow director at the BBC and his friend, a literary critic, both of whom had open sesame to this and other salons. The owner was dark, feline, almost excessively beautiful and, it seemed, as I looked around with all the connoisseurship of a twenty-four-year-old to whom privately owned grandeur had been hitherto a small suburban semi-detached house acquired on a mortgage with much difficulty, she was the proprietress or chatelaine of an urban palace. There were beautiful and real paintings and sculptures and rugs and furniture and well-connected people, many of them artists, including Paddy Leigh Fermor and Francis Bacon. I went several times, oscillating between brash and nervous, wondering when the recent patina of Oxford and the powder of the BBC Arts Department would wear off and reveal the working-class northerner with one good suit and nothing but his often over-forcefully expressed opinions to sustain him.

Perhaps Francis seemed to me then to be as much of a sore thumb as I felt. That was based on what I thought of his paintings. It was a mistaken assumption. He was not above claiming direct descent from the previous Francis Bacon, natural philosopher, chancellor, scholar and sexual adventurer of Elizabethan and Jacobean England. He could be an accomplished lounge lizard and was an initiate of the wealthy. He was also, though I had no idea at the time, a brutal masochist, a prince in the London homosexual world. I liked his paintings and I sailed in and asked him about painting and told him the Egyptians were my favourite artists. I remember that because he exploded into an eruption of agreement. They were, he said, the *only* great artists. The years 3000–2500 BC were the greatest years in the history of art.

Twenty years on, in the film we made, he was to repeat all of that and more. But what mattered in that overwhelming house in the sixties was that I had, by chance, found someone to talk to without feeling hedged in by the apprehensions and uncomfortable indecipherability of wealth and class and breeding. Quietly, modestly present: but still too strong to be able to ignore. Yet I think I exaggerate retrospectively, or analyse with unfair hindsight. It was a courteous, welcoming group, funny, unpretentious and oiled to have a good evening on equal terms with whoever turned up. Even so, I felt that of all of them, only to my friends and to Francis could I talk honestly. To Francis Bacon I could talk directly. The Egyptians were the key. Rameses lived on in Knightsbridge, London, England and Francis Bacon carried a torch for him and so did I.

Outside the Knightsbridge salon, Francis had a circuit of which I knew only a little and to which I never aspired. I knew some of them individually as time went on and circles overlapped. As in any cluster, there were the good, the bad and the dull but the circle was the swelling and contracting Soho-based swirl of artists, collectors, art historians, critics, hangers-on, drunks, drugs, rough trade, aristocrats, layabouts and criminals. Many of the company were gay when gay was queer and queer was homosexuality, a crime punishable by imprisonment.

It was not my swirl. In many ways it was as distant and strange as Pluto. The Francis I knew, on and off, over the next two decades, was someone met occasionally, by chance, and always there was a crash conversation, perhaps rather adolescent, about Great Ideas. It was pursued more like animals closing in on prey, terriers on a rat or leopards on an antelope rather than by any academic method or manner of discussion.

And so it meandered on. A metropolitan acquaintanceship the occasional encounter, happily shallow.

His paintings had disturbed and puzzled me, more the latter than the former, when I first encountered them. I was still struggling to absorb the manifold transitions from the Sistine Chapel ceiling and Rembrandt and Turner and Constable through the Impressionists and Fauves, to Futurists and any number of isms. Francis seemed to me to come almost, if anyone can, out of 'nowhere'. References could be made to Goya and van Gogh and others by those more learned than I but to me his *force*, which was, if it is possible to say this, more important than the paint, the figures, the structure, his *force* was a blow that stopped me in my tracks. As it does still.

In 1965 I was editing an arts programme on BBC2 and I persuaded the presenter, Julian Jebb, who knew Francis, to approach him ('he's totally opposed to that sort of thing') and do an interview. It was agreed. The interview was done by Julian and Francis was spellbinding and serene charm.

Some time later David Sylvester interviewed Francis on television and the result is a substantial programme in which the critic and the artist cover the spectrum his work.

There was, however, I thought, another sort of film to be made. More Francis unleashed. Francis on the loose. I was editing *The South Bank Show* then and I approached him at the turn of the eighties but he wasn't interested. He had done enough. He would do no more films he said. So we had a drink and left it at that. There is little point in trying to drag someone to the altar.

Two or three years later I saw a film on Francis made, I think, by a young American. I did not admire the film. I thought it did Francis and his work little justice. I was furious that he had, in a way, broken his word. I went to see him and told him this and I'm sure I added that if *this* was the way he wanted to be remembered and represented in a film then it served him right. Words to that effect.

To cut to the chase he agreed to a film. But cutting to the chase was one thing. Catching the fox was altogether different and chase as I did and amiable as Francis was, somehow we were not in business until his friend John Edwards entered the frame.

We started the film with Francis and John Edwards walking through Piccadilly and Soho. Francis is smartly dressed in a two-piece double-breasted suit, very likely new, the fastened central button being put to the test by the slightly too fattened stomach, a fashionable coat open and swinging a little like a cloak, a black polo-necked sweater. John, much younger, is in a sports jacket, flannels, Aran sweater, camera slung over his shoulder. He is taller than Francis, black curly hair neatly barbered, a handsome gentle intelligent face. Francis left everything to John in his will, his paintings, the drawings, the property, everything. John was ripped off ruinously and died young of drink, a few years after Francis.

'He's a real East Ender,' Francis would say with pride, 'from Brick Lane. Some of his brothers are boxers.' And worse than that, John might add, splayed in a chair in the Groucho Club, late at night after the umpteenth glass of champagne, wholly engaged in watching the world go by, seemingly content and yet, I sometimes thought, wholly adrift in private aimlessness.

John took a liking to us and to the idea of a *South Bank Show* film and quite simply nagged Francis into keeping his word. I have no idea what went on between them. It's a fair guess that sexual fidelity was not a requirement. I would speculate that to Francis sex was a commodity, a need to be served as and when like any other. Companionship was the gold standard, and friendship. In company together they exemplified both. John had an independence every bit as tough as that of Francis, but perhaps – enter psychobabble? – there was something of the father-son in there as well. Whatever it was, John had an influence, he took to us, and eventually we were on our way.

Before the filming began, Francis decided to take us to lunch at Wheeler's in Old Compton Street in Soho. It was here that Francis had eaten in his early days and here, it was reliably said, that he had paid for his meals by running up an account and trading in a painting. He arrived with a wad of £50 notes. (In 1985 cash terms £50 is probably about £200 today.) A £50 note was peeled off for the cloakroom attendant to whom I was formally introduced, £50 to the maître d', to whom I was formally introduced (i.e. name, designation, thumbnail c.v.), £50 to a man whom I swear was just returning from the Gents and £50 each to the wine waiter and the menu-bearing waiter and then Francis sank down into his seat bursting with pleasure. 'Champagne,' he said, 'of course. Brut.'

The menu at Wheeler's, a fish restaurant, is exceptionally big and exceptionally detailed. John scanned it in two seconds and snapped it shut. 'Quick,' I said. 'What are you having?'

'Caviar and lobster.' He leaned forward. 'Thing is I can't read or write. Francis is teaching me to do my name to sign things. But they always have caviar and lobster in this place.'

'What are you having, John?'

John told him.

'That's good. I'll have the same as John,' said Francis. 'Beluga.'

Suddenly they were two scamps. One from the East End, another from the horsey stables of Ireland, whooping it up in London Town and loving every moment.

And so we manoeuvred towards the filming. Before that, though, I think it is worth attempting to describe Francis's manner. Broadly there were two: one when sober shading to merry; one when drunk darkening to savage. The sober Francis spoke rather mincingly, with something of an upper-class drawl picked up, I'd guess, in London and the south of France in the thirties. He had also copied upper-class manners and could be effusively polite: in fact his politeness was not skin deep; even blotto he could be courteous. He was vain, especially about his face, which was regularly cleansed with baby oil, and his rock 'n' roll fifties' quiffed hair which was clipped carefully and combed compulsively. A friend of mine once saw him late one night at a party so desperate in his attempt to find his inside jacket pocket in his search for his comb that he took a short cut and ripped out the silk lining.

He had no qualms at all about seeking out a mirror and primping himself up. He was stocky, and he walked in a leisurely fashion. His face was broad, well carved, strong-boned, sunken eyes not quite symmetrical – one had practically been gorged out in a lover's tiff. He often ended statements abruptly with 'Well, there it is,' and left the other to pick up the pieces. He loved talking and arguing and the more emphatic the better, it seemed to me, when good manners would be interpolated with 'and then she said' to refer to a male or 'the cow' sometimes a female, or richly biting sarcasm again given traction by that then fashionable upper-class drawl. Dead drunk but still steady he would go out on to the streets like a beast prowling for prey. But up again the next morning, at the easel, and then lunch at Mario's, bright, polite, even twinkling. And repeat the day.

And so we did the film and it began at 9 a.m. in his studio flat in a mews in Kensington. You went up a steep and narrow staircase. To the right was his studio so small we could scarcely fit in our crew. To the left a sitting room/bedroom equally small. Between them a galley kitchen in which, at 9 a.m., were arranged in a line six bottles of champagne. I had been in the north, in Cumberland, writing and sober for more than a fortnight, but I knew that if I did not drink glass for glass Francis would suspect I was trying to get the drop on him. So I forced myself! And we did the interview in the studio and I was still sober. But then we moved on to Mario's and had lunch with red wine while the crew set up and got shots of the full restaurant and later had lunch again for the interview with red wine only in the empty restaurant. And then we moved on to his favourite drinking den in Soho.

Francis was born in Dublin of English parents in 1909. His father was a breeder and trainer of horses. Tales from the stables of violent equine beasts and randy stable boys have been called up as the making of the man. In 1914 his father moved to London to work in the War Office and early life was split between the two cities. Francis was asthmatic and had no regular schooling. He went on to become a designer and his work first hit print in the early thirties, as 'a young English decorator who worked in Berlin and Paris and is now well known in

London'. He painted and in 1933 his first *Crucifixion* was included in Herbert Read's *Art Now*. He entered paintings for a surrealist exhibition but he was rejected for 'not being surrealist enough'. His first exhibition failed and he took to gambling, which became a lifelong habit, at times an addiction. In the early forties he destroyed most of his paintings and there was no reason for anyone to think this young decorator would ever make his mark.

But in 1944 he produced his *Three Studies for Figures at the Base of a Crucifixion*. The snarling, distorted bodies of almost mythical beasts struck a post-war nerve and both reflected and helped form the zeitgeist. In one bound he was launched and although it took time to build his great reputation, there seemed to be an inevitability. When we did the film in 1985 he could be called 'the greatest living painter in the world' and he had just been offered the rare honour of a second major retrospective at the Tate Gallery.

We filmed in a vast empty storeroom of the Tate in which we had set up a screen, brought in a projector and invited him to comment on his own and others' work. He arrived immaculately turned-out and began with his 1949 study of *Head and Mouth*.

'I wanted it to have all the beautiful colour of a Monet landscape,' he said, 'but I didn't succeed. I just didn't happen to get it.'

Velázquez's *Innocent X*. 'That is one of the greatest paintings in the world. I became obsessed by it. Then I made a very great mistake.' He made his own Innocent X. 'I never got the colour. I tried to get the Pope screaming. It never came off.'

Next, another of his paintings showing a distorted female body splayed on a bed and nailed to the ground with a syringe. Here he displayed one of his several experiences of mockery. 'You've said that you de-form and re-form reality in your paintings,' I said, as I thought providing a simple tee-up.

'I would say there was some de-formation there, wouldn't you?' he laid on, a touch heavily. 'I don't think you've seen a human body *quite* like that. They said, "Why a hypodermic syringe? Is she supposed to be a drug addict?" I just wanted to impale her on the bed. I couldn't use a nail.'

Velázquez again, *The Toilet of Venus*. 'That's a very beautiful painting. But you see one's had that. I try to make concentrations of images.'

At times Francis talked as if he were nervous, almost hesitant, but always, when he wanted to say what mattered emotionally to him, he would pause, physically steady himself, look directly at me and be emphatically clear. 'I try to make concentrations of images.'

His own *Study for portrait on Folding Bed*. 'That's a disaster. It just doesn't work. I wish they'd burn it.'

A Jackson Pollock. 'I've never really cared for Jackson Pollock. Of course he's a hero in America. And you know, I said a most terrible thing. Some old cow asked me what I thought and I said it was like a bit of old lace. It went down very badly. I've never been liked in America since.'

Rothko? We showed two maroon carpets of paint. 'Rothko has always completely escaped me. I always thought that with abstract paintings at least you'd get a bit of truly vibrant colour. But I hate that dirty maroon colour. They have a whole room of them here. If you want to be depressed you can go there. Or you could go to a carpet shop and ask them to roll out some maroon carpet.'

Van Gogh's *The Night Café*. I read from van Gogh's notes: 'The café is a place where one can ruin oneself, go mad or commit a crime.' He wrote: 'There's a bar, a billiard table, lights, chairs, one or two figures, violent colours. It's one of the ugliest paintings I've done.'

'I love it said Francis. One of the inventions is the way he's done the lights.' Around each bare light bulb are concentric circles of yellow. 'He's made the light turn around the bulb. Without that the painting wouldn't have that extreme intensity.'

'He called the painting ugly. Some people have called your paintings ugly.'

'I'm genuinely pleased those sort of people don't like them. If they really hate them it means there might be something there.'

George Dyer and Francis were together for some years. Dyer was a handsome, well-built young man, a 'real Londoner', Francis said, who took to drink and drugs and while on a trip abroad with Francis took his own life, discovered on the lavatory seat, syringe at his feet. I think it was John who told me that Francis had gone to the funeral but stood apart from the other mourners, which may have been a wise move as several of the male members of Dyer's family around the grave discussed whether or not to beat him up. The studies of George Dyer have an exceptionally powerful presence.

We showed him *Two Studies of George Dyer with Dog*.

'Can you remember what you felt when you painted that?'

'I didn't feel anything. There's nothing to feel. I rather like the dog. It looks as if it's had a fine run, that's why its tongue's out.' There's an image, rather like a bust, plumb in mid-foreground. 'I'm glad I put that image down in the front. I like it. Because it's really artificial, the more artificial the better. I couldn't think of what to put in. I couldn't put in an awful vase of tulips or something.' The smile was wicked. The object was David Hockney and this, I thought, was the smallest revelation of acres of the envy & vilification indulged in frequently by many artists. Francis, I'd guess, was a master of the form.

On now to the treat of this private film show – the Egyptians. Instant unqualified vehement praise. 'That's the greatest art that's ever been done: 3000 to 2500 BC. The very greatest art that man has ever made. It was made by artisans. There's religion behind it all. They were an attempt to defeat death. You may say we all do that. We make images. They may live on. The Egyptians live on. They look more grand now, just as good now as they ever did. Well, there it is.'

Finally, one of his own. *The Seated Figure*. 'I particularly like that "thing" coming out of the blue sky.' He ignored the figure and pointed to a weird mythic animal figure hurtling towards a window, vengeful and out for blood. 'That's the Furies. Guilt. Not that I suffer much from guilt. I wouldn't care if I did.'

'That's from Aeschylus. You often refer to Aeschylus.'

'Yes.' Emphatic once more, direct, once more. 'Because it gives me exciting images. The violence brings up images. He writes: "the reek of human blood smiles out at me". What could be more amazing than that?'

A couple of days before the filming in the Tate, we had filmed in that mews flat in which he lived, up the narrow staircase, past the champagne guard of honour and into the studio just about big enough for the two of us, one cameraman, one lighting man and the director, huddled a few feet away. We stood. There were no chairs. 'It's a kind of dump. No one else would want it,' said Francis.

He was wrong. It has since been transferred to Dublin and can be seen there in all its dump glory. Dump does it no justice. Tip might be better. Lino, thick layers of oil paint on the floor, dead tubes by the score, bottles, fag packets, finger-thick dust, books stacked in crazy towers, frozen bristled paint brushes stuffed into jam jars long ago and forgotten, the walls daubed with paint. 'These are my only abstract paintings. I use the walls to test the colours.'

He looked around and smiled with proprietorial fondness. 'I like chaos. Chaos for me breeds images.' He himself is once more immaculate in a glistening expensive black soft leather jacket, newly purchased. It's tightly belted.

Work? 'Regularly. Inspiration comes from regular work.'

No art school? 'Thank God! I'd have been taught old techniques. I had to find my own.'

How? 'Trial and error. By just trying to do it. That's all.'

'When you come to a blank canvas, do you have any idea in your head of what you want to do before you start?'

Often, when talking, Francis fidgets with things, or looks away – slyly? Nervously? Seeking, I think, a way to pull together his concentration. But then he plants his feet, stares and carefully delivers.

'I have an overall idea. It's in the working that it develops. It's a very difficult problem. I'm a figurative painter. You can't any longer make illustrations better than a camera.' He begins to stumble in his sentences. 'I thought you might ask me that. I thought about it very clearly this morning and wrote it down. Now I can't remember. Can I use it?'

Blushing a little, he unzips a pocket and takes out a scrap of paper and reads. 'Not illustration of reality but to create images which are a concentration of reality and a shorthand for sensation.' He smiles. He tucks the note away.

'Any drawings beforehand?'

'No. If I drew it I'd just be making an illustration of the drawing.'

'You like to let your unconscious take over?'

'I like to think so. There's this deep sea of unconsciousness and I do think I can draw from it.'

'At the same time you like to see things deeply ordered?'

'Yes. I believe in a deeply ordered chaos in my work. I work very quickly.'

'How do you do it?'

'Until the images come through you're not in control. When they come up you have to control them.'

'So you come up with an overall image which you don't want to define except by working towards it?'

'Yes . . . no . . . yes, that's exactly how it is.'

'You've thrown paint at the canvas?'

'Once or twice. I couldn't stand the sight of them so I just threw a pot of paint at them.'

'You put yourself at risk.'

'You have to, otherwise you're an academician.'

'If it doesn't work?'

'I destroy the canvas. I work on the unprimed side of the canvas so it can't be rubbed out like the usual oil.'

'Why do you work on the unprimed side?'

'I was in Monte Carlo and all my money had gone so I couldn't buy any canvas so I painted on the back of those I had. And it worked. Because once you've done it, it can't be changed. It's indelible.'

'When is a painting finished?'

'I know instinctively when it's finished. There it is . . . I'm always hoping chance will work in my favour. I don't want to tell a story. I've no story to tell. I like the starkness of the image. I want it to give me a sensation. Shock, you could say. It's a form of experience. A visual shock.'

'What does your painting mean when you've finished?'

'Nothing. Except what people want to read into it. Nothing.'

At that point John came into the studio to join us. In fact on our finished film, John appeared to come into the studio to join us. We had hoicked the camera around, stationed John in front of the big bare canvas on the easel and filmed him taking rapid shots of us. The sound of his camera clicked in a series of photographs. Birds and beasts of prey, shots of violence from news stories, stills from Muybridge's books on movement which showed in one frame after another the strange distortions of the body. And the bodies of wrestlers, boxers and rugby players at moments of hard contact: these and other photographs were intercut with some of Francis's paintings. The photographs led us back to the galley kitchen. The table was heaped high with photographs.

'I've collected every type of photograph. I particularly like wild animals.' We see a rhinoceros. 'The movement, the structure of it, are stronger than the Muybridge photographs. I like movement taken at the time.'

'Is it because that particular thing is happening at that particular time and nothing else and there's something about that instant indelible fact that seems to be more real than anything else?'

'Yes! I think you put it very clearly. There it is. It is itself and nothing else. I would like my paintings to have the same immediate effect as you see in this photograph of a lion just after the kill.'

'And the Muybridge photographs – the naked men wrestling where you see bodies as if distorted, men clasped around each other as if in sexual passion or drowning or fear or ecstasy. Or wrestling.'

'In the Muybridge there are all sorts of exciting things you can use. He did studies of deformed people as well which I like.' He spread out his arms across the unordered heaps of photographs. 'These are my models. These are my subject matter.'

From the models it can be seen clearly how the bestial, the animal and the human converge in Bacon's visual reality. There is no hierarchy and no sign of join. The connections are seamless. As are the 'borrowings'. There are Bacon paintings of disabled children walking on all fours taken straight from Muybridge and many a growling mouth comes from a leopard. While the structure of the head is classical, the 'distortion' on the face can often be tracked back to a photograph on which there is just such a 'distorted' face; a boxer's jaw, for example, skewed out of kilter by a heavy blow, or the flailing upturned legs of a dozen rugby players, headless as they dive into a loose scrum. Other deformations are all his own. There is no sense in which there is mere 'copying'. But I found that to discover something of the roots of some of his work in those battered heaps of photographs was an important reference freely admitted, by Francis himself.

And then we went for lunch around the corner, to Mario's. The real lunch. Then the filmed lunch. A corner table by the window.

'I don't think I'm creative. I'm one of those people who received a lot of luck, a lot of chance.'

'Why is chance so important to you?'

'Because I've made images the intellect could never make.'

There is a magnificent painting *Hanging Carcase 1949*. In the background is the hanging open bloodied carcass of a cow. In the foreground a man under a black umbrella.

'I tried to make a bird falling out of the sky into a field of grass. But all the marks on the canvas went another way and came up with this image – a dictator with the meat around him. It's one of the most unconscious paintings I've ever done.'

'Some people say your paintings are too full of horror.'

'What horror could I make that would compete with what goes on every single day? If you read the newspapers or look at the television, what could I do to compete with that except that I've tried to re-create it?'

'So you paint the real world?'

'Yes! Between birth and death has always been the violence of life. I paint images of sensation. What *is* life but sensation?'

'Do you think anything exists outside "the moment"?'

'No. I believe in nothing. We are born and we die and there's nothing else.'

'So what do you do about it?'

'I do nothing about it. I just drift.'

'You paint.'

'Yes, but my own life is just going from bar to bar and drifting, that sort of thing. I'm an optimist. But I'm an optimist about nothing. I was born with that nature.'

'Why are you so intrigued by the mouth?'

'In Paris I bought a book on diseases of the mouth. Hand painted. Very beautiful. Rather like a Turner. All those beautiful colours. All those beautiful vibrations of colour between the tongue, the lips, the teeth . . .'

'But Francis! Most of your mouths are black!'

'I've never been able to make a really successful mouth. There it is . . .'

And then we talked of Ingres, Michelangelo, flesh and sexuality.

And after that, in that late afternoon, we heaved over to the Colony Room Club (Members Only) in Soho. Established in 1948 by Muriel Belcher it's up a narrow staircase like hundreds of other narrow staircases at that time and some still today which led to the rooms of prostitutes, the dens of pimps, the lairs of gangsters, the offices of film makers; and restaurants, some now fashionable.

Soon after it opened 'Muriel offered me £10 a week and free drink if I would bring my friends. It was very helpful for me.'

He has been a patron of the Colony ever since and, once the club soared and his enlisting services were no longer required, he became its most spendthrift customer. Mostly champagne. His lifestyle challenges the asceticism of the modern archetypal artist and his drinking and self-indulgence fly in the face of all sober and scholarly contemporary taboos.

So we roared into the Colony, and talked, but came back another day to talk without the howl of the pack, the ceaseless piano, the multitude of wide-open mouths, shouting, drinking, packed together and swaying in the small room as if on deck on a stormy sea or a sinking ship or in Dante's circle of hell.

There were occasional overheard sentences. 'They've been giving him a really bad time. He likes being given a really bad time. There's a lot of men like that.'

His £50 notes crossed the bar and bottles of champagne were shuttled back.

'People come in here and lose their inhibitions,' he said, a little superfluously as a crimson-faced old friend yelled out, 'Can I have a £50 note or two, Francis? No? Oh. I thought you and I were doing a bit of whooooring together.'

Somehow he found the space to stand in front of a mirror and comb his hair. Then I heard him, loudly, 'I never use make-up! Keep your make-up for yourself, you old cow!' He came across. 'I am not one of those made-up poofs. It's very old-fashioned, you know.'

We had begun on the drink at 9 a.m. We had been in Mario's for approximately four vinous hours. Now Muriel's.

On another day in the club he said, 'I've always done portraits of people I know. But even then I work from memory and photographs.'

And, 'I'm not a do-gooder. There are far too many people.' I would say he was not of the liberal tendency in politics; while in private life the licentious tendency might describe it best.

The roar of the Colony was growing in my ears like a mighty tide, rising and crashing with a powerful but queasy rhythm.

'Are you surprised at your success?'

'Yes. I never thought I'd sell at all. I always thought I'd have to take some other job. That's luck.'

Yet again he raised his glass. Yet again I did likewise. But whereas he would go on to Charlie Chester's Casino, with John, to play roulette – 'they say it's the silliest game,' he said, 'but when you *win* . . .' – I managed, who knows how, to navigate a passage back to north London, contentedly, and slept.

David Lean

David Lean was and remains the most successful and, for some, the greatest British film director there has been. In critical awards – twenty-six Oscars – in the admiration of his peers and of a younger generation of film makers, in takings at the box office, the introduction to the screen of actors who became stars, in his indisputable technical mastery and the rigour of his final cut he outsoars all but a few in the world of English-speaking films.

Brief Encounter, *Oliver Twist*, *Hobson's Choice*, *Great Expectations*, *The Bridge on the River Kwai*, *Doctor Zhivago*, *Lawrence of Arabia* – these are a magnificent seven.

For this interview, I followed him through the making of *A Passage to India*. We filmed on location in India as well as in his cutting room in London and in various locations with the art director and the composer. This took months, and allowed us to interlace a biography with the process of making *A Passage to India*, showing how he had arrived at this film, in his mid-seventies after a fourteen-year gap.

Our film started with the opening night in Los Angeles, crowds, cheers, the film about to reap rewards from critics and public alike. David was uncomfortable but correct in his dinner jacket and smiled through what for him was a triple ordeal: the usual first-night fears, the apprehension over a film that came after a fourteen-year absence and the fear that, as with his last film, *Ryan's Daughter*, the critics might savage him.

David Lean is one of the few subjects I got to know well privately. A couple of years before our *South Bank Show* I wrote a script for him. The film was made eventually, but by others. During the writing I spent a good deal of time with David.

Save for the very occasional enforced dinner jacket or a rare necessary lounge suit he was always dressed in the same outfit. It was a uniform. The white shirt was always freshly laundered, buttoned to the neck; the slacks, navy blue, the shoes slip-ons. He might have had his hair cut every day so neat and regular was the cut of the silvery grey.

This uniform was as happily constant throughout our filming as it had been throughout our script conferences: an elegant navy blue cardigan might ward off a cool evening but usually he was on parade impeccably the same. This says something about him, I think. First that having got a style that was comfortable and elegant he stuck with it, no fuss or decisions to be made in the mornings. Secondly, he knew how well this simple outfit suited him. He was an exceptionally handsome man and seemed to grow more handsome the older he got. Along the way many people – especially women, he married six – must have told him so.

'One thing about the cinema,' he began, in a very controlled thirties' middle-class English, gentle, often throwaway, only rarely breaking the surface to reveal strong emotions, 'you were in the dark and it was very private. I used to turn around and see the beam going through the tobacco smoke and it still holds a fascination for me. I don't know why. Part of a magic show, I think. And the beam showed me places I thought I'd never visit. I've been terribly lucky and I have visited them. And it showed me characters that I'd never have met in my ordinary dull suburban life.'

He was born in 1908, son of a London accountant. On his father's side were academics and painters, on his mother's Cornish inventors and engineers. He lived in Croydon, a prosperous Edwardian London suburb. He had a younger brother, academically gifted, who was to go on to a brilliant career in public service. His father left his mother when the boys were very young: a divorce. Both parents were Quakers and David went to a Quaker boarding school where he was always academically overshadowed by his young brother. His school report, with admirable but harsh Quaker honesty, replied firmly in answer to the question 'Has he shown aptitude for any particular subject?' '*No.*'

'I was a complete dud at school . . . my life changed when an uncle of mine gave me a Box Brownie camera.' He played the air with his hands, making, shaping the camera and smiling at the memory. 'It was the biggest compliment I'd ever been paid. They always said I would never be able to take photographs. And I went out and started to take pictures . . . and they came out . . . it became a great friend and . . . I found myself rather good at it.'

And by that time he had been allowed to go to the cinema.

'I began to realise there were people behind the camera doing things. In *The Big Parade* by King Vidor, they were saying goodbye and the woman was standing while the army went past her. I never forgot it. I captured it almost exactly in *Zhivago*.'

He left school and worked in his father's office as a clerk.

'After a year, I couldn't bear it. I went to my father and said, "I'd like to go into the films," and he was *very* good. He introduced me to an accountant friend of his who worked at Lime Grove. I remember looking at the cameras and thinking, *That* camera might have photographed *Roses of Picardy*, one of my favourite films of the time. I remember touching it and thinking I was in some wonderful magical world and I just loved it. And they took me on and paid me £1 a week and I did *everything* – humped cameras around, pulled focus. I was an assistant director. I had a brief spell as wardrobe mistress and I went into the laboratories and I finally eased my way into the cutting rooms. These were the silent days. It was a world of magic.'

The cutting rooms are where often many hours of film is cut to its final comparatively short length, and shaped and given finished form. It was there that he made his first reputation and learned a key craft that has underpinned the whole of his professional life. He became a film editor: a 'cutter' he called it. His work on silent films gave him roots in simpler but in some ways more demanding techniques. When the talkies came along and he moved into newsreels, other lessons followed.

'In the cutting of newsreel you learn *speed*. You *had* to make decisions. There's no messing about. You've got to cut it and have it out in two hours. Lots of people look on movies as some kind of dreamy job. It isn't. It's intensely practical. You have to be pretty imaginative as well and very often the imaginative doesn't go with the practical. I think that's why there are few good film directors.'

By the middle of the 1930s, David Lean was Britain's highest paid film editor. He made £60 a week, twice as much as anyone else in the business.

As in many success stories, there are 'the breaks' and 'the big breaks'. In 1941, he got 'the big break'.

'One day I was asked to see Noël Coward.' He does a good imitation. ' "My dear, I'm going to make a film about the British Navy." ' (*In Which We Serve*.) ' "Would you come and help me direct it?" And of course,' said David, in an accent not too distant from that of Coward and with 'The Master's' stiff upper-lip understatement, 'it's quite a bag of tricks, directing a film. You'd got to know about technique, and Noël had gone around asking, "Who's a good technician?" Three or four people had said – me. That's how I became a director.'

We saw Coward, on the deck at the height of the major sea battle which was to sink the ship he commanded. It was the first film in which Richard Attenborough appeared – he made an immediate impression as a boy paralysed with fear: some critics thought his acting stole the film.

'Acting was a mystery to me and Noël was simply wonderful at that. I took over the technical thing. Noël took over the actors. I was lucky because Noël became terribly easily bored and when he wasn't acting in one of the scenes he wasn't there, so I handled the whole damned thing. Great piece of luck.'

David went on to make other films with Coward – *Blithe Spirit*, *This Happy Breed* – and then came *Brief Encounter*, originally a play, reworked by Lean into film, and the first Oscar nomination for any British director.

Ronald Neame, his cameraman, who later became his producer, said, 'He's completely and utterly single-minded. Once he's dedicated himself to the film there really is nothing else in his life. *Really. Nothing.* If he heard that his best friend was dying he would say, "I'm sorry. I'm working on a scene." Every line of dialogue and description is studied and worked out. David takes at least a year on a script.'

His preparation was seen again and again in the scenes we shot from the making of *A Passage to India*. In one scene – which was to last for three and a half seconds on screen and involved a car almost knocking over two cyclists and throwing up a storm of dust – he said, after several takes, 'Well done. The dust was almost perfect. Let's do it again.' A second later the description said that in the following car the women's scarves were 'flying in the wind'. This proved impossible to organise. He was visibly upset.

In order to get complete control he had bypassed a real town and built streets and a bazaar in the grounds of a Balmoral-type maharajah's palace in Bangalore. The film looks sumptuous and grand – even, in some scenes, epic – and yet at a time when 'big' movies were regularly costing $50 million, *A Passage to India* was brought in for $16 million.

I spoke to him several times on location. One key interview and several on the hoof. Rather like his attitude to film-making, after we had talked and discussed the project over several weeks and he had met the producer and the director and listened to our outline, he then decided to go ahead and give us unlimited access. But it was often the script he returned to in the interview ('it's all in the script: I tell them – read the script!') On the set, it was always the script, in the keeping of Maggie Unsworth, as his scripts had been in many films, that he called for between shots. His shooting script was, he said, 'in fact a blueprint. I may alter it at the time but . . . it's a frightening job doing a picture because you have hundreds of people around you and a lot of highly paid technicians and the money people practically looking at their watches – there are tremendous pressures. My script is something I can lean back against.'

David, like so many others in this book, abides by what seems a common pattern: a very early passion which quickly became an adolescent obsession which became an adult single-minded struggle to have it realised – a struggle often seen in terms of a life-or-death battle to survive as the person they were – and, if achieved, the grateful addiction to the fuller and fuller expression of the talent.

David's obsession is with 'pictures'.

'I said to an actor the other day, "Quote me some lines of dialogue that you remember from a movie." There was a pause and I said, "Here's looking at you, kid," then the Clark Gable "Frankly, my dear, I don't give a damn." Now – think of visuals, pictures – and of course you're flooded with them. People remember *pictures*.'

One characteristic of David's career after he broke away from Noël Coward is that, though nervous of his intellectual ability, he was dauntless. He took on two of Dickens's long and richest novels – *Oliver Twist* and *Great Expectations* – cut them down without losing the story or the sense or the mood and made them into cinema classics. And he added. In *Oliver Twist* for instance, the opening sequence, in which the pregnant young woman battles through violent weather and barren moorland to the refuge where she will give birth to Oliver, lasts for five minutes without a word being spoken. It could be seen as David's ultimate tribute to his days in silent films and his bold notion of Great Drama.

Similarly in the opening of *Great Expectations*, when the boy Pip is going across the desolate empty moorlands to take some flowers to his mother's grave. Here he introduces Magwitch, the brutal convict.

'I had to have an entrance for Magwitch. How? The only hope I had was to frighten the audience as the convict frightened the boy.' This he did by showing fear in the boy, then, allowing a moment of calm (the planting of the flowers) and then relief (the boy turns to go home) and then – Magwitch 'appears' out of 'nowhere' and threatens to slit his throat if he cries out. An entrance much copied.

Another unforgettable picture is that of Bill Sykes's dog frantically scraping the door, trying to get into the room as Bill clubs Nancy to death. We 'see' and 'feel' the viciousness, the horror of the murder entirely through the dog's frenzy of panic, the thuds off screen and Nancy's dying cries.

And in *Hobson's Choice*, which starred Charles Laughton ('I loved working with Charlie: slightly over the top, some of it, I ought to have brought it down, but I loved working with Charlie'), we have the sequence where, drunk, he sees the moon in a puddle, tries to work out how it got there and then walks on – to stamp on it? Catch it? – only for it to disappear, then reappear in another puddle. Once again – save for the music – a silent sequence of genius, on a par with Chaplin or even Keaton.

David Lean seems essentially English. In his clean-jawed dashing looks, in his accent and his manner, in his association with Coward and above all with British films and actors, including his third wife Ann Todd, with whom he made three films. Yet the roving longings first felt along the nerves in the cinema in Croydon stirred into a life that changed his career utterly when he went to Venice with Katharine Hepburn and made *Summer Madness*.

'It was wonderful! I'd never had such glamour in my life. Out of the hotel in the morning. Up the Grand Canal in a boat to the location!' He was bitten by it. After that, every film he made was on a foreign location. The next one was *The Bridge on the River Kwai*. It was seen by more people than any other film had been. It won seven Oscars. Colonel Nicholson's obsession to build the perfect bridge for his captors caught the world's imagination.

It was both tightly located and an epic. The bridge itself and the railroad took eight months to build. The landscape in which it was set was vast – a feature of all his films from then on. The hero a tiny figure in nature, both chastened and given heroism by this juxtaposition. When he discovered the gigantic block of rock in India which would become the Malabar Caves, he told the producers, 'This will be a much bigger film than I'd thought.' Scale in itself began to matter greatly to Lean as a director. He was aware of the pitfall.

'You have to be terribly careful not to let the landscape swamp the people. There's a fine line.'

Lawrence of Arabia is the film that most emphatically demonstrates this new development. It was shot in Jordan, Morocco and Spain as well as England.

'I loved *Lawrence*. It was a wonderful picture to make. They were some of the greatest days of my life. In a caravan, out there in the desert, I saw some wonderful things.'

'What drew you to Lawrence?'

'Well, I'm fascinated by those . . . nuts. They're both nuts. Nicholson is certainly a nut and so was Lawrence – in a wonderful way. To get out there and lead a band of Arabs and have as a bodyguard one of the biggest thugs he could find. Most extraordinary. The thought of an Oxford don on a camel. Wonderful.'

David worked with the same core team for decades. Maggie Unsworth was in charge of the script. Eddie Fowlie, who helped him hunt locations and turned forest and a plateau from summer into winter with the help of thousands of tons of crushed marble, is his best friend. John Box, who won two Oscars on David's films, has been his art director over a long period. He got together his own travelling troupe.

For *Lawrence*, he employed the British dramatist Robert Bolt.

'He's just got a sense of *style*, Robert.' Often, when David talks about those he admires and works with, you are aware of an undiluted boyish hero worship. 'In a way he was rather a younger brother to me. He rather resembled my brother whom I admired enormously. He was very intellectual and I'm *not*. Robert and I did some quite good things together. It seemed to work.'

Yet one of the most memorable scenes in *Lawrence* combines the big landscape and the character of a silent film. It is when Omar Sharif comes out of the desert towards Lawrence and his companions at a well. As it turns out, *his* well.

'Was that influenced by William Wyler?'

'In a way. He once said to me, "If you're going to *shock* an audience, get them *almost* to the point of boredom first." '

Omar Sharif was picked up as a black dot in the far distance. They shot about 1,000 feet of film. There was the effect of a mirage, the desert turned to water, the screen shimmered, and we, like Lawrence, waited and waited as the sound of the camel's feet grew louder.

'In fact I lost my nerve,' said David. 'I had Omar coming through the mirage at twice the length and it was better but I lost my nerve and cut it quite a bit. I wish I hadn't.'

Sam Spiegel, the producer, said, 'I think this is the *only* shot I can think of in which a man enters in such a spectacular way. It is not only his entrance into *Lawrence of Arabia*, but the entrance into a new career for a man who thought he'd be the best bridge player in the world.'

I came up against Sam when I wrote for David. Robert Bolt had written a new version of *Mutiny on the Bounty*. It had extended into two films. There were rumours of great scenes and great strain and then Robert had a severe stroke which put him out of action for some time. David asked me to take up the script.

It was a strange business. I had written six feature films at the end of the sixties, early seventies, and four of them had been made – *Jesus Christ Superstar*, *Isadora*, *The Music Lovers* and *Play Dirty*. I'd worked with Sam on a script based on the disgraced Victorian politician, Dilke, but it was not made. There had been good times and great people but I didn't like the film business and went back to do television arts programmes. But the call to work with David Lean was irresistible. And Sam Spiegel was an extraordinary man: he's produced some fine films – including *On the Waterfront*. He was a European Jewish intellectual, a man of great taste and wisdom. There were five or six months which seem now like a fantasy and need not intrude on this portrait except as they help illustrate David's working methods.

David had not lived in England for thirty years and he took a suite at the Berkeley Hotel on the edge of Knightsbridge. The suite was distinguished by a big terrace and by the furnishings: David had thought the furniture too fussy, had it removed, and bought simpler stuff. Nevertheless, it was grand. He was with Sandy, many years younger than him. She had been brought up in India, was devoted to him, somewhat of a pupil, quietly very clever, and they were clearly 'mad' about each other. While we worked on the script in the main room, which we did from ten until about five most days, Sandy read in another room and now and then joined us for lunch, which was served in the main room.

I found it excruciatingly intense and wished I'd worked with him at the outset of my career, because he was the charming but seriously tough taskmaster you needed. I remember one scene where Fletcher Christian, after the ship had anchored in Tahiti, came back on board to confront Captain Bligh – Christian with a few others was living on the island and enjoying the sex. Bligh stayed at his post.

We went through that scene to the point of head-bursting weariness, day after day, until it was like a sore on my mind. David paced it out. Acted it out. Rearranged the furniture. Spoke my lines. Spoke them again. And again. Until I *knew* they were inadequate. And the next morning – after I'd made one or two small changes to the brief scene, we would repeat the process.

We had one big disagreement. I read around the subject and concluded that far from Fletcher Christian being a young liberty-loving brilliant Lawrence of the Ocean, he was a bastard. He was selfish, vicious, prepared to condemn Bligh and his few loyal supporters to a horrible death and later he proved to be a butcher of the native population. David did not like that information.

Bligh, on the other hand, was sensible – the man who introduced exercise and fresh fruit and vegetables to life on board long voyages, one of the world's greatest navigators, honourable and, when he got back to London, the object of a vile influential campaign by the friends of Christian to blacken his name. This campaign was set up to redeem the reputation of the mutineer, Christian, whom the British Navy were pursuing and who, if caught (he never was), would have been hanged. David was not interested in that.

Fair enough. His film. But as I kept trying to edge in my view, these meetings next to the hotel's roof terrace grew increasingly tense.

That apart, we became friends, rather surprisingly, and were keen to keep up even after the film collapsed. There was a World Heavyweight Championship Row in Sam Spiegel's apartment in the Grosvenor Hotel when the two of them stood toe to toe locked in opposition. I sat across the room watching the *Bounty* sink. It was a pity, I think. A remake of the *Bounty* as the 'real story' could have been . . .

His instincts are keen, his decisions often seemingly simple. *Doctor Zhivago?* 'I wanted to do a love story. It was a wonderful love story, I thought. And so it proved. That's why the public liked it so much. It was such a success. *Zhivago* has made for me more money than all my other films put together. And I didn't do it for the money. I just liked the story.'

There is a sequence in *Zhivago* where the Guards, on horseback, charge an unarmed crowd.

'How do you do it?' said David. 'Everybody's seen men on horseback slashing innocent people. I decided to concentrate on Omar. He was on a balcony, watching. I cut to him and went in on him. I played the cries and the slashing over that. I think it's much better because the audience can imagine something much better than I could do.'

Omar Sharif said, of that sequence, 'He whispered in my ear . . . what you have to convey, it's like you're making love to a woman and you're about to climax and you're holding back . . . I still don't know what he meant.'

One of his most constant stars was Alec Guinness, to whom he gave his first starring role as Mr Pocket in *Great Expectations*. 'I can see him bounding up the stairs now. He was quite wonderful.'

'He guided me,' said Guinness. 'I was very self-conscious. I still am. He would pretend the camera wasn't running. But then I cottoned on to that.'

Those sentences contain the ping-pong that went on for fifty years.

'Alec wanted to play Fagin. Fagin? He was a boy. He said, "Give me a test. One thing. Don't ask me anything. Don't see me until I come on the set . . ." Then this extraordinary thing came on . . . I didn't change a thing.'

Guinness got an Oscar for Nicholson in *The Bridge on the River Kwai*, but they fell out badly as to how the part should be played.

'Alec came and he started talking about it in a certain way and I saw we thought of it in different ways and I made a fatal mistake. He said, "Now tell me about this chap," and I said, "Well, if he came to dinner with us now we'd both find him a bit of a bore." A terrible look came over his face and he said, "You're asking me to play a bore?" We had difficulties along those lines.' They were adamantine personalities, horn-locked.

Sam Spiegel was the producer. 'David came to see me – most, *most* unusually – with tears down his cheeks because he couldn't convince Alec he was destroying the picture and he was so frustrated that he literally shed tears. I mediated between the two of them for some time until they started talking to each other again.'

Just as David is the hardest man I've ever worked with, Alec Guinness, of whom I did a profile some years later, was by a league the touchiest and most worrying.

'On the whole I'm not sure actors like me very much,' David said. 'They think I'm rather tough. I have a one-track mind. The part's in my head and there are the actors and I have to try to make them measure up to the image I have of the part.'

We then saw a scene in which Lean was directing Victor Banerjee in *A Passage to India*. Lean gave us total access and the process was grinding. Victor had to come into a room, say a line of dialogue, sit on a chair, admire the bookshelves, say another line of dialogue and take out a collar stud. David's energy could have directed the chariot race in the Colloseum in *Ben Hur*. The *effort*, the *force* of personality, the patience required of the actor and the almost painful obsession of the director – 'Again, this way, let's do it again, good, once more, clever bugger, but why don't you? Again, again, again, hurry up, the light's going, hurry up! No, why don't you . . .' On the screen the scene flowed like a stream.

It was in this set that we did the key interview in India. He was pressed for time, taut as a bow-string, fussed by the 101 factors and irritants which gather around a film director like flies around a horse's tail. Yet he kept his word. We stood outside the set for some time while he unwound from the morning's filming and I grew more nervous. Inevitably he noticed that and commented on it in a way both flattering and yet almost guaranteed to make it worse.

'Nervous?'

'Yes.'

'Good. Alex's always nervous before a take.'

'Is he?'

'Anybody who's any good is nervous before the take.'

'He has enviable authority,' said Guinness. 'He can't disguise his feelings – which is a good thing. His strength is his imagination. It's always slightly unexpected. He looks for selected moments.'

We saw Lean in the cutting room, white gloves, sparkling, cutting, cutting 'so that it *appears* on the screen as one shot. It isn't. It's six. At speed.'

His next film? *Ryan's Daughter* was hated by the critics and it had a crippling effect on his life and career.

He now blames himself. 'I wanted to give the impression of somebody being madly and hopelessly in love in that heady atmosphere. I wanted it to be wildly over the top – that's how Rosy was – bluebell woods, clouds along the hills . . . the fault that I made was that I didn't tell the audience what I was doing. I should have pointed out that this was Rosy's romantic vision of love.'

Spielberg, one of Lean's greatest admirers, says, 'It was a movie that was a little behind the times. At least in America. *Woodstock* had come out, *Easy Rider*, low-budget movies – suddenly this warhorse of a classic movie comes out. The thought it was out of step.'

'That may well be true,' said Lean, 'but they didn't have to hammer me for it. At worst I made a mistake. It ran at the Leicester Square Empire for a year. Not bad.'

David, as Alec Guinness observed, does not disguise his feelings and over the next few minutes he seemed to relive what had been a most bruising encounter. This man, of twenty-six Oscars, had been totally humiliated, publicly, by a bunch of American film critics in one of their sessions in the Algonquin Hotel, New York. It was sad to watch him on the screen. His head dropped. His voice was much quieter. He did not look at the camera. He was distressed. But he went through with it.

'I sensed trouble from the moment I sat down . . . First Question: "Mr Lean, could you explain to us how the man who directed *Brief*

Encounter could produce this . . ." I forget what word he used but he meant "rubbish". It carried on from there. They're very good with their tongues. I was there for about two hours and they just took me to bits.' You can see it, the polite Englishman, unafraid but *never* 'good with his tongue' – bears and baiting come to mind. 'In the end I remember saying, "I don't think you'll be satisfied until I do a film in 16mm and in black and white." And Pauline Kael, the critic of the *New Yorker*, said, "No. You can have colour." That was the end of it. Horrible. It had an awful effect on me. For several years. In fact I didn't want to do a film again.'

Nor did he, for fourteen years.

'You begin to think, Maybe they're right. You begin to think, Why on earth am I making films? I don't have to. It shakes one's confidence, terribly. I find it very difficult directing movies and one's awfully easily shaken, you know.'

Shelley claimed that Keats was 'killed by a critic'. Many others have been bruised; some, like David, damaged, and yet the going rule is that critics must be free to say whatever they like in whatever form they choose. It allows for spite, envy, ignorance and the formation of pack mentalities. Sometimes, of course, they are right. Yet few artists 'escape whipping while the critics go blamelessly unwhipped. But: I can't think of another system. Unless artists can regularly claim the right to answer back? As V.S. Naipaul said, 'Take it on the chin and move on.' Sometimes some people can't.

When David was eventually persuaded out of his self-imposed exile, he refused to go to New York for the opening and, I saw it, took no pleasure at all when *Time* magazine put him on its cover, declared *A Passage to India* a masterpiece and David a great director. The article was written by one of the most vicious of the Algonquin critics.

He came back to live in London but chose not to plant his new roots in the traditionally fashionable areas: Mayfair, Belgravia, Kensington, Knightsbridge, Chelsea. He found two large abandoned warehouses on the Thames in the East End and enjoyed getting hold of old London bricks and appropriate beams from churches under demolition. It was grand, but with no swagger: unexpected. He even gave a few parties there.

He worked on a script of *Nostromo* . . . but he never made it.

At the end of our interview, unbidden, he said, 'Movies have been my life. I love being behind the camera. I love putting images on the screen. I love seeing a sequence cut, putting music to film, getting the dialogue balance just right. I find it immensely exciting. It's been my life.'

Eric Clapton

This is based around two interviews: one in 1987, the other in 2007. The Assyrians recommended two meetings on a serious matter, once when drunk and once when sober. He had been drunk and on drugs for the twenty years before that first interview; soon after it, no connection, he had gone dry and clean and stayed sober since, twenty years on. Unfairly, in 1987 he looked blooming with health, even fresh-faced, even bright-eyed; in 2007 there was a lean and rather grizzled look, still a handsome man, but much calmer, little of the loose-cannon vivacity which had characterised him in the first interview. Yet while some of the still photographs and snatched news footage of the young Clapton showed a deeply depleted, exhausted man, a face falling into ruin, now, whatever the context, he is consistently alert, a successfully restored businesslike self.

We met in his London house, in a discreet street in Chelsea, the place impeccable, Clapton trim in black T-shirt, dark jeans; bespectacled.

When we transmitted the film we intercut between the two interviews.

(2007) 'We did an interview about twenty years ago. What was happening to you then?'

'I can't remember, to tell you the truth. I can hardly remember our work. I think that was at the end of my drinking career.'

(1987) 'But when it gets to two bottles of brandy a day, it's beyond having a good time. That's punishment.'

'I did one gig lying flat on my back with the microphone lying down beside me.'

'Because you couldn't stand up?'

' 'Cos I could stand up. I tried to stand up to begin with and then lay down and I thought, Well, they don't care so why should I care. They had a good time.'

(2007) 'I remember you and I drank. That's probably the only way you'd have been able to stay with me. Shortly after that I went on a tour to Australia and during that trip I came to the conclusion that I had to pack it all in and try again to get sober. I thought that last year I'd had a lot of fun, playing cricket and going to the cricket and going out with Beefy [Ian Botham]. But when everyone else went to bed I'd just carry on and get blitzed until I passed out and have really dark thoughts about myself, suicidal thoughts. It got pretty grim.'

'Do you look back and see your life in two parts?'

'Three parts. Until my twenties I was skating on thin ice now and then but it wasn't really an issue. Then there's this whole long period until my early forties when I was in the grip of all kinds of compulsions and powerless. Then the last twenty years – sober.'

'Powerless? Helpless to resist?'

'Helpless. And hopeless. And compelled to do whatever my instincts drove me to do.' (He ticked them off on his fingers.) 'Sex, drugs, drink, relationships, with absolutely no inclination to disengage – just' – he threw up his arms – 'go for it.'

It became part of the culture of the rock generation. There is nothing new in musicians, notably jazz musicians, taking drugs, getting drunk, chasing women, but in the sixties drugs became the infection of a generation and musicians of the status of Eric Clapton became, were expected to become, the leaders of the pack. Sex, drugs and rock 'n' roll it said on the label. To light up, get smashed, and score was all but obligatory. There was the competitive compulsion for those generally decent and well-mannered, often suddenly rich, young men to behave badly and, when the opportunity was there, scandalously. They were the new young bucks, the new bloods on the block.

(2007) 'When I came back from treatment the first time, I couldn't sleep with my wife. I just couldn't perform. I didn't understand it. Then it occurred to me I'd *never* had sex without being stoned. *Ever*. In my life. If I thought about having sex with somebody, I'd get drunk first.' (He threw back an imaginary drink.) 'Usually I'd be guided through it. And when the drink was removed, all of those things which are normal everyday things to most people, become impossible.'

One of the key ways in which he fights against a recurrence of the addiction he said is to get down on his knees every morning and pray.

The drink began before the drugs. Eric Clapton grew up in Kingston upon Thames, a suburb of London but very much its own place in his youth, with a strong working-class culture which embraced drinking.

'I think it was genetic to a certain extent. There was definitely big drinking going back all the way on my grandmother's side, from her father, my uncle, even my mother. We often all drank together. I spent a lot of time drinking and not seeing a lot wrong with it.'

'You quoted William Blake in that last interview.'

(1987) ' "The road of excess leads to the palace of wisdom." That's it. Yeah, I believe in that.'

(2007) 'And that meant a great deal to you.' I said 'Many artists have thought that taking drugs, drinking, excess, has opened the doors of perception. Was that really happening?'

'It's a great justification! Fantastic rationality! I think the road of excess is too often a short cut to something we really need to be putting a lot more *labour* into. Spirituality is a hard road. We can sometimes cut a few corners by taking the right substance but unlike *genuine* spirituality, it fails when the drug wears off.'

'Did fame become a drug?'

'Not for me, no. I was always very cautious about fame.'

There was a widely distributed photograph of words painted in big black capitals on a wall of corrugated iron: CLAPTON IS GOD.

(1987) 'There's nothing you can do about it except think, They've gone too *far*. I'm not lumbering myself with that. I never accepted the fact that I was the best guitar player in the world. I always *wanted* to be the best guitar player in the world but that's an ideal.'

(2007) 'Wasn't there some vertigo about it? After all, you were a lad from Kingston: at eighteen you were in a group and those who knew their stuff were already serious fans. Didn't it have a dizzying effect?'

'Very much. But it was something I was always trying to sabotage. It baffled friends and family who said – what's wrong with the guy? He's got what we'd die for and he doesn't want it. I would feel I didn't deserve it. So I would try to dismantle it in some way.'

'Has your music changed over the last twenty years while you've been clean?'

'I was lucky to find a direction from very early on which stood me in good stead.'

'The blues.'

'And I still rate them as being the most powerful . . . healing agent. The blues had an incredibly restorative effect on my teens and my twenties and I put that in the bank. And I draw on it. I never really get far from it. When things got so bad, it was just there, waiting to be picked up again.'

'Why decide to publish your autobiography now?'

'If I didn't do it now I won't remember it. I've started to experience memory lapses, you know . . . the whole middle period of my life is plagued with the blackest patches. I needed a great deal of help.'

His four-year-old son, Conor, fell out of the window of a New York apartment block. Clapton found some relief in dealing with the practical side of things and then he wrote 'Tears in Heaven'.

'I couldn't do the public grieving thing. It's not English, is it? I was trying to console myself by writing these songs and they got me right inside myself and started some sort of healing. "Would you know my name, would it be the same, if I saw you in heaven?" The thing of an afterlife is a mystery to me. I live in the moment as much as I can but I do half believe we've got to be moving around in some other area, that all this energy just doesn't stop.'

Eric Clapton was already thought to be, in the language, 'up with the greats' when he was eighteen. A self-taught guitarist, he had driven his talent on the electric guitar to such a pitch that at eighteen he was a professional musician and was asked to join The Yardbirds. You see film of him then and he stands rigidly still, totally concentrated on the music. To that generation the electric guitar made the sound of their lives, obliterated all other instruments, made redundant all other musical instruments save the drums and became wired in to what it meant to be new, free and powerful.

Clapton's command of it gave him a devoted fan base. As did his grave demeanour, I think: the blues were serious, they moved you and could rock you but mostly they came out of pain and yearning and had to be respected. Clapton personified all of that. He was tight-lipped. Not a grain of flamboyance. His unrich, unprivileged, working background was, more often than ever before, the seeding ground of a number of great artists in the twentieth century. As the decades unfolded, they saw doors of opportunity open and shot through them. This made him easy for similar young men to identify with – which they did. They loved his integrity. He *was* their god.

(2007) 'What did you get from The Yardbirds?'

'We were craftsmen. We listened. What I was doing was hitting the road and honing my craft and every so often it would be a money obligation to make a record. I moved from one band to another, sometimes with disastrous consequences.'

'At one stage you thought people were getting too commercial and you didn't like that?'

'That's right.'

'At another stage you got fed up with touring?'

'The one constant reason was my mind root. I had to be true to my vision, my mind vision.'

'And that was?'

'To honour the blues. If I sensed that the situation was going in any way in the wrong direction I would sabotage it.'

In 1965 he joined up with Jack Bruce and Ginger Baker to form the world's first supergroup – Cream.

Despite its phenomenal success, Clapton was restless from the start.

'I seemed to be the lowest man on the totem pole in terms of author- ity and decision-making. I was the youngest. I was the least informed about this kind of life. I was green. There were moments when I thought I was at the absolute top of my capabilities, when being in a trio was the best place in the world, and two days later I'd think: I'm tired, I don't want to *do* this, this music is *rubbish*, I can't stand these guys, I want to go *home*.' And he laughed loudly.

In an interview in 1978, he said of his time with Cream: 'It would have been better if it hadn't happened, really. Cream was just aggressive music. It wasn't honest, either. We weren't being faithful to the audi- ence we were playing to.'

(2007) 'What we ended up doing was a little nucleus of a repertoire we worked to death. But we weren't sensible enough to stop and say, "Wait a minute, this is worn out." '

'And you thought the only way to change that was to break it up?'

'Just walk away. I wanted out.'

They disbanded after being together for two years but it was at a Cream concert that Clapton met Pattie Boyd who would dominate his life for the next twenty years. She was beautiful, sexy, clever, stylish, and married to Clapton's friend George Harrison.

'I was in love with Pattie, I'm sure of that, but lust was a very big part of that picture. And lust, unleashed, is dangerous. It doesn't really have concern for other people's feelings or circumstances. The fact that George was my friend and a very famous person had no bearing on it whatsoever. I give myself some credit for the fact that I didn't just snatch her. There was a long period when I was almost in mourning for a relationship because it was taboo. It was only when George was clearing out of the picture that I made the real move.' And 'I was a full- blooded practising alcoholic from the day we got together.'

'People would say some great songs came out of it.'

'They did. "Layla" was about Pattie.'

Then there's 'Wonderful Tonight'. This, a tender, doting love song to Pattie, tells a brief story about a couple going out, the girl saying, 'Do I look all right?' the singer replying 'Yes you look wonderful tonight' and after the last verse 'My darling you were wonderful tonight.' Clapton blues purists were not won over but to many it is the epitome of his feelings for Pattie.

(2007) 'People think it was written in the throes of great passion and adoration. But it was written in irritation. She was late getting ready and I went to the piano and started to play and it was there. It doesn't matter. That's the amazing thing about music. You can listen to it. You don't have to know how it was written or why it was written.'

Eric Clapton was at pains to point out that there were resentments and vendettas and troubles in his drinking years. 'The thing is that when you are in turbulence you attract turbulence.' Photographs of him at this time – alone or with Pattie – veer from the druggy sentimental to the dangerously disturbed. In 1976 he caused great resentment and controversy when he supported the views of a leading conservative MP Enoch Powell, who had spoken about the disruption that would flow from immigration. Powell said 'The sense of alarm and resentment lies not with the immigrant population but with those among whom they have come and are still coming.' There was more than enough in the speech – 'I seem to see the river Tiber foaming with much blood' – he added. This caused deep unease, gathered support from white extremists and cast Powell as an irresponsible provoker of violence.

Eric Clapton's support for him at a concert in Birmingham enraged many of his fans and made him something of a pariah in the music world. He was persona non grata for some time until his appearance at a Live Aid concert set off a movement of forgiveness.

(2007) 'It was fairly normal behaviour for me to come out with inappropriate speeches – usually they were in private or in the pub. That one made the papers. I didn't think it was that important. I can't remember what sparked it off.'

'I think it was the reference to Enoch Powell and the black "colony".'

'I was concerned that the government's attitude to immigration was corrupt and hypocritical. I thought Enoch Powell was somehow telling the truth. That there would be trouble and of course there was and is. But it's not a racial thing. I mean how could it be for me when I've always identified so strongly with the black community?'

Eric Clapton is convinced that there is an essential distinction here. And he underlined that defence by a reference to Muddy Waters, his hero.

'From the time I first heard him, I realised he was the king of that situation. It was to do with where he came from, out of the Delta. Muddy took me under his wing and I did my best to honour that.' Muddy was not the only guru.

There is film footage of a concert in 2004 with B.B. King and Eric Clapton playing alongside each other. B.B. King is so relaxed, literally laid back in his seat, looking around and then striking his commanding chords, open, free. Beside him, Eric looks very much the earnest student, sitting at a lower level, hunched over his guitar concentrating so hard, the whole teacher-pupil image accentuated by the fact that Eric is wearing shorts, calf-length, fashionable but still, shorts.

'When you started to sing, who did you want to sound like?'

'Muddy. Or B.B. King. Or Buddy Guy. But Muddy.'

It is a striking cultural crossing over. A young white youth is mesmerised by sounds and rhythms which come out of American slavery and not only plays that black music but imitates black voices when he sings. There are some who accuse white singers in the USA, in the UK, everywhere in the American-music-speaking world, of ripping off the sound and sanitising it, through their whiteness, for the bigger and richer audiences and bigger commercial deals. There's no evidence that occurred to Eric Clapton. He saw in the pain and hope of the music, in the visceral rhythm and the dark drive of it, a description and an explanation of his own state of mind, and having found it, he has hung on to it, often for dear life.

His female model is Rose, his grandmother. She brought him up and gave him 'unconditional love'. We talked to her in 1987. She was shy in a sweet old fashionable grandmotherly way but clear in her thoughts about Eric and very steady in giving them voice in her gentle south London accent.

'He was a bit of a loner, really. To start with. He used to have an imaginary horse and all those sorts of things, you know . . . He used to sit on the doorstep and play with snails and there'd be snails everywhere . . . He was a lovable kid, you know; he still is.'

(2007) 'I'm glad she isn't around any more so she can't read the book. Things like going off to Guildford and vandalising trains and stealing. It would have broken her heart. In the depth of my addiction she was there and didn't really try to effect a change in me. She never gave up on me.'

(1987) 'His really favourite song of mine is "Dear Lord, Give Me Strength". He came back from the pub once and said he'd lost a fight, said he always lost fights. I said, "You've won your biggest fight." He got over that awful business. "You've got strength." '

Soon after he was born, his teenage mother went to Canada and left him in Rose's care. When she returned he was nine and for a considerable time he was asked to believe she was his older sister.

We talked to his mother in 1987. She was nervous, her eyes avoided the camera, a finely shaped face and something of a film star look about her underneath the apprehension at being interviewed. 'I'm sure he knew,' she said, sadly. 'He was confused by me coming back. Undoubtedly.'

(2007) 'My mother suffered from guilt and regret. She lost her stepson and that was the beginning of the end for her. She frittered away her life after that.'

In photographs and in the film there is a weight of sadness clearly pressing down on her, as if she thought, continually, that she had wasted her life. Perhaps he absorbed that from her. Perhaps he got the blues from her.

Clapton married again in 2006: he has three daughters. His wife 'reminds me of Rose. She loves me for what I am, warts and all.' He lives a country life, hunting and shooting and securing his outdoor wear by buying the most exclusive and old-fashioned country clothes shop in Piccadilly in London. The rock star still peeps through with the collection of cars, but the dutiful dad is a new fixture.

And he even got together again with Cream.

'I have to play music with people. Left alone I'd just go shooting and fishing. Why re-form Cream? *Selective memory!* I'd forgotten how bad it was! People talked to me about them. I realised I'd missed them. It was really my call because I'd walked out on them. Then I thought, We *can* do it. We're all still *alive.*'

Back to 'Sunshine of Your Love'.

David Puttnam

In 1988 I went to Greta Garbo's house in the Hollywood Hills. It was at the time rented by David Puttnam, who had left Columbia Studios after no more than a year in charge. He was the first English film producer to be invited to run one of Hollywood's great movie principalities. His arrival and his departure were equally dramatic.

Just as I happened to interview Francis Ford Coppola at what I think was the peak of a career which continued after *Apocalypse Now* but never matched the glory of that time, the two *Godfathers* and *The Conversation*, so I think in his life as a film maker, I met David Puttnam at a similarly climactic moment.

A creative film producer can be as influential on a film as a director. William Wyler, the director, said that the three most important ingredients in film-making were 'casting, casting and casting'. A good creative producer casts the director and has as big a say as his personality allows in the casting of the actors, the crew and the often replaced screenwriter. He also controls the purse strings, having been the man who acquired the money to fill the purse. It's unlikely that films such as *Midnight Express, Local Hero, Chariots of Fire, The Killing Fields, Bugsy Malone* and *The Mission* would have been made in anything like the shape and form they were made without Puttnam's underpinning vision, control and expertise.

He left school early and was soon an agent to a like-minded clutch, a gang of young London photographers – David Bailey was the star – who took a vertical lift-off to fame in the sixties and dominated the better magazines. He moved into advertising with Charles Saatchi and Frank Lowe where the young directors who cut their teeth included Alan Parker, Hugh Hudson, the Scott brothers. He helped lever them into the feature film world when he got going as a film producer.

His was a dizzying success story, and also typical, it seemed, of that stream of a skilled working-class, lower middle-class force which stormed London in the sixties, a wonderfully optimistic regiment of talent from all parts of the United Kingdom.

And David won the most glittering prize of all. The call to Hollywood. Not just any old call. This was an offer to run one of the most successful dream factories in cinema history.

I had known David for years before that 1988 encounter. There was a close generational kinship. He was also as impossible to miss if, as I was, you were in London working in films or television. At one time I wrote screenplays, for Norman Jewison, Ken Russell, Karol Reisz and others, including David Lean. There was a general mêlée of this loosely connected cluster of like-minded young artists who kept bumping into each other.

Over the last twelve years I have got to know him well. We see each other regularly in the House of Lords in which he plays a vigorous and effective role. There's a seamless move from his work in film to his work in the legislature and in the other organisations he works in – universities, arts funding, UNICEF . . . He was my 'monitor' when I was appointed to the Lords and that both sealed and strengthened what has become a friendship.

I feel like writing 'and I should like several other previous convictions to be taken into consideration'. It's a declaration of interest intended to clear the path. As with Beryl Bainbridge and Francis Bacon and a few others, the personal connection was not the reason behind the choice of the subject, but it is as well to state it. By any standards, David Puttnam was not only a good but an inevitable subject for *The South Bank Show* and I think we happened to get the timing spot-on.

Greta Garbo had a large Hollywood swimming pool which featured for a moment in our film as we slowly paced around it (being filmed) to establish we were overlooking Hollywood from Greta Garbo's large swimming pool. Then we went indoors and cut to David Puttnam, speaking rapidly, as he does, emphatically focused as he always is, but reflective and rueful after what some saw as a fall from the pinnacle of producer ambition.

'Sooner or later a film maker has to come to Hollywood. Either it embraces you or you don't like it and you go back to make your way in your own country.'

Coca-Cola, who owned Columbia, had given David an extraordinary deal. Even so, he had been worried and 'I insisted I would only come for three years. I made a lot of that. And Patsy [David's wife] said, "When you're fifty-five, wouldn't you regret you didn't take it and wonder what you'd have done if you had?" '

His reluctance came partly from the security of his base in London, the acclaim which so much fine work had brought him and the intoxicatingly high regard in which he was held in the British arts world and in the world of movers and shapers, and the great and the good. All of this mattered to David, whose ambitions were not confined to making extraordinary and successful movies. And there would be envy and there would be mutterings of 'selling out'. But the deal on offer was exceptional.

'I would have the autonomous right to run a studio. I could make twelve to fifteen films a year and be responsible for worldwide marketing. More importantly I set out a list of obligations to make the studio more global and adventurous.' There was a feeling of David and Goliath with David, blessed with talent and fortune, capable of taking on Hollywood – because that was his battle plan – and, with a slingshot, winning a famous victory.

'There are only three ways to run a studio. One is that you are a Baron. You hand it over to producers and directors. That had been Columbia's way. They had handed it over to what I called 'The Baronies'. At the centre was a very weak government. Another way is to revert to the thirties and forties where the studios ran everything. Disney's very successfully done that. Finally you can try to mix the two.'

The Baronies were agent-driven. Generally, a screenplay would go to the writer's agent who would pass it on to a director on his books and show it to a star, also on his books, and bring the package to Columbia, who would only have the input of suggesting a producer 'simply to get on with the ugly job of putting the film together'.

'What were the disadvantages?'

'You don't grow an esprit in the company. You don't grow your own talent. Soon you can't grow your own talent.'

'What did you find when you got there?'

'A company far more divided than I'd expected. It no longer believed in itself. It was a very sad place, empty corridors, people working behind closed doors. I wrote to Patsy and said – This is supposed to be a creative enterprise, it's neither creative nor enterprising.'

'And outside the studio, in LA itself?'

'I thought there would be a potency, a groundswell, for better work. I underestimated the fear factor. People would say things privately, but not under pressure in public. I hopelessly underestimated how fearful people were. I walked into a straight right.'

Puttnam's experience of clearing the hurdles in London, of taking his own gang of talents and his ethos of film-making into the heart of the establishment and then taking over the establishment had given him the confidence that he could repeat it 6,000 miles to the west. But he had worked with a small like-minded group of buccaneers. In Hollywood he faced a mass of bureaucratic lifers. And if all big organisations are plagued by the fear factor, it is especially true of those in which it is impossible to measure value.

When he arrived at Columbia he was alarmed by how few films were under way and as an emergency measure, called in old pals – John Borman, Ridley Scott, Bill Forsyth – as well as making sure that Columbia held on to Bertolucci's new production, *The Last Emperor*.

At the same time he set in place his strategy. Because of the time-table he had set himself – three years – he felt he had to work quickly on all fronts. He told me these first three months were the hardest and most joyless in his life. Patsy and the family had not yet joined him and the atmosphere of acceptance and adulation which he had created for himself in London was not there. Nor was the fun which had oiled the engine.'

'So how did you tackle the studio?'

'I found that there was a core at Columbia, a creative core which was very good. I set out to embellish them. First with people I knew. Then I set up programmes – one for young directors and writers, another for minorities, the disenfranchised, women and blacks and Hispanics – who were hopelessly under-represented.'

'Were you looking for a particular attitude?'

'We've talked about this many times. I don't believe in "either/ or", that a film is commercial or idealistic. I'm utterly convinced that cinema has a huge social role. It has an obligation to be entertaining *and* it has an obligation to address an issue.'

'But sometimes they clash head-on, don't they?' I said 'Take marriage. Traditionally, all Hollywood films, like thousands of romantic novels, portrayed marriage as the fulfilment of life, the crown of happiness. We know that often and sometimes interestingly, it isn't like that.'

'TV is the great medium for dealing in that sort of reality. Cinema and TV are different and complementary.'

'Because TV is a lie detector?'

'I've never looked at myself on television without learning something . . . But cinema is different. There's the big screen. People are in darkness. They drift off, in a positive way. That is the moment to feed them with ideals. It's very important to tell people that good men behaving properly will prevail. I know that's what happened to me as a kid.'

'So you wanted to turn the studio back to that sort of film?'

'All I could do in three years was to build a team for 1990 and a studio for 1995. After the first few months I thought I was getting somewhere. I didn't enjoy it. I never enjoyed the job. In many respects it was the most uncreative part of my life.'

'Around town, as I understand it, you affronted and effectively disenfranchised the "package" men?'

'My dad told me that a man was not only judged by the calibre of his friends but by the ambition of his enemies . . . I was attacking people's incomes. There were a *great* number of people at Columbia alone earning over a million dollars a year. To cut that in half, or less, did not go down well. I didn't make friends.'

There were powerful enemies. Ray Stark, Dustin Hoffman and Warren Beatty, who blamed him for the flop of *Ishtar*. Most of all, Bill Cosby, then at the zenith of his pan-American success. The $4 million-a-year 'face' of Coca-Cola, who owned Columbia. He was a big investor, he was a friend of the management.

'Cosby had agreed to star in what was to be his first comedy since his fame. The script was rubbish. It shouldn't have been made. With hindsight I should have battled that through and stopped it. I let it drift and it was a catastrophic film and it led to a catastrophic relationship with Cosby.'

'Do you think, after playing golf, on the nineteenth hole, although I'm sure they didn't drink, they said, "It's Puttnam or Cosby"?'

'Maybe.'

'What had the management to do with the films?'

'There's a positive side. They'd given me unlimited resources. They were personally extremely agreeable, bright people. On the negative side, they had very strange, whimsical attitudes. It was two different worlds. My failure was not to grasp it.'

'Was there something else? By insisting on three years only, didn't you rather insult them; wasn't it a stick they could beat you with?'

'They should have said five years and made it a deal-breaker.'

'Was it helpful or wise to be so bullish about your own objections to Columbia, and to Hollywood?'

'I'd been very critical of Hollywood. I had tremendous concern that people – like yourself – would say, "There's old Puttnam, off to Hollywood and changing his tune." I wanted to be true to myself. I had the problem to get across very quickly to what I saw as the artistic community this version of a different type of studio. I wanted to do that over the heads of the agents. It was very important for me to leap that barrier. It comes back to the three-year business. I didn't have enough time to find out who my friends were. I didn't have time to persuade and cajole on a day-to-day basis. There were friends. Jane Fonda, Robert Redford, Michelle Pfeiffer – but others were too unsure to rally round.'

There was a movement of the old guard to isolate Puttnam and get him out. It can't have been comfortable and the whole town looked on.

'Then Coca-Cola merged with Tri-Star – which effectively broke their contract with you.'

'I realised the new company would curtail my freedom. I said I'd work in a smaller stockade but with even higher walls. The final straw came when they wanted to bring back something I thought was completely at odds with what I was doing. I thought, We're talking about two different visions of the future. Better I go in a seemly way. Maybe they were quietly delighted. Two or three days later it was done.'

'Did you still think your sort of film could be made in Hollywood?'

'Yes, but it needs change. And change can only be brought about by people. There has to be a debate and it isn't an atmosphere where debate can occur very readily.'

'What's left of what you did?'

'Nothing. They went back to the old style. At the end of my year we got eighteen awards – more than any other studio. Then *The Last Emperor* got nine Oscars. But – nothing.'

'Do you think you are leaving the movie capital of the world?'

'When I came I thought I was arriving in the movie capital of the world.'

'You've been here a year.'

'The opportunities are in Europe. There's the talent and a vigorous creative environment.'

We exchanged the pool in the Hollywood Hills for the Wiltshire countryside. David and Patsy had found a place with its own water, a stretch to be rowed on. He had come back and straight in to revitalise his company Enigma.

David is always utterly occupied on something. Extending or improving a house, reshaping a room, building a path, being enthusiastic and persuasive on the telephone, arguing, catalysing, planning, nowadays more than ever, but even then, in 1988, the urgency for activity and achievement was compulsive.

He had put together a rolling fund of £30 million – the biggest investment in the European film world – half from the USA, the rest from Japan and Europe. He wanted to make four films a year with that – it would be a revolving fund, profits would go back into it – and his idea was to find a 'niche': films costing about £8 million, at that time far beyond the films for television and even beyond those mostly made for the British cinema.

'I see myself as an international film maker,' he said. 'I want subjects that will appeal across the board. Britain has been starved of capital for more ambitious films – in scale, in metaphor. Something more than large-scale action films.'

He was at the beginning of another great adventure. This time on his home turf, regrouping in the West Country, deep in Saxon England. There was no doubting his conviction and commitment.

'Again and again people have praised the talent and potential over here,' I said. 'Again and again it's been a false dawn. Good people go "over there" (the USA) Are we kidding ourselves? Why do you think it has never happened?'

'Someone said it was poverty of ambition. Film people here have been continually let down. Sooner or later any sensible creator works in a framework which is visible. It's for people like me to open doors.'

'One argument is that the good film makers here have been working in television. What's wrong with that?'

'Nothing if you only want to travel from Basildon to Edinburgh. But if you want to travel abroad, France, Germany, your television film is not part of the conversation. And when film makers go to festivals they want their films to be shown around the world. You can't do that through television.'

I suppose I think that if local is good that's good enough. If international 'comes naturally', fine. But making it good is the prime aim and as often as not the bigger the stretch the thinner the substance.

We concentrated on television.

'Cinema is important,' David said, and then, rather surprisingly, 'but it is now subsiding. Television forms our attitudes.'

We moved on to public service broadcasting, a subject which both of us have engaged with since, in radio, television and films, in the press and in Parliament.

I saw what was in 1988 an emerging polarity between public service broadcasting and broadcasting as a lucrative business opportunity. Since the 1920s broadcasting in this country has been a cultural force, tightly focused in the beginning but growing in reach through the decades – especially when challenged by ITV in the sixties and seventies and eighties. Its cultural reach and its well-funded capacity to nourish many varieties of broadcasting made it unique in the world and all the evidence shows that the British people liked it and were rather proud of it.

The situation is in far sharper relief now than it was twenty years ago, but the arguments are much the same. David, a former advertiser, said of advertisers: 'They are not part of the cultural mix. They have no responsibility. They just want money. And they are being allowed to have the only voice in the argument. It's completely undemocratic. I came out of advertising. Let me put this to you.

'Today wherever you look there's a restlessness and dissatisfaction with society. They're bewildered by the place they live in. I came from a group – with Charles Saatchi and Frank Lowe and others who control the big advertising world now. We went to the same night school. We read the same books – Vance Packard for instance – and over the last twenty-five years we've made better quality advertising than anywhere else in the world. We were taught to do things very differently. Before us you put out the goods and slapped a price on it. We were taught to make the customer feel inadequate if he or she didn't buy our product.

'Maybe what's happening is that after twenty-five years they know these things are unattainable and not affordable and maybe that creates an anger and frustration. Instead of being arrogant, advertisers should face up to a broader responsibility. If getting rid of or cutting down on documentaries and arts and classic plays and long-term news is the policy of high-level advertising – it's too big a price to pay. What we'll end up with is second-rate ads between second-rate shows. We must get business to understand there is a broader social responsibility.

'If we're going to leave behind better than we found we must make good TV at affordable cost and not be squeezed out by business priorities. We have to get them onside to make them see their ultimate aim must be to leave behind a legacy, to affect society for the better. I see this great narrowing of choices in the USA at the same time as there is a broadening of the delivery system.'

'And that threatens us, here?'

'Totally. If you don't see it it's because you choose not to see it.'

Twenty years on, the jury is still out although some would say that doomsday is creeping up on us. Twenty years on, having left the film industry, David is still urging on the arguments, calling for a better public debate, for more voices in the debate, for a culture which helps deliver the society promised in those fine but also upstanding films he saw as a boy in north London.

David Hockney

From the start of his career, David Hockney stole the affection of the public and the admiration of critics. It was partly the cheeky look and sound of him, the grin, the slow Bradford drawl and the hair dyed blond because he'd read a sign 'Blondes have more fun'. It was partly, of course, the high quality of his work which was original and amusing, modern but accessible. And there were the times, the sixties, much applauded, much derided but undeniably a time when young artists, musicians, actors, directors, writers felt they could rule the roost and crow about it. There was a swell, especially in London, of a new classless culture, sexy and delighted with itself, confident, style-setting, daring, crossing bridges and David was quickly recognised as a star turn.

In 1988 the Tate gave him a major exhibition showing a selection of his work over thirty years. I'd known David for a long time. He had talked about Picasso and Wallace Stevens on one of the first programmes in *The South Bank Show* run and I'd made a documentary with him about his Joiner photographic works and about his visit to China to examine Chinese scroll painting. He is remarkably consistent in his openness, cheerfulness and loquacity. He loves to talk and talks well. I've found him to be someone very sure of his ground and grounded and willing to be caught up in a novel idea which he will worry about, sometimes to death.

His Joiner photography was one instance. Then there was his obsession with the way Canaletto produced paintings of such 'photographic' accuracy. There were the tulips. The opera sets. At present it is the landscape near Bridlington in Yorkshire with a painting of trees filling a vast wall of Tate Britain. He is a very public smoker of cigarettes and misses no opportunity to proselytise on their behalf. And the charm has not worn thin, the cheerful provocation, the incessant talk about art, the obsessions are unslackened. The slow Bradford drawl has been made even more attractive by its top layering of Californian – little is now liddle, city now ciddy – as Yorkshire crunches into Hollywood where he made his most famous paintings.

We took a long morning's walk around the Tate's retrospective. We had the gallery to ourselves, just us and the film crew, and began with the first painting, a portrait of his father. He is in a dark suit, a tie ('he was always rather smart'), leaning forward and looking down, a heavy presence.

'It's the first oil painting I ever did. I was about seventeen. Father bought a canvas at a jumble sale and I painted over it. I sent it into an exhibition at Leeds. It was the first picture I'd exhibited. Somebody wanted to buy it so I rang my father up. It was his canvas. It was his picture. He naturally thought they wanted to buy it because of him! And he said he could always get another canvas and he would pose again. Twenty or thirty years later I bought it back.'

'What do you think of it now?'

'It's painted the way they were beginning to teach you to paint at Bradford. That's what you have to do at art school. He thought his face was a bit dirty.' (It *is* rather grey.) 'Perhaps he was right. It's just a little dull art school picture.'

David seems to have had the most amiable relationship with his parents, with his brother and sister, his teachers once he got to art college, the city of Bradford, London when he arrived there, California when he took up residence there, with his friendships, his sexuality, his hardworking but rather louche life. He is a great advertisement for a fine artist not needing adversity or angst. His pictures appear to have been entirely self-sought – the subject matter, the form, the quizzing of where painting is today and what he can do about it.

The painting *We Two Boys Together Clinging* was begun in 1961 when he was at the Royal College of Art in London. It is undeniably 'modern': the two 'boys' are upright rectangular slabs, the heads are almost turnip-like, the arms held out to enfold in a chunky outline, the legs are matchsticks and the canvas crawls with words from the poem which yielded the title: and the impact today is still fresh. We stood opposite each other, the painting between us in full view of the camera.

'I left school at Bradford and for two years I worked in a hospital – in place of military service – so I didn't go to the Royal College until 1959. I thought they'd all be very good. I was just a little provincial boy coming up to London. I thought, Well, now you have to deal with modern art. All the lively people were painting in a kind of abstract expressionist way. I did a few paintings based on abstract ideas – not very satisfying to me, so I slowly started putting lettering in pictures. It's from a Cubist idea. I realised that as soon as you put in a word it was a little bit like a figure. You were forced to look at it, to read it, and in the end I started to paint pictures about things I *knew*.' Like a painting of a packet of Typhoo Tea. 'Not just things I'd *seen*.'

The lines come from Walt Whitman's *Leaves of Grass*, a book which he borrowed from Bradford Library. It set him off on a poetry-reading spree which has not ceased. 'One of the lines was "We two boys clinging together", which I thought could be interpreted in all sorts of ways. It was even sexy and so I made a painting of it.'

'Did it feel bold in 1961?'

'A little cheeky perhaps. Yeah. I did all my painting in the RCA. I couldn't afford a flat which allowed me the space to paint so I grabbed a space in the RCA and people passed by so you'd also get a little exhibition space. So you would deliberately do cheeky things – or I would.'

'Is this the first painting telling people about *yourself* as a painter and as a person? Things that were being said more openly in 1961.'

'Well, I think you became aware of homosexuality so you start dealing with that, telling people in a sense to piss off about it, that's what you're doing.'

'And bold to bring in the literary side?'

'Yeah. But you have to remember we were all wanting to do things bold. Twenty-four years old. Wanting to do exciting things. At that time to be able to push Sickert away, to push away that tonal painting was very exciting and they were doing it now not from Paris but from America.'

We went into a room in which were hung several 'pool paintings', all done in Hollywood. He moved to California in 1964. He's been called 'The Piranesi of Southern California'.

'What drew you there?'

'Well. Sun. It's always sunny which means it's always sexy.'

Sex, liberated gay sex, was also a factor. In the previous film on his Joiner photographic work, he'd shown us American magazines full of photographs of handsome, well-built young men, posing never entirely nakedly, the fig leaf always in place. They were usually in the shower or beside a pool and David became intrigued by the location – it was in LA – and wanted to take a closer look. So he went and sought it out. If that helped to get him there, though, it was the light that held him.

'It's light that's full of colour. I just had a hunch it was a place I would like. I just went there. I didn't know a soul there. I thought it was three times better than I'd imagined when I got there.'

'Why the pools?'

'I remember flying down over LA. You can see the city very well and you see all those little blue pools – they're not a luxury as they would be in England. Even a cheap apartment block had a pool. I paid about $90 a month and there was a pool outside the door. I thought that was great. I was the only one who kept swimming in it in January. It wasn't heated but the idea of being able to swim in January! But you start looking at pools and I noticed the patterns the water makes and you see this dancing light. And I was also aware it only happens on the surface of the water, this thinnest film. How thick is it? Does it actually exist? So I made a few paintings. Not many. About twelve. I was painting water in different ways.'

'What were you doing in *A Bigger Splash*?'

'Bigger only refers to the size of the painting. The splash itself was painted from a photograph of the splash. You can't quite *see* a splash.

It lasts such a short time. It amused me that it took about two weeks to paint the splash – lots of little brush strokes – to paint this thing that lasted no time.'

Hockney is an obsessive photographer. His father was very keen on it and perhaps that rubbed off: then there are its uses in his painting. He'll often photograph a friend who will model for him for the painting and then work from that and of course his knowledge of that friend. But it goes even further. He has scores of beautifully bound albums of photographs on his shelves – arranged in regiments of navy blue and the gilded letter names JAN–JUNE 1964, etc. It is a way of seeing that he has both brought into his painting and used in his lengthy attempt to find ways to give photographs value – especially with regard to time – as paintings.

We moved into a room in which there were double portraits.

'What attracts you to the double portrait?'

'Twice as interesting as a single portrait.'

'Necessarily? Rembrandt's "single" portraits . . .'

'A double portrait is about a relationship as well. In a sense it's not quite a portrait. It's what's going on between two people.'

We stood at the double portrait of *Mr and Mrs Clark and Percy.* Percy was a white cat sat on the knee of the seated Mr Clark; Mrs Clark stood – on the other side of the room, a long window of light between them.

'This is a portrait of friends of mine who'd been married about a year and a half then. I saw a great deal of them. So I decided to paint a picture of them. Ossie [Clark] was a fashion designer. Celia designed fabrics. Their relationship did rather fascinate me, actually.'

Perhaps I should not have left that hanging in the air.

'Are *you* in the painting at all?'

'Partly . . . I did drawings, took a lot of photographs. It's the reverse of what should be happening. He's sat down in the chair. She stands. The window is a big source of light. I wanted the two figures in very clear space like Fra Angelico or Piero della Francesca. Later on I gave it up because I couldn't *do* it.'

'Is it important to you that they look as they *do* "actually" look, let's say "photographically"?'

'In the long, long run it doesn't matter. If it lives who knows what they look like? But when you're *doing* it, it does. In the end I think portraiture is an instinct. It's something you can't quite teach. I'm always interested in doing portraits. There are periods when I do a lot, periods when I don't. I *do* want them to look *like* the people.'

Another couple. An old lady upright in a hard-backed chair. Blue dress, fine grey hair. A man, her husband, bending over a book. There's a chest of drawers between them, a mirror and a vase of tulips are on it.

'First of all it's your parents. My mother poses very patiently. My father, the moment he sees you're not actually painting – with a brush – he'll pick up a book – in the end I realised his fidgetiness was something I should put in the portrait. When my sister saw it she thought it was a very accurate portrait. That pleased me more than any art critic.'

'You often use the word "pretty" about your paintings and other things. It's not common. "Serious" art critics might take exception to it, see it as rather frivolous. Do you purposefully use it to deflate the critical language and to get their backs up?'

'To a certain extent yes. I know some paintings are beautiful but I know a lot of pretty pictures that I love. Wonderfully pretty pictures. Bouchers are pretty pictures. I was talking to an architect the other day and he said, "I prefer beautiful." I asked him, "Wouldn't you like to live in a pretty house?" "I do," he said. But he wasn't building one for someone else! They think that "pretty" can't be serious. I've never understood that.'

Sometimes I think that although David is always among friends, always in a small community of his own making, there is a longing in the painter, outside the couple he is portraying, looking in at a world he would like to join, to be part of a double portrait.

'I struggled with a portrait of George Lawson and Wayne Sleep for six months and then I abandoned it. I couldn't paint like Fra Angelico or Piero della Francesca. I'd just got disillusioned with it. I moved to

Paris and I only did three or four paintings in two years. I did a lot of drawings.'

He had a large flat just off the Boulevard St Germain and when you went there the first thing that struck you were the drawings. They were all over the room. Many of them of the young men who drifted in and out of the room. He seemed to me – but he always does – full of beans, content with his lot, but it was at this time that a touch of luck helped him out.

'In 1972 I was asked to design *The Rake's Progress* – Stravinsky – for Glyndebourne. I went back to Hogarth for ideas and one of the books I found was a book on perspective by Mr Kirby, and Hogarth was saying if you don't know about perspective "great blunders will be made". My painting shows the blunders. A woman leans out of a window and lights the pipe of a man standing on a hill. She couldn't *do* that. I show it by bad examples. The trees and the sheep get bigger as they go away. I liked it. It made a good pattern. And it broke the rules. I liked that.'

He went on to do more operas – three for the New York Metropolitan Opera House. He broke the rules of perspective here too. In Los Angeles he made a move to the Hollywood Hills which took him away from the clean lines of rectangles and wide boulevards of LA and into an area of winding roads wriggling over the pass and often baffling visitors. This led to the huge and colour-packed *Mulholland Drive*.

David is constantly thinking aloud about painting. He is a most careful and articulate man about his work, almost always, I've found, starting with ideas and working them through the paintings. For someone whose work can appear so easy to read, he is a very industrious and intellectual artist. He reminds me of Robert Graves who, when complimented on the clarity of his prose, pointed out the effort of time, and work it took to achieve that clarity.

We had made a film about him a few years earlier on his Joiner photographs. For at least two years he gave up painting and, instead, worked with a camera. He said, 'I may be one of those people who in the end will say, "The only thing I ever *did* was all these photos. The other stuff is just pointless.'

Hockney, with those 150 bound volumes to prove it, had been an ardent photographer all his life. Now he turned his artist's mind to it.

'The main problem was this lack of *time* in a photograph. I'd become very aware of this frozen moment that was very unreal to me. The photograph didn't have life in the way a painting or a drawing did and I realised it couldn't because of what it is. Compared to Rembrandt looking at himself for hours and hours and putting all those hours into the painting – there's many more hours there than you can give it. A photograph is the other way round. It's a *fraction* of a second. So if you've looked at it for four seconds you've looked at it for far longer than the camera did. It dawned on me that all this was visible. This is a terrible weakness. Drawings and paintings do not have that.'

There are flaws in the line if you want to find them. A photograph can take many hours to set up. Many hours do not necessarily a great painting make. A glance can be a sufficient appreciation. And so on. But, by and large, the previous statement is what David had arrived at and he put his energy, his work and to some extent his career behind it as he tested it some would say to destruction.

His solution was to build up a picture by taking a series, often scores of photographs of the same subject, close-ups, long shots, profiles, full front, details, many details, changes of expression and of position. When he got the prints back – in Hollywood it was from his local launderette which had a developing service – he would deal them out on a table, like playing cards, and begin to make patterns, 'joining' them together. He did not cut or in any way crop the photographs but for instance laid one halfway across another and arranged the whole series in a pattern which forced the eye to move, to shift around, to check 'back' and glimpse 'forward' as the swirl of photographs led on the viewer. He had built up this technique slowly over some years but not followed it through until he launched himself on the project.

He did one for *The South Bank Show*. It was a simple scene. A woman coming down the stairs from his home into the garden to hand over a cup of coffee to another woman who was sitting by the pool working on a tapestry. He took six rolls. Then he made a shape. He varied the composition from 'frame' to 'frame', as it were – half faces, quarter faces, hands, the cups, the tapestry, feet, faces . . . And he brooded over the composition for hours.

'I'm not sure exactly what I've done . . . there's a lot of possibilities I haven't explored . . . narrative possibilities mostly . . . the stories can be very tiny.'

'Do you see the photographs as more important than the paintings?'

'I don't really think you can separate them. It's just picking up another medium and using it. At first – not very good, very limited technique . . . what I was trying to do was to *extend* it and it seems to work . . . it's more serious than I thought.'

'Are you saying you can eventually get all the impact of a Rembrandt self-portrait?'

'No, I don't think so.'

'Neither do I. But why not?'

'Because of the unbelievable scrutiny that Rembrandt is giving with his hand and eye and himself, and frankly from what I've done so far you can't do *that* much with a camera. That's when you begin to paint again. But I've done more than I *thought* I could so I'm not *sure* yet.'

His last Joiner of a highway in California, with the signs often in close-up taken by standing on a ladder and games with perspective that threw the picture into different dimensions, was, I thought, very like a painting.

'People kept telling me not to waste my time. I thought, It's for me I'm doing it, not for you anyway. The pictures got more complex. This is the last one I did and when I finished it, my friends in LA said it wasn't a photograph it was a painting. For instance, I'd changed the colour of the sky several times. After that I went back to painting totally.'

And to finding new contexts to feed the painting, like the trip he did to China. This was to see and examine the long scrolls, stories of journeys through towns and landscapes unrolling as you unrolled the scroll. And time was again involved in a way which intrigued him.

He designed sets for *Tristan and Isolde*. He made portraits. And then there was Picasso.

'He's a great artist. A wonderful artist. He did twenty masterpieces which is twenty more than most people. His invention is staggering. Artists have made whole careers out of little portions of Picasso. The amount of work means that it's of varying quality. This doesn't matter for art's sake. I love being able to look back on Picasso and make quotes about him. People try to bury Picasso. But he won't go away. You have to deal with him. The moment people started painting the visible world again you have to deal with Picasso. I'm not afraid if my paintings become Picassoesque. So what? You have to do that before you can proceed further.'

We started the grand tour in the Tate Gallery with the first oil painting, of his father. We ended it in front of an oil of his mother. I think that his drawings of her are his finest work.

'I wasn't interested in drawing people I didn't know *really* well because only then would I know what they *really* looked like.' The painting seems very simple. Single, seated, facing straight out, a presence. 'I painted and repainted that face about twelve times. Other people might have thought it was my mother but *I* didn't until that one, the last one.'

'What about the hands?'

Big, red, knotted, clasped tight together.

'She hates me painting her hands because she's got arthritis.'

We were done. At times he is like a teacher, passing on his essays into the understanding of art. For a man so physically at ease in himself and calm, there is a surprising restlessness.

'Do you think the Tate Gallery runs to a drink?'

'Yes!' he said and led the way.

Martin Amis

Over thirty-two years I interviewed Martin Amis three times on *The South Bank Show*. Because of his work, of course, and also because of his almost fatal facility of quotability on such a range of subjects – most especially, though, on literature. He became the acknowledged leader of a new pack of novelists which began to seize the high ground of London literary success in the seventies and held that position for a generation. They became a formidable gang. As well as Martin Amis, there were Ian McEwan, Julian Barnes, Christopher Hitchens, Kazuo Ishiguro, Craig Raine, Salman Rushdie and James Fenton. Clive James was a guru as were Karl Miller and Terence Kilmartin, the Literary Editor of the *Observer*.

The younger critics welcomed their own generation to the top columns of the literary pages. They were very intelligent, amusing, astonishingly self-confident, bristling with literary ambitions and references and connections and on the move. One of their base camps was the Greek Street pub, the Pillars of Hercules, at the court of the poet and editor of the *New Review*, Ian Hamilton. Others were at the *Times Literary Supplement* and in the literary pages of the *New Statesman*.

Martin Amis's first novel, *The Rachel Papers*, was rightly acclaimed and his talent for interview was soon on display. The hounds of the cultural press bayed at his scent. He also defined a mood and manner of his time more boldly and humorously than anyone else. More than that, he stands up for literature and is unafraid to examine his own motives and progress as a writer, somehow both fitting them into the zeitgeist and making them relevant to an influential number of the novelists of his generation. He has a unique pedigree and is neither fussed nor fazed by it. Kingsley Amis comes into the conversation as frequently as Nabokov which is high praise: Nabokov, practically known by heart, is one of Martin's masters.

Another is Bellow. Then there's Updike. And more – he is consumed with literature and with the literary project. His conversation steers its way through the lives of writers and the works of writers and it can be as studied as his prose style. Sometimes when I'm with him I think he's using a conversation as a first draft of a written paragraph. He once told me, 'I don't want to write a sentence that just anybody would write.' This became a point at issue between Kingsley and himself, part of their public generational tug of words and fiction.

I've always liked him. He is polite, funny, good company and charged on all cylinders in the drive of his intellectual curiosity – the dying planet, the political experience of twentieth-century Russia, as well as the poetry and novels in the western canon, traditional and recent. He's a warm companion, prone to obsession on fruit machines or darts. Football is a constant.

We began to know each other when I edited and introduced a paperback book programme called *Read All About It* in the seventies. I modelled it on a television panel game but the panellists included Gore Vidal, Antonia Fraser, Clive James, Martin et al., *and* people outside the literary ambience. The footballer Rodney Marsh, the actor David Niven.

It had a swing to it and delivered what it set out to deliver – a lively programme, accessible but well-informed, sharp on opinion, often criticised for not being sufficiently austere. The idea of mixing genres was new and resented by some in the literary world. Martin became a regular and a dab hand. Through Ian Hamilton we kept meeting. He became, Ian Hamilton said, after his novel *Money*, the 'main man'. Kingsley and Elizabeth Jane Howard came to live a few doors down the street from me and we would have a drink and sometimes Martin would be there, usually disagreeing with Kingsley on the merits of Nabokov.

I've concentrated on *The Information* which came out in 1995 chiefly because it is about writers and Martin talks well about his take on the task of writing. There was a fuss around the pre-publication of *The Information*. Martin had found a new agent, the American Andrew Wylie, who had secured a £500,000 advance – way above the reach of any literary novelist in England. That caused stir enough. Further oil was poured on the flames by the rift this move to Wylie entailed. Martin left his agent Pat Kavanagh, who was married to one of his closest friends, Julian Barnes, who cut off the friendship, which was, I thought, a great shame for all three of them. But it was done and the lit-buzzards had lots of fun.

I'd been to Israel with Martin and Julian and a few others on a literary trip and seen how much they enjoyed each other's company, even basked in it. I think Martin was shocked by this unanticipated consequence of what must have seemed to him a sensible commercial move. I mention this because the novel, *The Information*, concerns the friendship/rivalry between two novelists and the background noise in the book's reception was coloured by that.

A.S. Byatt, already a grande dame of Metropolitan Eng. Lit., had attacked Martin for 'turkey-cocking', for taking an advance he might never be able to pay off, for a 'literary lottery fever'. That too was in the background of the interview which took place in his small writing flat near the Portobello Road, a bachelor pad inhabited overwhelmingly by tumbling stacks of books. And a dartboard. And a pin table.

There are two novelists in *The Information*, a dismal failure and a bestseller. The failure, Richard, is beset by tears shed through the night when he dreams of disasters and yet when comforted and questioned by his wife as to what is happening, always replies 'nothing'. He is about to hit forty and this was important to Martin's interest in him. He himself was forty-five at the time of the interview, an age, he would assert, which was the crucial crunch.

'There's a certain age when you realise there's nothing you can do about your tiredness. No nap or cuppa is going to perk you up any more. It's the tiredness you get from your time you've been on the planet. That makes you worry . . . the gravity bearing down on you.'

'Would you claim that was a universal condition – you – your character – but more generally?'

'Yes. The whole gamble in writing is that what you come up with is of universal application. That's almost a definition of literary talent, I would say. I didn't have a didactic purpose in mind but I did think – this is what I know about it – this is my information on it. It will be exaggerated and dealt with comically for the most part because that's the way I write. But here it is.'

It might be useful to say here that there were some points – not many – along the way where I wanted to take issue with Martin, or qualify his opinion. I thought, as I often have done in these interviews over the years, that such a stance would not serve the purpose. The point was to make a portrait of Martin Amis and his writing, 1995. My job was to be the painter not the subject and in that way to give the viewers the chance to make up their own minds.

'The trouble with Richard' – the failure – 'is that he isn't doing what he wants to do all day. He is a "slave" in his own life. He isn't a writer. He hasn't made it. I worked in offices for eight or nine years – the *TLS* and the *New Statesman* and I travelled on the Tube twice a day surrounded by people who didn't like going to work, and there's no question that piles on the years. The book is very much about that. It's a very sapping world, not deserving the envy it gets from women who want to be in that world. This is not male rage or male self-pity. It's saying – we're all in this together – look at the results. Look how emotionally straitened men are – what a dull repertoire of emotions they have. This is all to do with just grinding it out on the job.'

'So doing what you don't want to do presses the life out of you?'

'That's right. And you're running out of time.'

'And that starts around forty?'

'Yeah . . .'

It's perhaps a useful historical note that Martin rolled and smoked cigarettes throughout the interview. I don't think it was nerves. He was already too much of an old hand for that. But the layering of fragile tobacco in those flimsy little rectangles of paper, the careful, rather animal licking of the glue, the lighting up, were all useful forms of punctuation. It is likely that when this and other smoking interviews I've done are repeated in a few years' time or used for schools and universities, the cigarette will be airbrushed out and there will be this strange hand-mime baffling the tobacco-foreign viewers.

'The writer has two parallel lines of time he is following. One is his own span, the other is the historical span, the span of the planet. The self changes. The middle years are different. They were for my father, for various reasons. The younger writer is always telling the older writer, it's not like *that*, it's like *this*. There's a wonderful example of this – the disaffection between an older and a younger writer – in a quotation on the back of *Lucky Jim* from Somerset Maugham. It goes something like, "There's a whole new generation of people coming up from provincial universities. Mr Amis's eye is sharp and he has captured them exactly." The quote on the Penguin ends there. But in the original statement the next line is "And they are scum. They have no understanding of art, aesthetics, etc.!" ' He laughs: he laughs a lot.

'I bet the publicist had problems cutting that.' I said.

'Yeah . . . shall we cut it off here? But there is always that thought from one generation to another. There's another familiar relationship. Between contemporaries. Richard envies his phenomenally successful friend Gwyn Barry and his worldwide bestseller. He's deeply envious of him. Early on it's envy of the house particularly . . . He envies Gwyn his share of the universe. He envies him the fact that when he goes into his study, he comes up with what people want. Gwyn's books are, as I hope I make clear, worthless. As Richard says, they would only be remarkable if Gwyn had written them with his foot. They don't offend anyone. They're programmatic novels for the age of political euphemism "we are all equal"; "there are no differences between us"; "no one's better than anyone else"; "no one's prettier than anyone else". So he's trapped in a syllogism here because if Gwyn's stuff is shit, as he keeps saying it is, but it's what people want, then the universe is shit and the world's a joke. That's what he's trapped in.'

'You say that Richard's troubles are intractably *literary* and nothing would ease them except readers or revenge. Why does revenge come in?'

'We're going to start talking about the writer's ego. Literary envy is something we usually just splutter and bluster over.'

'But it's common' I said.

'It goes with the job. Various monstrous deformations of ego go with the job and if you haven't got them, you're not in business, really.'

'What others?'

'Oh . . . huge vanity. You might as well pack up and go home if you don't think you're the best, I think. You may pretend you don't think you're the best and you may put on a good impression of someone who's very happy being in the same first division as his peers. But if you don't secretly think you're in a special class then I think you're not ever going to have a chance of being that.'

Martin is unafraid of potential public risk in speaking his mind in such a memorably abrasive manner. And he doesn't mind being pushed on it.

'Why does that have to be the path, the way of it? Why is it imperative?'

'It's just a very strong hunch. There's a story we could never tell about William Golding until now. I don't think it at all diminishes him. Golding was at some party and everybody was amazed by how modest and ordinary he was and then the clock struck ten and he had the fifth glass of wine and suddenly there was this great scream from the corridor: "I'm a genius!" ' Martin laughed and went on. 'When Conrad was showing a lady journalist around his study she noticed that he was weeping with rage and she panicked. He said, "Aren't you going to ask me to sit in the chair where I wrote *Nostromo*?" And she said, "Yes," and he immediately calmed down. I think these things bubble up and maybe get out of hand later on!'

'*The Information* is about writers and writing. In what sense is it autobiographical?'

'There's no doubt there'll be speculation about that. The answer is there's only one writer in the book who is real – that's Salman Rushdie, who gets two mentions. Apart from that, there's no one. Richard and Gwyn are both me and that's very obvious in the end. The nature of Gwyn's egomania is such that nothing's enough. You are trying to plaster yourself all over the world in the form of words and there's always something you're not getting. It's a bit like male sexuality in your middle years. You're tormented. It's your genes. You're making half-hearted attempts to propagate yourself all over the place and suddenly – I've spoken to many men in their fifties – they can't get down a street without having fifty different sexual thought experiments about every girl they pass – but you're not going to get them all, forget it, you never will. But the writer does want to get them all, all the readers.'

'Back to the book. Autobiography. How are you going to handle the speculation?'

'One of the subliminal reasons I wrote this book was I'd done a lot of interviews over twenty years and I felt all the interest directed at *me*. The truth is we are more interested in writers than we are in writing. So I thought, If you're interested, here's a book about writers, so you're getting it in the book and in the person at the same time. What I do is what I often do in my fiction – is to take two elements of my own character and imagine there was nothing else there. It's a serious enquiry into the plain fact that there's no way of distinguishing good writing from bad. We all know bad writing when we see it. But there's no way of pinning it down. Take two lines of Wordsworth: "When all at once I saw a crowd" – that's obviously a weak line. He just put in "crowd" to rhyme with "cloud". Then there's a great line like "thoughts that do often lie too deep for tears". Even though he puts in "do" to make up the numbers.'

'It's a great line.'

'It's a great line. Richards, Leavis, the big critics, they all killed themselves trying to find out why good lines were better than bad lines, good books better than bad books, but it can't be demonstrated. The more you read Milton and the more you read – I don't know, Blackmore

– you're going to find that Milton is more rewarding to study but all you can do is to labour that point. You can't actually clinch it. So it's *time* that decides these things, time sorts these things out but you're not going to be around for that, so it's all up in the air; we can't tell and we're at the mercy of contemporary taste.'

'One of the ways people value books is through the money earned,' I said. 'The American phrase: "if you're so smart why aren't you rich?" So – this advance of £500,000 for the novel. To a few writers – not huge; to the majority – very large indeed. Why do you think so much fuss gathered around it?'

Martin, for the first time in the interview, took his time, rolled a cigarette. Maybe he didn't want to answer. He didn't have to. This was not an interrogation. There was no crime. In the bonus culture of the City of London, £500,000 was commonplace. But as, I believe, Henry Kissinger said, 'The reason there is so much competitiveness in the literary world is because the stakes are so small.'

'Did it surprise you?'

He was ready now.

'Let me just say that the book is 500 pages long, took five years to write, and that advance is for two books. As for the fuss, it surprised me. I think what it did tell us . . . no American and no European I spoke to at that time could tell what it was about. It couldn't be explained to them.

'We're talking about English stuff here, an English phenomenon. English people basically don't trust writers. Nobody minds anybody getting £500,000 for crap because that fulfils a need, but when they start getting well paid for stuff that's supposed to be serious, fabulistic things happen. They think that publishers are nice old boys who love literature and just want to run their little businesses and here come the greedy bigheads who are trying to destroy the whole thing. They haven't realised that most publishers are owned by Andrex Toilet Paper and that they are businesses in the modern world just like any other business. We both know that if publishers pay a lot of money they will try harder and sell more books and get more readers and that's what we want, is readers.'

'Do you think it soiled the whole thing?'

'It seemed very mild compared with the mud that was slung at me for my last two books. For *London Fields* I was accused of misogyny. For *Time's Arrow* I was accused of being anti-semitic. That's serious. That's like someone daubing something on your door. Having survived *that*, this seems trivial and transient to me. I don't think it matters.'

'A.S. Byatt went for you. She wrote of "turkey-cocking", she said you'd never earn the money back, therefore there'll be less for other literary novelists, advances should be earned out, like hers. She presumed, or it was assumed, she spoke for others.'

'She's got an absolute right to say that. I would say she spoke for *no* other writers. The reactions I've had have all been the other way, including rookie writers as well as older writers. Every other writer in England, as far as I could tell, was behind *me*. It happens in this book I say every writer in England votes Labour. A journalist checked up on this and said I was right. Every writer in England *does* vote Labour. Except A.S. Byatt who has an admiration for Mrs Thatcher which traps her in a contradiction. Anyway, the fuss is England's problem. Her remarks are her problem.'

One theme of the book consists of reflections on the state of the universe.

'There are several passages about what's going on out there. Are you deliberately pitting your universal themes against the universe itself?'

'Well, I expect there to be a paradigm shift in the next century once the discoveries of this century enter the consciousness. And the main discovery of this century was made by Edwin Hubble in the thirties and forties. Until then, everyone believed, even Einstein, that this was *it*, the Milky Way was the universe. Hubble discovered that various shady nebulae in our galaxy were in fact other galaxies. We've been continually demoted as astronomy and cosmology have advanced until we're now a contemptible speck at the end of an unfashionable part of a galaxy in a local group. We'll soon be asked to take on board that there are infinite universes, so, a real facer *there*. I expect that to have an effect. It would be a kind of liberation.'

'What would be liberated?'

'This is a sub-atomic dot of life in what seems like a universal morgue. Everywhere you go the universe kills you. It's that hostile to life. It should tend to make us think – let's not get lost in local concerns. Border wars – so what?'

'That's quite idealistic.'

'Yes it is. And it will surely in the end spell the end of religion. I think the revealed universe is so much more fantastic than any religion. We'll grow out of it.'

'The religious stories are quite fantastic.'

'Christianity is quite fantastic: all you've got is a big shepherd with a big beard somewhere up there. We refuse to give up the idea that we are at the centre of things and that the universe is about us. You'd have thought modern astronomy would mean that astrology would just curl up and die. Not so.'

There was then a reading from *The Information* which began, 'nothing ever happens to novelists . . .' and catalogues a life of birth, illness, marriage, death, and ends, '. . . nothing ever happens to them, except the universal'.

'Again there's this gamble that what is true for you is true for others. I say of Richard he's always got the blues playing in his head. We've all got the blues, that's what we're hearing all the time and we struggle to connect with others. The writer has a discipline of doing that. What's happening to me as a writer is that probably if you start young, you're saying to your readers "Hi" and then, after a certain time, when the curve turns down, what you're really saying is "Bye".'

'You're only forty-five. You look pretty fit. Your father's still functioning as a writer.'

'Novelists' stuff does tend to give out. It's not like being a footballer. But you're not much cop after sixty, usually. There are exceptions. Conrad's one, Bellow's one, my father's one. But on the whole it's not a long career. A friend of a friend, about my age, went to see a doctor and he said he felt terrible all the time, everything hurt, but there was nothing wrong with him, but the doctor said, "Nature's through with you. What do you expect?" And that's what happens.'

'What about sixty is the new fifty? Fifty is the new forty, all the diets and regimes. Better and better.'

'Better and bette . We all know that's bullshit. What the mid-life crisis is, is an overreaction to the sudden conviction that you are going to die. It was just a rumour but now it's solidly in your sights. The thing about middle age is you don't know anything about it. When I was thirty-eight I thought I'd got everything pretty well summed-up. There was nothing I didn't know or understand about people. Then you're borne on this wave and you crash into the beach and you look around and it's unrecognisable. It's a completely new world and you don't know *anything*. Kundera says that this goes on throughout your life but I think – this is the crucial one. When you get to your fifties it's not so different. Maybe there's a final vision when you're about eighty, but the big one is around forty. And I wanted to be true to that and perhaps I exaggerated it. I look for the comedy in it.'

There is about Martin, and as far as I can remember there always has been, a certainty and wit about discussing the life and craft of being a writer. It must have something to do with the example of his father whose routine was rigid – at the desk every morning, including Christmas Day – whose range was wide – essays, tabloid journalism, anthologies, poetry, literary reviews and the novels – and whose memory for poetry was prodigious and even in drink accurate. And there was Elizabeth Jane Howard, a serious and successful novelist, Kingsley's second wife and, in his teens, a mentor to Martin. She encouraged him to read Jane Austen. Then the literary hive of the *New Statesman*, still in Martin's time boasting V.S. Pritchett and run by Claire Tomalin. Even so, the confidence with which he does it and the sense he talks are rare. And the insights are often valuable, however much you want to challenge or qualify them. He is still the leader of a pack even though the pack has always had its own opinions too.

'Writing is a permanent state of infidelity to everyone. You're an impostor in your own life much of the time. The only time you're faithful to anyone is when you're alone. 'Cos you're never going to give anyone a hundred per cent of your attention *ever*. There's always going to be your writer's pilot light left still burning. So in that sense you're not being true in your dealings with other people. Even with your children, because you're watching them, as a writer does.'

'Do you think that's unique to writers?'

'To artists perhaps. I think, again, it's part of the occupation.'

'Could this not just be part of the human condition?'

'When you read a literary biography, you have to be interested because you're interested in the writer, but you have to discount everything he does in his life because how could anyone who behaved so stupidly and selfishly and egotistically produce anything you'd want to read?'

'Isn't the private-public disjunction common to some schoolteachers and factory workers and people who don't or can't write at all?'

'Well . . . It's by virtue of the contrast with the public work which is ordered, which is moral, etc. So you say, writers are hopelessly irrelevant to what they write otherwise you don't have anything there. If a writer's life contaminates his writing, we haven't got any literature.'

'Why's that?'

'Writers tend to fail as human beings.'

'Do you include yourself?'

'It's a difficult ledger to draw. But one thing my life hasn't been is orderly. Milton when he went blind taught his daughter to read Latin, but not how to understand it. He didn't need her to understand it. So she sat there, four or five hours a day, reading this stuff she didn't understand. Now Milton wrote the central English poem. If being a bastard and a tyrant says goodbye to *Paradise Lost* . . . I can't do that. So what you have to do is separate the two things.'

'What *is* the Information?'

'The Information is Nothing. Meaning, something called Nothing. Meaning the void. Meaning what the rest of this universe almost exclusively consists of and where we will end up. We will rejoin the void.'

'So where does that leave you now?'

'I don't know if I'm good long-term. I don't know whether what I write will renew itself. Any worldly bauble or advance is not going to clarify that. There are psychologists who believe that the urge towards immortality is the most powerful of human urges. It was certainly why Milton wrote.'

Martin has pitted himself against tough opposition since that interview. He has no hesitation in courting the cliché by taking 'the world as his parish' and the world now and then resents his boldness on its various territories which they see as an encroachment, an impertinence. I like his boldness. I like his literariness. Every new book still creates an epidemic of reviews and interviews and conflicting columnist comments.

I shared a platform with him a few months ago in Manchester where he has a visiting chair in creative writing. He was as always very polite, generous, gracious, and as always nose to the page. Nabokov was still a dear reference. On the way back to the hotel after a rather heavy dinner he quoted from Nabokov and said, 'That sentence makes me proud to be human.'

Dame Edna/Barry Humphries

Not a transvestite; not homosexual; not camp, not really; not androgynous; not hermaphrodite. So who is she? *He* is a collector of rare books and paintings, a metropolitan intellectual, a reformed alcoholic, an amused observer of the scene, publicly mute. *She* is, as she says, a megastar, an icon of loud vulgar bad taste, glamour and bling, sometimes a cruel or a taunting tongue with her audiences who love her despite the insults. A couple of weeks ago, as I wrote this, she packed the Albert Hall, having recently blitzed Los Angeles, ever onward, surfing success. Who are they? Only their eyes are the same; when you stop the film and look closely – the same wicked twinkle, the same calculation.

I thought the best way to find out was to interview each of them, separately, and crucially I asked them the same questions. Sometimes I reported what the other had said, and collated the comments. Each knew the other was doing it.

I talked to Barry at his house in Hampstead, grand but by no means star-posh; an extraordinarily rich library with boxes of rare books still unopened, recently arrived. The walls were the walls of a connoisseur, paintings and drawings from a specific period, mostly first half of the twentieth century. Barry walked slowly down the grand oak staircase and paused at two or three of them as we filmed him.

We talked in his drawing room. He was dressed in a dark blue suit, tasteful tie, black hair brushed flat: a man comfortable in his own skin, oozing calm, ready to strike.

'I've always thought of myself as rather a dilettante and always felt a little bit guilty about that. I always knew I was an artist of some kind . . . perhaps a writer, or a painter.' We cut to some of his paintings – landscapes, seascapes, Notre Dame – bold. 'And yet my efforts at painting have not been successful. I'm just a cheerful amateur with a style somewhere between Winston Churchill and Hitler with a bit of Noël Coward thrown in. There's nothing sadder than an artist manqué or more dangerous when you think of Hitler. A disappointed artist is often an unstable neurotic.'

I interviewed Edna in her dressing room. She was in full superstar fig – the upwardly swooping spectacles, costume jewellery dripping from her neck and ears, rings on her fingers, gladioli behind her, a deep pink dress gleaming at the camera. Her face was wildly expressive.

'Did he compare himself with Hitler? A frustrated artist is sometimes a very, very dangerous person in the country? I don't know where I got that idea. I could've picked it up from him. Sometimes, you know, I do.'

'I wanted to be a magician when I grew up,' said Barry, 'and the big advantage of being a magician is that you make people disappear . . . very sinister, isn't it? Yes.' (He smiles – perfect Barry/Edna teeth.) 'Now I make them disappear by turning off the lights in the auditorium.'

We go back to Edna in Drury Lane in performance – teasing the people high up in what used to be called 'the Gods'. To Edna, the cheap seats. 'Hello, paupers! . . . all the way up there . . . right the way up the top at the back. Cling on!' She looked up and then back down to the stalls. 'Up there we have a slightly poorer type of person.' They begin to laugh. 'Hi, paupers! Hear their wistful cry. It's steep up there, isn't it, paupers? It's like the Wall of Death up there. Cling on! And when you clap – use one hand . . . I'll glance up there from time to time. I will. I will – in strict proportion to the amount you have paid.' She waves and abandons them. 'Goodbyee! . . .' And they applaud – at Edna's vim as a performer, at the truth of it, a rueful recognition, a sense of just good fun? They applaud.

'It's quite a common quirk,' says Barry, without my asking it.

'Do you think the character of Edna has taken you over?'

'It's a terrible thought.'

He began to play with the notion, the unlikely twinning, the Jekyll and Hyde of it, the sense of it being more than just 'an act'. 'I think it's very unlikely. If I found myself lovingly arranging a vase of gladioli one day . . . unlikely . . . It's still an act . . . on the other hand I feel it's an evolution of a real character and not an impersonation. Somewhere out there, Edna *does* exist.'

We cut to row upon row of Edna's shoes and dresses.

'Here's me in my dressing room. Please don't think these dowdy frocks are mine.' She is putting on a deep red lipstick. 'These dresses belong to Cilla Black.'

'I've always been more interested in collecting things than in doing things,' Barry said. 'In accumulating books, where I still follow early enthusiasms.' We see a copy of *The Autobiography of Alice B. Toklas* in Edna's dressing room. 'The authors of the twenties and thirties. I still think it would be a life to track down the work of one particular artist, to become obsessively interested in the artist's life and career. To find the rarest creations. And then to *acquire* them.'

'I think,' said Edna, 'he's a little bit – on a minor scale – like that Russian – Diaghilev. He can bring people together. I think he has a bit of an ability for that. I think he's got a bit of a talent for orchestrating the gifts of others.'

Now and then Edna's high phrasing is uncannily like that of Barry.

'I always thought of myself as a minor character,' said Barry. 'I was always more deeply interested in the work of minor artists than I was in major artists.'

'I wonder if he really is as he represents himself,' said Edna.

'It was a form of affectation,' said Barry. 'Also a kind of literary snobbery. People would be talking about Conrad and Wells – I would rather like to introduce the subject of Marmaduke Pickthorne.'

'Well of course,' said Edna, 'I too was always very difficult to penetrate in my early years. But Barry, I think, takes the prize. Is there anything *there*, Melvyn? That's the question you and I can ask.'

'I'm also,' Barry went on, 'interested in periods in history and in artistic history which preceded some great catastrophe, pre-war cataclysmic art – in Europe just before World War One . . .'

'He would put up a front,' said Edna, 'like a lot of my fellow Australians. I think I'm a notable exception – he *parades* a kind of new-found knowledge. Did he give you the sort of literary thing? The artistic thing?'

Edna's fluting voice is layered in wickedness, glee, a touch of malice, teasing yet somehow demanding to be taken at face value.

'The art of Weimar before the Nazis ruined the world . . .'

'Know-all Know-nothing was a phrase my mother used to use and I think that could apply to Barry. I don't mean to sound catty.'

'I'm only interested in *modern* art' says Barry '. . . and what I do in my own job seems very different – my jests about cooking and disabled toilets – people's interior decoration . . . It's something else . . . it's a way of describing my background. It takes us back to Melbourne.'

'He's still exploring his own background,' Edna said. 'His own childhood and trying to understand it, explain it.'

'I felt a sense of frustration. After all I was quite bright. I'd started reading precociously and I was making all kinds of invidious comparisons. I must have been rather insufferable.'

His spoken prose is literary and rather Edwardian. Edna's stage prose is demotically contemporary. Both are well studied.

'Some people were late developers,' Edna suggested. 'I think Barry was. I think behind all that know-all – I shouldn't say that; well, erudition shall I say? – albeit superficial, is a questioning person and therefore he's rather moving. Finally I think he's a bit of an old-fashioned person. He's rooted, culturally, in the fifties, in an Australia which is no more.'

At this point we showed film of suburban Australia which could have been propaganda for the quiet, orderly virtue of suburban life. Neat rows of houses; bicycles; clean broad streets; cheerful purposefulness.

'My father was a successful builder. I wasn't interested in that. I would sit in my parents' sitting room playing English music, generally by Vaughan Williams, imagining what it would be like to be in

England, picturing the English countryside, wishing I were there and not stuck in Melbourne. I felt frustrated by the philistinism of that kind of life.'

There is, now and then, a frisson, even a touch of vertigo, at the gap between this quiet elderly scholar ruminating in his artists-lined den in intellectual north London and Edna, almost glowering with bling, in the West End undermining her begetter.

'I began to feel that things I was good at were things I couldn't talk about. I had to invent a character for myself.'

'He *was* an outsider,' Edna said. 'As a child.'

'I went to Melbourne Grammar School and I was unhappy for at least two years. Then there was pressure to join the cadets. I'd been reading Bertrand Russell on conscientious objection. I said to the headmaster I couldn't join the cadets – much as I would like to – because I was a conscientious objector. He was so astonished to hear this from a school-boy that he instantly exonerated me from all military responsibilities and called me "Barry" thereafter and not "Humphries".'

Edna went straight in.

'He had a tendency – only Les Patterson would use a word like this – to brown-nose his way into the good books of people.' Edna turned directly to camera. 'Isn't that an uncalled-for thing to say? I'll never say it again!'

He went on tour with a rep company – much to the concern of his parents – and his life changed when he walked on stage as Orsino in *Twelfth Night*.

'I had that wonderful line: "Yes. If music be the food of love play on . . ." But somehow I got a laugh on it. Something to do with my tights – too baggy at the knees – I tried to stand behind the furniture. My first line – a titter around the audience . . . I thought, I've blown it.'

'I'll say this for Barry. There's talent there. I'd love to see him play Ibsen and Strindberg – he'd be good – if people didn't giggle. Because there's something a little bit ridiculous about him.'

But his luck was in.

'After every performance there was a little supper in the church hall. And the Lady Mayoress would give a speech about culture. How grateful she was to us all, how we'd brought this wonderful play by Shakespeare to Wogga Wogga . . . So I impersonated this Lady Mayoress. I did her voice and I more or less reported exactly what she'd said. It wasn't all that jokey and everyone was vastly amused by this character. It was a running gag on bus trips. At the end of the season the director, Ray Lawlor, said, "What's that character's name?" I said, "*Edna*." I'd once had a sort of nanny called Edna. "Other name?" I hadn't thought. "She's a very average sort of person. So Edna Average." "Write a sketch," he said, "for the Christmas Revue." "Who'll play her? I'll do the voice from the wings." "Oh no," he said, "*you* do it." So I said, "All right." '

'I don't know if he's told you the story but he'd invented a sort of housewife character dressed up in kind of Oxfam clothes. He looked a fright. More like a clown and he *wrote* to me. Out of the blue because I'd just won the "Lovely Mother" contest. And he said, "Give me some clues, a few little ideas about what Melbourne housewives are thinking." I said, "Ask your own mother." He said he didn't want the family to know because they were very opposed to the idea of him doing show business at all . . . so I went along to a rehearsal. I saw him up there on stage. It was embarrassing, Melvyn. It was very embarrassing. In the end I leapt up on the stage myself and said, "I *think*, *this* is what you were trying to do." And from that sprang the legend, and I think it persists to this day, that when people see me on TV they think that it's Barry. That's a compliment in a way to him. That he could impersonate a real person.'

'At the start,' said Barry, 'Edna was a very simpering, shy kind of woman, rather genteel and she described in *exact detail* the house in Melbourne in the 1950s when people were just learning to put three ducks up the wall and the colour of the venetian blinds and the sofa – everything was described, and the more I described it, the more the audience laughed. Because they'd never heard their houses described in the theatre. People went to the theatre to learn about another world. But life had served them up suburban Melbourne – so it was the *novelty* which produced the laughter – of recognition rather than funny – it was a "gasp": and that astonished me.'

He came to London at the end of the fifties and into the 'swinging sixties'. Girls wore very pale lipstick. Eyes looked like darns in socks. Everything was "soooper". And I rented a bedsitting room in Holland Park and I lived in expectation of becoming a star.'

He earned his living as a jobbing actor. Despite his success in Australia and his humorous records – he made no headway until Peter Cook heard the records and took him up and in 1963 put him on at the new Establishment Club in Soho.

'The jokes that really worked were jokes about Harold Macmillan and I didn't make political jokes. And only on the first night did I real-ise there was something *very* very wrong with me being there. I didn't *feel* funny on that stage, looking down on an audience expecting jokes about Harold Macmillan. And when a comedian doesn't *feel* funny, he *isn't* funny. You've got to feel funny.'

He was however making progress in another smart establishment, that of the Oxford-based mafia in English intellectual life. It was conducted by the Warden of Wadham College, Maurice Bowra, and Barry used to go to parties there.

'I remember Osbert Lancaster when I met him at a party at Maurice Bowra's at Oxford, and Osbert said, "Oh. You're Australian, are you?" I said yes. He said, "Oh, God, save us from some of your citizens." What do you mean? He said, "My friend Betjeman sent me to this terrible club in London, I think it was a brothel of some kind, and there was this terrible drag queen – it was the most excruciatingly boring evening I've ever spent." Well, he was in too deep. I couldn't say, "I'm afraid it was me." I said, "Yes, I saw that too. It was awful, wasn't it?" I said, "We're not all like that." '

Despite his failure, Peter Cook kept faith with Humphries and teamed him up with the cartoonist Nicholas Garland. They created the Barry McKenzie strip of *Private Eye*. He was a rapacious, foul, drunken Aussie, living in Earl's Court. 'I could put my vast collection of Australian slang to use, some real, some invented, which gave the *impression* of Australian speech. Barry became a cult, then a hit, then two films. And Edna appeared in the films. But Edna was the character that had the longer life. Largely because my livelihood depended on it. And *I, was, Edna*. I had to constantly guard the development of the character. I became increasingly aware that the character had a life of her own.'

'It's a paradox, Melvyn. He assisted *me* early on in my career and now, if it weren't for *me*, I doubt if he'd be anywhere, little Barry.'

It was on the *Russell Harty Show* that Edna, the new brash Edna, the Housewife Superstar, hit the audience. 'British audiences respond very warmly to anything that is funny. The British are wonderful comedy audiences. And that studio audience enjoyed her. I felt funny. I thought, Perhaps it might work now. It's all about confidence – and talent of course – and it became a West End success and I just keep doing it.'

She became a megastar and her clothes grew to magnificence. 'I brought in designers. Women came to see the show – "we can have a good laugh at Edna" – only to find that she's wearing what they're wearing, only better! I decided to make her very smart – still over the top, a parody of real clothes – but she gave the impression of being a SUPERIOR figure.'

Edna then began to tell the audience about her relationship with Mrs Thatcher: 'Mrs Thatcher rang me in tears saying, "What can I wear tomorrow?" The audience want to believe that Mrs Thatcher talks to Edna and when they see her on the front page of the *Telegraph* – they *know* it's true! The Ednaisation of Mrs Thatcher is a palpable reality.'

'Do you think you have power on the stage?'

'It's limitless,' said Barry, 'the audience want you to exert a massive degree of power over them. They deliver themselves into your hands. They know they're not going to be hurt. They're titillated by the possibility they might be. The ripple of fear when Edna selects a victim' – as she does, several 'victims' in her stage show: the victims are then mocked and humiliated – 'that is a *pleasurable* ripple – what's going to happen? It has a certain eroticism about it. Embarrassment becomes a benediction bestowed upon those people, generally women of a certain age. Edna's age. This vulture disguised as a bird of paradise. But I've seen the victims on the steps of the theatre afterwards being complimented on their performances.'

'I don't think he knows who he is,' says Edna. 'Does that sound a cliché? When Barry Humphries looks in the mirror in the morning – what does he *see* there?'

'On the surface,' I said, 'there seems quite a difference between what you are here, in this house, and what goes on on the stage.'

Barry paused, I think for the first time, and noticeably.

'I don't think anything is just on the surface at all.'

'He's changed a lot over the years,' said Edna.

'I don't see a connection between what I do in the theatre and what I'm privately enthusiastic about – the collecting – but it has in some submerged sense to exist. To do with . . .'

'Power?'

'Yes. I think it's a harmless exercise of power.'

The film was running out, literally, we were at the end of a roll and as the screen went blank, Edna's voice went on.

'Fleet Street editors say people like Melvyn and Barry and Edna have entered into a Faustian pact with success and deserve to be punished. I don't think that. If we're going to be punished, let it be by the—'

And the sound ran out.

Edna goes on. On and on. It is one of the wonders that it is so good. That it remains so popular. And that such an intelligent and gifted man finds enough in this one creation to occupy him year in year out for decades, to possess his time, his energies. She changes, though, through the years, as he does. She is the monster he has brought to life and must for ever watch over because without her he is not himself.

Seamus Heaney

I was in the BBC Canteen in Lime Grove when I first encountered Seamus Heaney. It was in the form of his first book of poems, *Death of a Naturalist* (published in 1966) and it had just come out. A friend of mine, the critic and old-term 'man of letters', the late Julian Jebb, put it in front me – a hardback I still have – and said, 'You'll like this. You'll like it *very* much.' I did, I still do.

In the territory of 'generational kinship' there are a few light connections. Both Heaney and myself were born in 1939. The rural Northern Ireland he inherited was not unlike my rural Cumberland, just a few miles to the east of him, across a small sea. There was the farm labouring inheritance in common.. His Catholicism, though more political than my High Anglicanism, had enough of an ecclesiastical and narrative similarity. There was more but the point is that reading some of those poems was hearing clear echoes from my own childhood. That recognition draws you quickly into a writer's world: what keeps you there are the qualities of the work which follow no laws. Heaney's work not only survived a resonant and authentic beginning, it grew and still it grows.

Prizes have been given the work – the Nobel Prize most magnificently. He is treasured among poets and has made a point of praising and nursing other poets, often from other languages, a passion and pursuit he shared with his friend Ted Hughes. His deep knowledge of poetry has led him to write prose which has its own springs of rhythm and beauty and bears re-reading, sometimes as much as the poems themselves. As a lecturer he is a spellbinder and as a reader of his own work there is the ancient bard about him.

Seamus Heaney seems to bring to the modern world the cloak and aura of the ancient high calling of the poets of Irish history. It comes partly from his respect for that history, partly from the soil out of which his imagination grew and to which it still returns, the ancestral soil of Irish land and legend. And there's something in his bearing. There is a modest grandness about Seamus Heaney, a sure sense that the poet is a man of serious worth with nothing to prove other than that which his work will show.

Over the years, since that encounter in the canteen, I've got to know Seamus and to know him is to feel great affection for him. He is generous in his appreciation of the work of others. He meets you with a smile. He comes straight to the matter – your family, your work, something recently read and enjoyed. He likes long talks and drinking. And yet he is watchful, noting, forever moving the conversation by way of finding more careful and exact language. And he has a tremendous laugh on him!

We did the interview in 1991, at the time of the publication of *Seeing Things*. We shot it very simply, a close-up of Heaney with a few cutaways to some of the questions. The poetry was read by the poet either directly to camera or, where relevant, there were images from the precise places referred to in the poem, which worked well, I thought. And once or twice the director successfully 're-created' the images of a poem – as when the boys were playing football 'in the dark'.

Had there been a sense of danger in the countryside in which he had grown up? It was a troubled and divided community with himself and his parents and the family of eight children in a Roman Catholic minority in a Northern Ireland still bound in a sort of spasm to the Protestant UK while to the south was the bulk of the island, Eire, Catholic, independent and home of the IRA.

'I did grow up in a divided community that talked across its barriers very gently and intimately. I think of our own threshold at home, and the negotiation for milk. A guy called Jim Gilmore used to come for the milk. There was just a milli-, milli-, millimetre of difference

between the conversation at the door with him and with someone else
– that's overstating it!'

'But it was there? Because he was a Protestant.'

'Yeah. The sense of difference was acknowledged . . . it wasn't
a barrier at that level but one was always aware of it. So. Yes. From
the very beginning of my consciousness, *almost*, there was a sense of a
divided world. I write about it very directly, kind of heavy-handedly in
'Death of a Naturalist', a poem set in Belfast; it was about Protestant
and Catholic neighbours in one called 'The Other Side', about engagement with the 'other', not a threshold but a stream – 'the other side'. At
the time the Troubles broke out, I was just remembering the other day,
I wrote a ballad which was not published, but there are various ways in
which, as Orwell says, why not say what happened?'

There had been comment about Irish poets that some had not sufficiently addressed the Troubles. The first part of our interview would be
taken up with this. He read *The Toome Road*.

> One morning early I met armoured cars
> In convoy, warbling along on powerful tyres,
> All camouflaged with broken alder branches,
> And headphoned soldiers standing up in turrets.
> How long were they approaching down my roads
> As if they owned them? The whole country was sleeping.
> I had rights-of-way, fields, cattle in my keeping,
> Tractors hitched to buckrakes in open sheds,
> Silos, chill gates, wet slates, the greens and reds
> Of outhouse roofs. Whom should I run to tell
> Among all of those with their back doors on the latch
> For the bringer of bad news, that small-hours visitant
> Who, by being expected, might be kept distant?
> Sowers of seed, erectors of headstones . . .
> O charioteers, above your dormant guns,
> It stands here still, stands vibrant as you pass,
> The visible, untoppled omphalos.

This part of the interview was Seamus at his most careful. The line between poetry and politics, the threshold, to use a word of his, was sometimes fine, other times a battlefield. He had his own position worked out but the often brutal, simple, often black and white context had to be taken into account also.

'I suppose I've always been aware that saying what happened is an angle of saying, the angle is important. What is expected is that you join a political protest. I did that with prose in the late sixties. I wrote in the *Listener* and places. There was plenty of exposure going on and I don't think poetry functions particularly interestingly on exposure and accusation.

'As far as I was concerned, as far as I still am concerned, poetry and imaginative writing in general is a way of giving a sense of the world through a temperament and you have to be true to your temperament. My temperament is not Brechtian. In fact, I've very little interest in politics.' This said with quiet apologetic conviction, emphatically.

'In early collections,' I said, 'like *North* or *Wintering Out*, you make discourses about what you call "cultural depth charges" in the language. What interested you there?'

'Toome is a place on the borders. It's situated near several megalithic sites where some of the first human habitation in Ulster occurred. It's got an eel fishery. It was a sixth sense. There were creatures here in mid-Ulster in 6000 BC. There's a depth of habitation, of belonging – to use a corny word. There's more to us being here than all this Orange and Green stuff. The word "Toome" itself seemed to have that old – not archaic but archetypical – invitation to dwell in it.'

> My mouth holds round
> the soft blastings,
> Too*me*, Too*me*,
> as under the dislodged
>
> slab of the tongue
> I push into a souterrain

> prospecting what new
> in a hundred centuries'
>
> loam, flints, musket-balls,
> fragmented ware,
> torcs and fish-bones
> till I am sleeved in
>
> alluvial mud that shelves
> suddenly under
> bogwater and tributaries,
> and elvers tail my hair.

'Did you resent the pressure put on you and other poets in Northern Ireland? The expectation that was being delivered to you: "Come on, you're in the middle of a civil war – write about it." '

'I don't think we resented it but we resisted it. Perhaps too prissily. But the thing in the sixties and seventies would have been – Let others come here and write about the melodrama of the Troubles – they don't know it as well as we do – we know the minor complications. It glamorises it and melodramatises it just to say it's about Catholics killing Protestants.

'What we knew was *true* but maybe it was too refined, maybe the times required something rougher. I think writers in Northern Ireland behaved properly and honourably in not being enlisted into the bally-hoo of the thing. A number of them were involved in civil rights movements. They behaved responsibly as citizens. As writers they worked within the orthodoxies of the lyric as they had been working. You mustn't become other people's mouthpieces.'

In 1975 Seamus Heaney's cousin was murdered by Protestants. He wrote about this twice. First an elegy and subsequently a longer poem in which the spirit of his cousin returns and reproaches him for glazing over the ugliness of his death.

'The first one is an elegy. The traditional elegy resurrects the dead one in a benign landscape and makes the dead walk again in a beautiful free way.'

The Strand At Lough Beg: in memory of Colum McCartney

The last part of the poem reads:

Across that strand of yours the cattle graze
Up to their bellies in an early mist
And now they turn their unbewildered gaze
To where we work our way through squeaking sedge
Drowning in dew. Like a dull blade with its edge
Honed bright, Lough Beg half-shines under the haze.
I turn because the sweeping of your feet
Has stopped behind me, to find you on your knees
With blood and roadside muck in your hair and eyes,
Then kneel in front of you in brimming grass
And gather up cold handfuls of the dew
To wash you, cousin. I dab you clean with moss
Fine as the drizzle out of a low cloud.
I lift you under the arms and lay you flat.
With rushes that shoot green again, I plait
Green scapulars to wear over your shroud.

'And then later,' I said, 'there's "Station Island", which shows a radical change of mind? Of heart? Of thinking? Another way to examine the same event. He comes back to accuse you, the poet of the elegy, of "confusing evasion and artistic tact"; he says the poet "saccharined my death with morning dew" . . .'

' "Station Island" is a poem in which the mystification of art, the lyric, is refuted. It kind of puts the boot into the lyric . . . "you whitewashed ugliness". It's a dramatic poem.'

'Is it a confrontation of your own beliefs?'

'It's an exploration. It's trying to open the fan of your beliefs.' (He spread out wide the fingers of his left hand.) 'This part of the fan says it's the function of the lyric poem to tell the truth, it's a poetic truth – that's one belief. The other concentrates on the unliterary part of yourself. The kind of ignorant refuser of consolation part says you should only record that the guy was probably shot by Protestant paramilitaries. We hear about the IRA all the time, we should show it isn't just the IRA, we should show it's also the UDR. You're caught between the two things.

'In a way the attempt we all make in our lives is to become *one* and not to be just a bundle of contradictions. Poetry is an attempt to bring the contradictions together in one holding field.'

In his new book, *Seeing Things*, there's a change of direction and 'Fosterling', I think, introduces this.

> Fosterling
> *'That heavy greenness fostered by water'*
> John Montague
>
> At school I loved one picture's heavy greenness –
> Horizons rigged with windmills' arms and sails.
> The millhouses' still outlines. Their in-placeness
> Still more in place when mirrored in canals.
> I can't remember not ever having known
> The immanent hydraulics of a land
> Of *gl*ar and *gl*it and floods at *dailigone*.
> My silting hope. My lowlands of the mind.
>
> Heaviness of being. And poetry
> Sluggish in the doldrums of what happens.
> Me waiting until I was nearly fifty
> To credit marvels. Like the tree-clock of tin cans
> The tinkers made. So long for air to brighten,
> Time to be dazzled and the heart to lighten.

'What brought on this change?'
'I thought there'd been a certain amount of wading deep in the heaviness, sullenly, without any lyric charm whatsoever, no light-heartedness, all barge-work. There was a simple desire to change.'

' "Poetry/Sluggish in the doldrums of what happens".'

'That's right. Behind that is a phrase that's been coasting around in the criticism I've done. The phrase is "the music of what happens". It's from an old Irish story — "the best music in the world is the music of what happens". You feel at times that it is the responsibility of the poet to address that. But there's the other music, the other worldly music, the siren music, the music of what might happen, the music of desire . . .'

'The crediting of marvels?'

'What I mean by "the crediting of marvels" is to let the balloon go up, let desire go up, let there be some sort of flag flown for openness and pleasure.'

In this new book of poems Heaney is still entranced by, even in thrall to, his childhood. He writes a poem about a boy spinning the back wheel of an upturned bicycle by driving the pedal with his hand and the whole movement entering into him, pressing him, in the childhood landscape of Antrim. Both his parents died in recent years. His father died while Seamus was preparing this collection. There are poems in the collection which are about him.

'What effect did he have on you?'

'There was a potency and distance in our relationship. He was always an archetype to me rather than a parent.'

'And those sayings . . .'

'His sayings were few. "Catch the old one first and the young ones will all follow." Therefore they were cherished, I suppose, and they were shared by the family — there were eight of us — the mythology of statements by the parent and his kind of intelligent put-downs. He was devoted to reducing the magnificent as much as possible. I suppose in some kind of way we were completely overwhelmed by him.'

You can see this in the first poem in Heaney's first book. There we see his father out on the moss digging peat, scarcely pausing to take and eat the food brought him by his eager little son. He is a heroic and unsurpassable figure in that landscape. His spade became the boy's, the poet's, pen. He would dig with that.

'There's just a whole series of literary and life events – death of a parent obviously – where the sense of the crossing the threshold experience, the rite of passage, whatever, was coming to be very useful. So I got started on a little series and I got the idea of crossings, just crossings, so, doorways, latches, stepping stones and so on. They figured both for themselves and for their metaphorical possibilities.'

'The title? *Seeing Things*.'

'I found this after coming on a boat to Inishbofin. I wrote that in my fear of water, fear of drowning and this memory of my father almost drowning and seeing him – the title came – *Seeing Things*. It was going to maybe be called "Lightenings" – a contentious title. But *Seeing Things* – so throwaway and so potentially visionary at the same time. We went on a great sailboat with all the family. One big sail. It was like a first journey. Like going to sea in a story. The boat was anchored out from the pier. We went to the boat in a rowboat. That was to me a *terrifying* moment. It was clear water, stillness, but the boat was full to the gunwales and you thought, One false move and you're out.'

'There's a poem called "Markings" about boys playing football late into the dark.'

'That poem was after me. I wondered where it was going. I wanted to address the minor miracle of children being able to see in the dark when they are playing football. They cross a line, from this usual light to the inner light – not a mystical thing, an observable thing. It seemed to me that was a metaphor for the possibilities that reside in writing and in artistic activity generally. There's a little play in the poem on the phrase "extra time", which is a football term, but "extra" in the sense of being outside time, time stopping. And then it goes into memory. What happens when the remembered is held up and is transfigured in memory. It says somewhere that they . . .'

' "Marked the spot, marked time and held it open".'

'Yes, I suppose that's a description of what I'd like to do with a poem. That it be not just pictured, that it be not just a documentary representation, but that it have an aura and a radiance and a sense of fullness and pressure and that it . . . marked time.'

We marked the pitch: four jackets for four goalposts,
That was all. The corners and the squares
Were there like longitude and latitude
Under the bumpy ground, to be
Agreed about or disagreed about
When the time came. And then we picked the teams
And crossed the line our called names drew between us.

Youngsters shouting their heads off in a field
As the light died and they kept on playing
Because by then they were playing in their heads
And the actual kicked ball came to them
Like a dream heaviness, and their own hard
Breathing in the dark and skids on grass
Sounded like effort in another world . . .
It was quick and constant, a game that never need
Be played out. Some limit had been passed,
There was fleetness, furtherance, untiredness
In time that was extra, unforeseen and free.

There's Heaney the scholar as it were riding shotgun for Heaney
the poet, or carrying the lanterns before and behind him. And Heaney
commanding his world, readers out there flocking to his readings which
are brimful of his lines, his welcome, his embracing good feeling. Like
his work, he is someone to look forward to, and also like his work, you
leave the encounter the richer for it, that spring of humour never far
away, that twinkle in his eye, that seizing on a word.

Rudolf Nureyev

The crew set out from Positano and made for one of the seven islands clearly visible from this destination of luxury in the lap of the Amalfi coast. These seven islands had once belonged to another dancer, Massine, who had built a house and a dance studio on top of the largest of these small volcanic outcrops which poked through the Mediterranean like monsters from the mythic deep, rearing up their heads.

We chugged across the choppy water, rather surprised that at last we had landed Rudolf Nureyev, who had bought the islands and found them perfect for his twin purposes: to be outside society and to be able to concentrate on his work. He had by then acquired six other homes around the world, each one, he told me, similarly located – outside society and a workplace. His acquisition of seven homes – some of them of oriental magnificence – can partly be explained by the unusual wealth he accrued by his talent and partly by a shrewd eye for investment. But there must also have been an element of revenge on his past, which in childhood was as spectacularly poor as now it seemed mythically wealthy. He is seldom in any home for long, but this was his key retreat.

He needs to retreat. He has given more performances and been seen by more audiences than any other dancer. His is one of the most dramatic and unlikely personal journeys in art in the twentieth century.

Although he was outside society, as isolated as any of the poets and politicians who have been self-exiled or banished to Mediterranean islands, society sought him out. We thought we were a unique landing party. But, over the days, others came, always, it seemed to me, people whose appearance was designed to show off luxury, affluence and privilege. It was mesmerising to see them surround him as he lay on a couch on the terrace, stretched out, like a cat in the sun, the fawning and obeisance, the public display of devotion and adoration. And all taken like one born to it. Like one of the princes he had danced so often, like a Roman emperor. As lush shrubs of dark grapes were passed around, the Tartar Muslim from the impoverished outer reaches of the Russian Empire took it as his due.

'I was born on a train on Trans-Siberian Railroad.' We sat on one of the terraces, on hard chairs, in the shade, sat for one then two hours of interview during which he was thoughtful, courteous, laughing, at ease. 'My father was on military service in Manchuria – he called my mother and three children to join him. As you know the trip is very long, about twelve days from Moscow to Vladivostok, and I was shaken out of the womb by Lake Baikal.'

After the visit, they went to their home town of Ufa.

'It was a very small city. The most haunting sound of the city was the sound of the train. We could hear from miles away, calling you, beckoning you to somewhere.' We filmed the railway line where it crossed the river: our vantage point was the side of a mountain which the small boy used to climb and watch the trains go by. 'I used to stay for hours on the mountain watching the trains come and go across the river, going to Leningrad and Moscow and then maybe to Hungary and Paris and London. My mind travelled on those trains. In middle of night you could wake up hearing wheels tapping the time in the distance.'

Rudolf was eight when his father – a political instructor as well as a soldier – returned home from the war.

'We have *one room*. Just *one room*. Twelve square metres. We share with two other families. No intimacy whatsoever. To go to the toilet you had to go through the street and in severe weather you would be – ventilated by hurricanes and snowstorms!' He laughed as if at a fond memory.

They had difficulty in the primary matter of getting money for food. 'We would gather water bottles, wash them, sell them back to the shop, things like that, and sell old newspapers. During war when Father would send sometimes chocolate, Mother would make cocoa and sell it in markets. I used to sell water on a hot summer day.'

He has said that his most abiding memory of childhood is 'gnawing hunger'.

His dream of extreme wealth was never to be hungry.

'Once, it was just before the end of war, we had *nothing* to eat. Mother gathered a shirt of my father and some fabric and went to the village and sold it to my aunts. She came back with goose and some flour. And she was attacked by wolves! It was about six o'clock in the evening. So she took the blanket she was wearing and set on fire and scared them off.' He laughed, delighted. 'Ballsy lady!'

'When did you first want to be a dancer?'

'Age six. My mother smuggled me into theatre. *Then* I decided. To begin with, before the orchestra began, there was a green velvet curtain, and different colours on it. The projectors threw light on the curtain – red and green and blue. I thought that already was magic. And then suddenly overture begins and curtain opens and there is big void and wonderful people and I thought, That's me!'

At his first school, the kindergarten, humiliation began on the first day.

'I didn't have any shoes. My mother carried me on her back to kindergarten.'

In these early stages of the interview, looking at a man whose face has been photographed thousands of times, whose world fame is secure and earned, it is like listening to a fairy tale. Yet it is a true story. Hard, and also cruel.

At school he joined the folk dancing club. At home his sister says he never stopped singing and dancing. His father, a war veteran, was alarmed.

'He beat me up. Each time he catch me. But I just went *on*. And my mother was an ally.'

When he went up a school, 'They had heard I was gifted for dance and I was dragged out for these performances – applauded and tormented at the same time.'

His old teacher, gap-toothed, strong features, serious, said, 'He was cocky. The other boys resented the fact he had talents they didn't possess. There was always a lot of friction. They used to pick fights with him and he would retaliate. He was stubborn and determined and pursued his goal. One day his father came to see me and said, "I don't want my son to become a dancer. After school I want him to secure some kind of technical training – an engineer. Please influence him." I didn't. Anyway it would have been futile. He was determined and more than anything he was very stubborn.'

Folk dancing can smack of good-hearted amateur frolics. Not in Ufa, not then, not now. We filmed a group of young folk dancers from the school, in gorgeous costumes, drilled, trained, passionate.

'Folk dancing is feisty dancing. Temperament is very important and command of stage. From early years I knew how to be on stage and how to command it. And how to *shine*.'

His luck began to turn. There was in Ufa a former member of Diaghilev's Ballets Russes – Anna Udeltsova, who had married an officer in the Tsar's army and consequently been banished to Ufa. When we interviewed her she was 101, straight-backed, a high clear voice, certain of every word.

'In 1948 I ran an amateur dance group for children. Rudolf caught my attention. Just a little Tartar boy, shabby. But he impressed me by his dancing and moreover it struck me that he had a perfect ear for music. He did his preparation class *wonderfully*. He stood out. It was very difficult for him to get on with his dancing because his father punished him. He believed it was scandalous for men to dance. After a year he had learned all I could teach him. So I sent him to my friend who had been a dancer with the Mariinsky Theatre. I guided his future training and my husband helped him a great deal with social graces.'

A few years later, at sixteen, he made the first of two decisions to leap across a frontier.

'I wanted to go to Leningrad school. I had to gather 3,000 roubles. I went to school and taught them twice a week the way I began myself.'

Eventually he gathered enough money for a one-way ticket to Leningrad. He arrived there at dawn in August 1955 and walked straight from the station to the Kirov, home of Pavlova, Nijinsky, Balanchine . . .

He was seventeen, but they put this 'unformed provincial boy' in with much younger students. He was not pleased. Within a fortnight he was at loggerheads with the director of his class.

'I saw he was not a good teacher. I tried to get out of his class as soon as possible. I went to see Ivanovsky who was Artistic Director of the school. I say to him – if I stay in *this* class, army will come in middle and take me away. It's better I move to another class. So that's what I did. Of course Director never forgave me and at any given moment he needled me.'

Nureyev landed in Pushkin's class. Pushkin was probably the greatest influence in his career.

'Pushkin was an excellent classical dancer himself. Probably not very attractive but he was one of the purest dancers . . . he made combination of steps very danceable, kind of irresistible, very delicious. It was such a joy executing those steps in that combination. He had the ability to make you go higher and higher. He brought together music and emotion. A particular step and gesture had to express feelings. He inspired my attitude to dancing – attack, musicality, time suspension, grace . . .'

There was one very serious battle with the school. It was run on party lines and the party discipline was enforced.

'My first year I went to theatre. When I came back, door was locked. They made me bang on door for a very long time. Then they let me in and say, "We punish you because you went to the theatre." They took my mattress. They made me sit on a window seat all night. Next day – no breakfast, no lunch – so I went to my friend to eat and I am late for class. Why? I said, "Yesterday I went to the theatre and this displeased the party. So I think next time if I make mistake like that they will whip me!" So' – huge smile – 'the Director went up through the wall. Then they had really such a horrendous meeting. They take words out of my tongue and out of my memory. "I didn't say that!" "That didn't happen!" I was sure that they were about to throw me out.'

But they didn't. Pushkin and his talent saved him.

Natalia Dudinskaya, a leading ballerina at the Kirov, says, 'What was amazing was that after only three years at school he was a fully made dancer. He was secure in style and form. Where did he get this sense of beauty? It emanated from within. I understood this was no ordinary boy. I decided to take the risk of asking him to be my partner in *Laurencia* – his first starring role. It gives me great pleasure to remember dancing with Rudolf Nureyev. For this I gave away a piece of my heart. He is not only dancer. He is very great actor.'

He was a success but suspicion of him had been aroused and would never be dampened. He insisted on going to performances by visiting artists; he knocked about with them. He made his opinions clearly known.

'They worried that I might leave when I went to Vienna. They interrogated my mother and everybody to get assurances I would not stay. I didn't have that on my mind. Not then!'

When the Kirov went to Paris in 1961, Nureyev refused to go on bus trips with the company and explored Paris on his own – save for the two KGB men on his tail.

His dancing caused a sensation.

The company was to go over to London, but at the airport 'somebody tell me, "You don't have a place in the plane." I thought that was extraordinary . . . the man who brought *enormous* success to the Kirov in Paris has no place on the plane? Then somebody said, "Khrushchev wants to see you dance at Kremlin." Oh? Who with? What costumes? "You'll find there," Ah! So I decide right then that I'm not going back. Goodbye time.'

But it wasn't so simple.

'I'd been told to walk very slowly, six steps exactly, and say, "I would like to stay in your country." And is exactly what I did. Just before that

I was hiding behind a column and for some reason all Russians in KGB run on to street – past me! The moment they passed I went straight to the two commissars, no hysteria – I say, 'I would like to stay in your country.'

'They sent me upstairs. They say, "You have to wait there forty-five minutes before you sign paper." So I went upstairs. They found a translator. Suddenly she turned on me: "You are a fool! What are you going to do here? You are going to be hungry, where work?" I said, "Shut up, you bitch!" She tried to walk me out. There is a bang on door. Some solid guys come. "We will take care of you if you go back to Russia . . ." There was a nurse; she had a syringe; screaming I was mad, I had to be given an injection. NO! OUT! ALL!'

Then he gave the first of many press conferences in the West. It was a world event. His leap to freedom. It seemed to signify so much about the 'liberal' West versus the 'closed society' of Russia; the freedom here and the lack of it there. And the boldness of it! And his savage-handsome looks. And, above all, the reputation, hatched quietly in Russia but now ablaze in the arts world after those performances in Paris.

When you see film of him at the time, you can see the bolt of lightning that he was. His athleticism is breathtaking, the leaps, the pirouettes, the *speed* of it all. The speed and the precision. But just as breathtaking is the grace, the feather lightness of his movement, the mysterious but 'observable' hovering in the air, the attack and total immersion in the interpretation of the character and the music. In an old black and white film from a rehearsal at the time, he flashes across the stage, dressed in white, like some sort of spirit – and my appreciation here is merely the foothills of the praise that he would meet with in the West where he utterly transformed the perception of the male dancer and the place of ballet in the scheme of things.

In Russia there was silence.

His sister said, 'We only found out about the defection when the other dancers returned and he wasn't with them. He did the right thing. The right thing.'

But from Anna Udeltsova came a contrary view. 'For me it was a terrible blow. His father a political instructor for the Red Army and suddenly his son decides to defect.'

The KGB hounded him. There were death threats. Calls from his family.

'They called me. I was in Deauville. I was annoyed my mother found me in Deauville. What does she know about Deauville? And my mother said, "Ah – your mama – your papa!" Then she say, "*Answer me one question*." I wait. "Are you happy there?" I said, "*Yes*." And the call was over.'

He was snapped up by the Marquis de Cuevas Ballet and offered a six-year contract. He accepted three months. 'I was planning to go to Balanchine and also to study in Denmark with Erik Bruhn, who I considered the best dancer in the world. First things first. I had to find out what made him tick and learn the ticking. So I went there and studied with him and saw all his performances.'

There is footage of them at the barre, doing their exercises, facing each other, mirrored twice, once behind and with the other facing. It's a small masterpiece in itself and again you are thankful that film and television arrived to record such moments.

While he was in Copenhagen, Margot Fonteyn phoned him and asked him to come and dance with her in London. He got off the plane and went immediately to her house for tea.

'He looked pale and pinched which I wasn't expecting. We sat down, eyeing each other up and then something happened and he laughed and I said, "What a relief that you laughed," and suddenly I felt – this is going to be all right.'

It became one of the greatest dancing partnerships in ballet history and much of it recorded so that decades on we can still see how remarkable it was.

Dame Ninette de Valois was instantly converted. 'His entry into the West was like a bomb dropped on to our world. Here we had a dancer of tremendous virtuosity who was also a marvellous artist – that was a combination we were not used to.'

At Covent Garden his first appearance was when he danced *Giselle* with Margot Fonteyn and the roof was raised. Together they would become part of the swirl of international superstars. Nureyev became iconic. People were dazzled by the looks (he became a 'face' of the times), his cross-gender sexual appeal and the mixture of what people loved to call his 'animal' qualities and his unsurpassable classical rigour. There was also the dramatic story of the Tartar boy and the epic journey somehow emblematic of the twentieth century. Then the mystery that always veiled him and the glamour he brought to the male role in what had seemed to many an art form locked in its own well-lit, well-upholstered but sidelined museum. There were those who would have preferred it to remain that way. Not Margot Fonteyn.

'As far as the big classical ballets went, he brought a great change. They were the ballerina's ballets and the prince had a subsidiary role. Rudolf didn't like that. He thought the prince had to be as important as the ballerina and he saw to it that he was.'

'We were feeding off each other and reading each other's minds,' said Nureyev. 'Of course there was a lot of rehearsing to do. Margot took all the advice I could give her in *Giselle*. On *Swan Lake* she was . . .' – he laughed – '. . . we had a more difficult time.'

The South Bank Show made a film on Margot Fonteyn. In it we saw the intensity of her relationship with Nureyev. The love and sex involved, his rage when she lost their child, the violence of the passion behind the impeccable composure of their public performance.

Fredrick Ashton created a new ballet for them with designs by Cecil Beaton – *Marguerite and Armand*, based on *The Lady of the Camellias*.

'It was four people! We improvised. We had very good time. Then I would ask – does anyone remember what we did? . . . So nobody remembered and I was getting frustrated and angry and Margot is so fluid and loves to improvise – but I want to know what we are going to do *on stage*! Finally I take it piece by piece. We *fixed* the pas de deux.'

It was the first time a ballet had been created for Nureyev, and the opening was glitz and sumptuous press, photographers, friends from 'high places', success, excess, a deluge of publicity.

Nureyev was not altogether happy.

'In Russia we don't have this amount of that kind of thing. There's a lot of stories about me not always correctly reported and that made me *very* upset. I tried to keep away press, refusing interviews, refusing to talk to them and so I earned very quickly the label of being very difficult, unpleasant, all that. I just didn't want to have that much written about me. Also my great ambition was to be part of the Royal Ballet and the Company and I thought with so much publicity I will not feel equal with them and they will not feel comfortable with me. Each time I try to go into society it doesn't work. I like the performance, then just get out as fast as I can. I don't fit.'

The drawback of the Covent Garden system was that it was a dual-purpose house and more opera than ballet. When the opera moved in, the ballet, in Nureyev's words, was 'kicked out of the theatre. There would be big gaps without work, without any security, not knowing where to go. So I started to mount productions – in Vienna, in La Scala, Stockholm, Zurich – and that gave me work when I was kicked out of Covent Garden.'

His need for work was permanent. He gave 200 performances a year and on top of that charity concerts and 'appearances', constantly travelling. There were over a hundred roles in his repertory. One night he would dance in Europe, the next in New York. And he went in pursuit of other ways to dance – in particular his long ambition to team up with Balanchine.

'He was the greatest choreographer. I went to New York. He came to see my performance. I said, "Can I join your company?" He said, "My ballets are very dry. I don't have pas de deux." He said, "Get rid of your princes and then come back." '

It was fifteen years after that initial approach that the two former pupils of the Kirov school worked together: Nureyev had persisted.

Nureyev was entranced by the way in which Balanchine worked and there, on the terrace across from Amalfi, he acted it out, luxuriating in his impersonation of Balanchine's gestures and style of conversation.

'Balanchine would work with a pianist and ask him to play the last climax. 'Can you play last climax?' The pianist goes – Tum-tum. 'Ah, what is this Tum-tum?' . . . then he starts working it out . . . "Now what is the previous climax?" . . . then he choreographs that . . . then "What is the climax before that one?" . . . so he goes on – *backwards*. And then he says, "*Well*, now we can choreograph the dance." So he weaves the dance around these Himalayan tops so he knows in advance how the piece is going to finish. I find that wonderful and witty.' (Nureyev, no other word, beamed like a boy, ear to ear.) 'I was very delighted he shared that with me.'

He danced Balanchine, he danced Paul Taylor ('new steps, new contortions'). In 1976 he made his debut as a film actor with Miss Piggy in *Swine Lake*. It was fun, and funny, but was he in the vortex he wanted to avoid? He was certainly striking out. In 1972 he directed his first film – his own production of *Don Quixote*: director, choreographer, star.

His most significant move in terms of ballet was to accept the post of Artistic Director of the Paris Opera Ballet in 1982. It was famous for its dense bureaucracy.

Sylvie Guillem was there when Nureyev arrived. She was twenty and at the beginning of what, traditionally, would be a long haul to become a leading ballerina in that context.

'When Rudolf arrived,' she said, 'he had the luck to find a young company with a lot of talent. It was not only a corps de ballet, there were a lot of good soloists and Rudolf knew how to use them. In Paris Opera there was a huge hierarchy so you have to climb slowly years after years and Rudolf didn't care about that. He thought, This dancer was young but good – give him a chance. Rudolf gave me my first star role in *Don Quixote*, then *Swan Lake*, *Giselle* – with Rudolf – a lot of things.'

Roland Petit outlined the difficulty of running the company – with four different directors to please . . . The administration either smothered him or was beyond him. One day he just left.

In 1987 he was allowed to return to Russia. The authorities' excuse was that it was a compassionate gesture – his mother was very ill.

'I'm happy to be here,' he said at the airport. 'I'm happy I'll go and see my mother. She isn't very well. That's as much as I can say.'

Two years later, twenty-eight years after the leap to freedom, he was contacted to dance again at the Kirov. Few people in the audience had ever heard his name. His career in the West had been completely blanked out in the Soviet Union.

As the interview drew to a close he became reflective.

'I want to figure out what I'm going to do. Am I going to be a man of leisure? Do I stay on the island or go to London or Paris or New York? Working or doing choreography or dancing, doing musical comedy?' (He has said that he would love to be able to dance like Fred Astaire.) 'But dancing is the thing. It keeps me in good spirits and in good physical condition.'

But the edginess was never far below the surface. He was learning to play Bach on the piano ('Before going to performance, I always had to put on records of Bach') and our director had persuaded him to be filmed at the piano. He was nervous. Undisguisably. It was to be a performance on camera. The director then decided that I should sit by the piano and ask a few questions before he played. I demurred. The director insisted. I was not prepared to have a row: the director knew him much better than I did and had finally secured the film but . . . it was clear he was nervous and he said – *no*. She persisted. *No!* Again? The piano lid was banged down, artefacts were swept to the floor, Nureyev made a storming exit and through the window we saw him circling the terrace spitting nails. Then he disappeared.

The filming was almost over.

This was a minor fit of the anger which had helped power him from starvation poverty and an apparently hopeless dream to great fame, opulence, the world his stage. There were stories of excess and there was to be a sad ending in Aids which become a public illness. But far the most important was his dancing, his joy in it and mastery of it, the way in which he had found a way to express all the dreams and ambitions of the Tartar childhood in Ufa on stage and in films and amaze audiences, for a generation, wherever he set foot.

The film ends with Bach being played on the piano. He had softened, later, and played though it was not filmed.

What we saw on the screen was a shot of Nureyev down at the base of a rock, white, slim, muscular, naked, basking. The perfect music went on and he sat up, stretched a little, turned towards us, high above him, and then slid into the sea and swam behind one of his islands, swam out of sight.

Luciano Pavarotti

In the second half of the twentieth century, Pavarotti became the voice and the face of opera. One or two others were considered by some critics to be better singers, other critics frowned on his later celebrity concerts, but the public loved him and the connoisseurs could not deny the beauty of his voice. He was the most celebrated tenor since Caruso and at his finest Pavarotti was undeniably in the Premier League. He would have enjoyed that reference to football.

When I was on a television link to Rome to introduce 'The Three Tenors' concert (Pavarotti, Domingo and Carreras) there was panic in the control gallery because instead of waiting on red alert in the studio I was in another room with my son watching the England versus Italy football match on television. So, I knew for certain, was Pavarotti over in Rome prior to making his entrance at the Baths of Caracalla. A little like Francis Drake who was playing bowls when told that the Spanish Armada had been sighted and is reported to have said, 'There is time to finish the game and then to beat the Spaniards.' In his youth, Pavarotti was a locally renowned footballer.

The name itself sounds like an opera – Luciano Pavarotti – out it rolls, lyrically soft and gentle with a little bite at the end. His mountainous girth typified for many what a real opera singer should look like. His Italian-plated English accent was perfect – not in the least comical and not to be condescended to but bringing in the lilt and tang of the Mediterranean. His charm and smile were boyish. And he was funny, often at his own expense.

His bigness was part of his charm as far as the public was concerned. His fatness. He carried it with nonchalance. That his white waistcoat when in full evening dress for a concert performance seemed as big as a starched tablecloth gave to Pavarotti a grandeur. Others would have emanated embarrassment. He fulfilled what had become a standard model: that great Italian tenors were men of girth. And despite his apparent uncaringness, it gave him a vulnerability which added yet another layer to his attraction.

There were those who saw in his stoutness the visible evidence of a certain coarseness but even among that salami slice minority there could not be any real quarrel with the quality and the purity of his voice. 'He's not x . . .' they could say, 'or w. . .' 'let alone a, b or c . . . but . . .' He was very good. And his voice carried drama even if his body could rather let it down.

For those, like myself, who saw no live opera until my early twenties, there was about him a generosity to the untutored audience which encouraged appreciation of the work. It is a democratic manner and tone which cannot be faked.

It is not enough to say of him that he brought opera to a large public. But among his many gifts that was one. And it came from his generous character.

I met him several times and interviewed him more than once but most memorably for me was in the summer of 1995 in Pesaro on the Adriatic coast, where he had a villa overlooking 'Luciano's Beach'.

We arrived in the late morning, with cameras, sound equipment, gear: a television commando unit white from England and already feeling the heat. Pesaro, a stylish resort, the birthplace of Rossini, had provided us with a decent modest hotel but little sleep as the boys on their motor bicycles buzzed round and round the town for half the night like horny wasps. But this was Italy, summer, the Adriatic, how lucky can you get? And there was Pavarotti, standing massively before us at the top of the drive up to his house. Legs planted apart, flowered shirt flowing, the Colossus of Pesaro: smiling.

'Bergkamp!' he said immediately. 'It is not a good buy for you. He was no good at Milano. You will see.' His smile widened. He loved to talk football and Dennis Bergkamp, the Dutch international, had just been transferred from Milan (Pavarotti's nearest big team) to Arsenal, the team he knew I supported. He was delighted that, as he saw it, we had bought a pig in a poke and the cunning Italians had offloaded this dud to the gullible English. I had no answer. I'd only seen Bergkamp a couple of times in international games. It was unfortunate that we did not have a time machine on tap. Fast-forward two or three years and Bergkamp would be acknowledged as one of the greatest footballers in the world and for my season ticket, the most intelligent player I have ever seen in an Arsenal shirt. And as time went on I pointed this out. But on that morning, it was Italy one, England nil, and he was very pleased.

Football mattered to him. I talked to some of his schoolfriends back in Modena – where he was born and brought up – and they agreed that he had been a very good player. 'He was extremely fast,' said one. The team photographs show a slim, fit but still wholly recognisable Pavarotti. 'It seems funny now. But when he was nineteen and twenty we won two local championships because he was so fast.'

While the cameras were being set up, we walked across the garden so that he could introduce me to three Middle Eastern, Saudi I think, horse dealers who were patiently waiting their turn in his day to sell him some stallions. He has built a racecourse near his place in Modena and he stables his horses there. The three apparently imperturbable men, drinking coffee in the shade, their shades like masks, were a calm oasis. Inside the house, Pavarotti's lawyers were drawing up new contracts with recording executives and there was a febrile atmosphere all about the place because of the news of Pavarotti's broken marriage, a marriage which had endured for more than thirty years.

His wife and family were back in Modena in their flat – only two or three blocks away from the small council flat in which he had been born. Pavarotti's affair with a younger woman was headlines. Paparazzi were stalking the villa. The young woman in question was in residence with Pavarotti and later came out for a quick swim in the pool. She was the story of the moment. We never mentioned it.

It is not always best to start at the beginning in an interview any more than it is in a novel or an article, but it can have advantages. In Pavarotti's case the early years made his destiny.

'My mother was nineteen when I was born and she had to work in a cigar factory so she left at 6.30 and I went upstairs to the flat of my grandmother, who was thirty-eight. She had just lost a daughter of twelve years old called Lucia and so I was Luciano. My grandmother make me work – grating cheese. When she was in the next room she said, "Whistle, Luciano." Because when I whistle I can't be eating the cheese! I was the only boy born in that block for six years and I was very much loved and spoiled.'

'He was so cute,' said his mother Adele. 'He used to stand on the table and sing and say, "I am going to be a little tenor." '

'My father was, is, a tenor,' said Luciano. 'Even now, eighty-three, he has an incredible voice. He sang solo in the church. Not in the choir. Solo. He is a real tenor.'

In Modena we took his father Fernando and Adele to a park to talk about their son. They sat side by side on the bench, Fernando hand-some, at ease, a big confident man; Adele black-hatted and -coated, black handbag clutched tight by both hands on strictly tight knees. Fernando had made up words about Luciano to the melody of 'O Sole Mio' and out it rang across the square and, such was still the force of his voice, probably across the whole of Modena. The theme was 'what a beautiful voice my Luciano has'. When he had finished, Adele applauded loudly and at length. 'My voice is more harsh than Luciano,' he said, with sorrow. 'His is more melodic.' Adele shook her head. But Fernando knew. He is a real tenor.

'He is the divo of the family,' said Luciano admiringly.

There was neither context nor money for Fernando to be trained as a tenor. He went into a bakery aged fourteen. He sang in the bakery, he sang at home and in a choir which won prizes even at an eisteddfod at Llangollen.

There were two events in Luciano's childhood that by any reckoning must have had a formative effect. The first was the war, which impacted directly on the boy's life between the ages of eight and eleven. 'People in masks would come into your home. I saw people hanged. Yes. One Deutsch killed, ten Italians hanged. We went to the country to feel safer. But we heard the aeroplanes coming every night. To bomb the Deutsch but sometimes they bomb the Italians. But we ate. My father was a baker so we have the flour, the bread, eggs, chicken and pasta because we had the flour. I got to know all the animals how they make love. I know most of the flowers.'

More personally desperate was an attack of 'a kind of tetanus when I was twelve years old. I was in a coma for two weeks. The priest came two times with the last rites. When you come out of something like that you are definitely a survivor. You say to yourself, 'If I make it out of this I will enjoy all life – the sun, the trees. So you see me very optimistic all the time.'

It is easy to see Pavarotti as a simple man although sometimes it can take a lot of wisdom to be simple. And as the only much loved child, and a boy! To see him as 'spoiled', which again, like 'simple', is more often a sneer than a compliment. Yet for someone who courts 'simple' and happily admits to 'spoiled', Pavarotti climbed to a pinnacle few have ever reached. He expressed for millions emotion they longed to recognise and sang often testing music with a rare accurate technical virtuosity. He gives a good name to 'simple' and 'spoiled'. Better perhaps to replace them by 'single-minded' and 'understood'.

After Llangollen, where the choir won first prize, a choir that included father and son, Pavarotti, then nineteen, came back to Modena and assumed he was going to be a tenor. His father worked hard to dissuade him – and Luciano was an obedient son. But his mother wanted him to do it. 'I followed my instincts,' she says. 'When he sang he made me cry.'

'My mother says, when you sing your voice is telling me something special. Your father does not tell me something special. My father was furious.' It was a crucial time. He was accepted at a teacher training college 'for maths and for sports'.

It is always tempting and satisfying to winkle out what might be the crucial turning point in a life. Reason usually undermines it by pointing out 'it is a slow accretion' or 'it would have happened anyway'. But this tussle in the Pavarotti kitchen might just have been one of those moments. The father was determined to deter the son from a career in which he himself had been thwarted; the son was determined to have the career his father had not had; the loving and devoted wife and the loving and devoted mother had to choose. She chose her son. Luciano had to win this to get on the bottom rung of what must have seemed a ladder which stretched into the clouds. Moreover, while on those first rungs he was asking his parents to support him.

His father turned defeat into victory by providing a teacher, an outstanding teacher, in Modena, Arrigo Pola whom we interviewed.

One of the most engaging characteristics of Pavarotti is his respect for and gratitude towards those who helped him. Of Pola he says, 'I was very, very lucky. He taught me the technique.'

To the young Pavarotti 'the technique' was all in all. He wanted the precision of a Ferrari to which he often alludes. Modena was famous for being the home of the Ferrari, proof that a modest provincial town could have an international voice and also the model and the measure of all achievement. Pavarotti would often say, 'When you go on stage the voice must be ready to go, *instantly*, in perfect gear, like a Ferrari.' But everybody in Modena knew that a Ferrari was created through great and assiduously applied skills: 'the technique'.

'Pola would say, do this. I would say, impossible to do it. But *he* could do it. So I say, if he is doing it, *I* can do it.'

Said Pola, 'The voice is a great gift from God and from your mamma.'

The easy and sincere compound of sentiment and Catholicism seems yet another layer of the kinder, more devotional aspect of Italian life. An Italian-ness of which Pavarotti was so proud.

Pavarotti, at the start, had 'a little voice'. Pola gradually grew it. He taught Pavarotti vowel shaping, how to open and then cover a note; he drilled into him that he had to sing with 'the heart as well as the voice'. For two years he worked him very hard. That, too, lodged. 'The most important quality is persistence. Other people do it ten times to be good. I do it a hundred times to be very good. When you go now I will vocalise in my study.' He moved on to another teacher, but the groundwork was done, in the voice, in the heart and in the mind.

In his early twenties he won an important competition and then, with a small but professional company, he secured the part of Rodolfo in *La Bohème*, a part made for his lyric gift, his flair for romantic theatre and his great ability to communicate passionate feelings. He was on his way.

'But there were ten, twenty good tenors ahead of me in that field,' he said, 'so I say, well, I have to fight. I choose operas the other tenors are not doing, they are a little too difficult or too rare.' It worked.

At this point he slapped his mouth with one hand and with the other reached out for a glass of water. 'Mosquito,' he said. 'When people ask why I am so fat I say it is because I eat mosquitoes.' He drank the glass and swallowed the fly and beamed.

I asked him at what point he had felt really confident in what he often referred to as 'the voice' as if it were a cherished younger sibling.

'It was when I watched Joan Sutherland's diaphragm,' he said. 'I saw how she rested the voice on the diaphragm.' He demonstrated. 'I am sorry but to show you I have to make like when you go to the bathroom.' There was a hint of a squatting posture, very deep breathing, a visible change from tension to relaxation. He put his hands to his neck. 'Relaxed,' he said. He patted his diaphragm. 'The voice rests there. Joan Sutherland taught me that.'

Later he developed the notion of relaxation. I have seen this in sport. The fastest sprinters and the most flowing middle-distance runners often seem somehow above the effort. It is as if their bodies and minds know that all the work possible has been done, that the machine is in perfect condition and they let it go, floating above it. Muhammad Ali used to 'Float like a butterfly and sting like a bee' and you could see that almost always there was a sort of distance between himself and the effort involved; you can see it in footballers when the best of them always have more time to make decisions to be 'ahead of the game', an unhurriedness in the middle of frantic activity. Confidence has its role alongside that sense of complete preparation. 'The singer has to be completely relaxed,' said Pavarotti. 'When you go out you are ready to start. Like a Ferrari. You start right away.'

But in the ten minutes or so before the performance, 'I am nervous like the first day. Nothing can be done about this feeling. The last ten minutes before my performance is truly painful. Why am I doing this? Why do I try this? I would not give this feeling to my worst enemy.' And as he talked he did indeed look anguished: as always in the interview his expression is the more than usual orchestration accompanying his words. So at this point his face calms down, there is a look of tranquillity, a sense of immanence, 'Then I hear my music . . . and I have to be alert.' And on cue, the expression switches to readiness. And then the singing consumes him.

I was lucky enough to see him in *Aida* in Milan. We were filming the opening night of the La Scala season. I had not expected the flashiness of the occasion, the parade of high fashion in the foyer, the social buzz, the sense that here was the epicentre of rich and civilised Italian life, still imperial and given to gorgeous display. I had been with him the previous day and he was especially nervous. After all, Milan was 'his' place, a few miles from Modena, the shrine of Italian opera which sees itself as the founder and prime keeper of the art.

But Pavarotti's relationship with La Scala was not happy. A few years earlier he had sung *Don Carlos* there which had been 'a massacre'. The audience had booed him throughout. 'I should have said "no",' he said. 'The big career is made by saying "no", not by saying "yes". *Don Carlos* was not right for the voice. I was not ready but it was La Scala and I did it to please a friend.' He shook his head sadly. 'The audience booed. Me. The production.' Then honesty broke through. 'Me.'

So the *Aida* was loaded with anticipation. The audience, as I discovered, was quite happy to 'get' him again. Perhaps the sophisticates of Milan resented the glittering global success of the baker's son from Modena who had achieved his fame without their patronage. Or maybe they had been right about *Don Carlos* and were not going to let Pavarotti off the hook. Whatever it was I can testify that around the back of the stalls there was something of the smell of the Colloseum. And around me were the senators ready to be judges. On the next seat, a walnut-faced man, well-suited, heavily spectacled like a scholar, accompanied by an equally sober companion, suddenly pulled out a whistle and blew on it, loudly. There was a restless ripple of applause and apprehension. He and others were ready for battle.

Pavarotti was preparing to tackle one of the hardest opening tenor moments in any opera: the aria 'Celeste Aida' occurs two and a half minutes after the curtain rises and makes serious demands on the singer whose voice has to be in perfect running order and whose conviction in the role has to be unquestionable. Pavarotti knew all that, of course, and had come back to La Scala, in an old-fashioned phrase, to 'show them'.

He did. He was at his all but incomparable best that night. La Scala went into pandemonium. He bowed, just a little, and smiled, again, not too much. And on and on they applauded him.

We had talked for about two hours in the hot shade of that garden. It was rather like a court with the petitioners dotted around waiting on Luciano's leisure. He was about to do *The Daughter of the Regiment*, with its nine top 'Cs' and explained how difficult it was with 'a full voice' (not a falsetto) and how much more difficult as he grew older and the voice darkened. I raised the point that he was criticised by some for lending himself to huge open-air concerts – a charge which he flicked aside. 'It is good for millions of people to see opera,' he said. 'If you have England playing Brazil in a World Cup Final do you not want everybody to see it?'

'If England ever played in a World Cup Final with Brazil, I would want the world and its wife to see it.'

'Ha! I knew. I make that on purpose! I make that on purpose!'

The paparazzi were still outside. Inside, the contracts were being restructured and the pasta was ready to cook. Before that the question of the Arabian stallions had to be settled. He wandered over to them as we packed our equipment. I would see him again in the evening. He felt he had been too rushed, but in fact he had been generous with time and honesty.

Soon he would be 'vocalising', up and down the scales, as he does every day, and they would listen down on Luciano's Beach as the notes drifted out across the Adriatic Sea.

Judi Dench

It's the range. Judi Dench has been Lady Macbeth and starred in a TV comedy series, she's been Cleopatra and also M in the Bond movies, in Chekhov, in Shakespeare, and in practically everyone's books she's 'our greatest living actress'.

Yet it is the extraordinariness of Judi Dench that she can seem ordinary. Perhaps only when she chooses to? A star but not a diva; popular though not a 'celebrity'; she has camouflaged her success in anonymity; her fame seems to count for nothing at all compared with her privacy. Her work shows her to be ambitious, daring, risk-taking, uniquely versatile. And she loves to laugh.

When I asked her, at the outset of our documentary with her, how she was preparing for the lead part of Desirée in Stephen Sondheim's *A Little Night Music*, she laughed loudly, larkily, and announced, 'I'm not at all!' And it was true. In life as in her roles, she is a truth-teller. And you believe what she says.

She was at the time starring in the West End in the emotionally savage hit *Absolute Hell*. One at a time? Maybe also that is where she starts. From a clean slate. And the clean slate is the rehearsal room.

I have seen Judi Dench in many plays. When I came to work in London in 1961, the big treat was to go to the Aldwych once a month or so to see Peter Hall's Royal Shakespeare Company, a troupe of glittering talents among whom was Judi Dench. It would not be true to say that she outshone others even then — it was a constellation; and though the theatrical context encourages hyperbole, they *were* a remarkable bunch.

But say she was not outshone. As the years, and the decades went by, she moved gradually closer into the spotlight until she commanded it.

I'd met her, in a general way, several times when I'd done work with the Royal Shakespeare Company or just around the place. Nothing much more than 'hello' but enough for a small acquaintanceship in that generally still vagabond world of actors and directors which in London merges with films and television in a moveable feast and famine of gossip and success and failed projects.

She is hard to fix. I think she saves herself for the work in the rehearsal rooms and the stage. The little that is left for public view is given the least effort. And there's a reserve. The private life is the motor. Even so, there is always about her one constant characteristic: her readiness to smile, her love of laughing and her speed of response, including seizing any opportunity to put herself down. It seems odd but her quickness, given her outward calm, is something it takes time to recognise.

Our film began on the first day of rehearsal of *A Little Night Music*, followed it through to the opening night and looked over her career inside that structure.

We started our film showing the day of the opening.

'I didn't sleep very well last night and I always sleep well. Everybody's frightened on the first day so it's OK. But I couldn't get one of the songs out of my mind. I've assured people I'm going to sing exactly as I speak so I suppose I'm all right.'

Then back to the first rehearsal. There's a similarity, in the character of rehearsal spaces. They are in austere echoing halls. The floor is chalked out, floor tape marks rooms, the props are few and shabby. Most of the actors dress down as carefully as first-nighters used to dress up. There's a primitive rolling self-service of tea and coffee. The director and the script group have a trestle-tabled HQ. They work hard and efficiently without tantrums but with no opportunity lost for a laugh.

We went on the first day of the rehearsal. 'I know Siân Phillips,' said Judi, 'and I know some of the others. We all tell each other, "We just have to get through today." I haven't done any work on the script at all and so it's all new to me. I hardly ever read a play. Tony Hopkins and I hadn't read *Antony and Cleopatra* so we didn't know who died at the end!' This time a wicked giggle.

'So how did it begin?'

Judi was born and brought up in York with its great Minster and its rich-flavoured and vivid history of the last thousand years still visible.

'We were taken to the theatre all the time. When the Mystery Plays came along' (plays by townspeople which take place around the cathedral-minster every year as they have done since the Middle Ages; the plays portray key stories from the Bible) 'Ma made costumes. Father was Ananais the High Priest. They came to the Mount and took some of us to be in them.'

'The Mount was a Quaker boarding school?'

'Yes. It suited me very well. I don't have much of quietness about me. I'm not good at being passively quiet. That atmosphere – and there was also this tremendous stress on spareness. I come back to "spare" each time.'

Her brother went to acting school at the Central School of Drama in London.

'But I only ever wanted to be a designer then. I went and saw *King Lear* at Stratford. It was the most amazing set. I knew I could never do that so I tried for Central as an actor. I went through the first year half-heartedly. There we were told we had to do the Mime.' [one of the tests]. 'The *Mime*! I'd totally forgotten about it! I was really taken aback. I did it on the spur of the moment. I got a wonderful crit for it.'

'Did that support from your teacher matter so much?'

A feature of her conversation – in interview and, it was even more marked, in rehearsal – is her decisiveness about what effect advice or support have on her.

'Yes. It changed my mind about whether I wanted to act or not.'

Again and again when I've interviewed artists, so many have picked out a teacher, the encouragement, even a moment – like this – which have switched the track of their lives, given them the confidence and the route to fulfil hitherto unarticulated, unimaginable ambitions.

The main interview took place in her house, idyllically located in lush English countryside, a river running through the gardens, pretty furniture glistening with polish, lawns mown in precise military lines by her husband, Michael Williams, a fellow actor. And we also snatched interviews in the rehearsal room.

'Rehearsal is a time you are allowed to make mistakes and make choices.'

Which is why I was pleased that Judi and the others had agreed to let us film them. The previous generation, the 'old guard', never did, seeing rehearsals as a vulnerable place, the more private the freer, the more free the greater scope for failing and then failing better.

We were filming the moment when an old lover came to visit her backstage. Judi-Desirée, he is touched and amused to see, is eating sandwiches 'like a wolf' as the script says. She really wolfed and again and again her lines were muffled in a mouthful of bread and flung aside by her laughter at this self-inflicted impediment. But she used it.

'It's a very curious thing. Sometimes you *know* there's a laugh there but you can't get at it. Then suddenly, in a performance, you get it. It's an instinct. It goes right down into your stomach. It gives you an electric charge.'

And, in that one small moment, we saw the bite of the bread become a savage wolfing become a sexual signal, become a parody of a sexual signal – and set off laughter in the audience.

'Do you see yourself as more instinctive than technical?'

'Only instinctive. It leads you a little closer to the edge and you think, That might be all right.'

'But do you pick up technical tips?'

'Always. That's how I got into the Old Vic. I went to the Old Vic the night before the audition to see how much projection was needed. I copied Barbara Jefford!'

'You won the Central Drama School Gold Medal. You were very young and instantly cast as Ophelia opposite John Neville. One leading critic wrote: "she tripped over her own publicity and fell on her pretty face." How did you cope with that?'

She paused and took her time, as she did on several occasions in the interview. It was a bit of a straight left but she didn't duck it.

'Hmm . . . I don't know. I got over it, I expect. We were rehearsing other plays – *Twelfth Night*, *The Dream*, *Measure for Measure*, the *Henrys* . . .'

'I guess it was good that you were in a company . . .'

'. . . and had been since 1957. It's a vital thing, a company, a group of people working together. I like the jokes bit! Especially in rehearsal. They break down people's inhibitions. If you can't laugh at yourself you shouldn't be an actor.'

Peter Hall saw her through the early years when he was the king-maker of London theatre. The directors and actors and technicians around him attracted casts that dazzled London and went on to enthral the cities over the world. 'I saw the young Judi Dench in Zeffirelli's *Romeo and Juliet* – she was very bouncy, very witty, very sexy. Frankly I would not have thought that she could become the towering great actress she has become. I was wrong. I think that what is extraordinary about her is the combination of wit and refinement and sexy earthiness. She inherits the tradition of Edith Evans and Peggy Ashcroft. It goes on in her.'

'Let's get back to technique.'

'That's your training. You have to get it over very quickly. Breathing techniques. Ways of not losing your voice. Voice projection. It distinguishes the professional from the amateur. And if you learn to read Shakespeare's verse from John Barton or Peter Hall or Trevor Nunn it will never go away.'

'*A Little Night Music* seems a different proposition.'

'I approach it in the same way as I approach Shakespeare. I draw on that training and the RSC. But it's the same approach. What you're doing is examining the possibilities, examining what is not right.'

The director of *A Little Night Music* is Sean Mathias. He tries to give his notes briefly and clearly. She pauses. Then, usually, says, 'Oh. Right. Let's try it.' And moves back into the part to do just that. 'She doesn't require intellectualisation of the text,' he says. 'She always asks a very significant question and she wants an answer.'

There was an example. Judi wanted to know what to do during two bars of music. Sean explained the scene. She listened. He talked about her words. She listened. Then, 'It's *those two bars* of music after the end of that before I speak. I don't know what to do in *those two bars*.'

He gave her a direction. She took her time. Clocked it. 'Oh . . . Right.'

In the 1960s and '70s Judi worked at the RSC, in rep at Oxford and Nottingham and in the West End. She was London's first Sally Bowles. Her reputation grew as her repertoire widened.

In 1971 she married fellow Royal Shakespeare actor, Michael Williams. They bought a house near Stratford. After their child Finty was born, 'three generations of our extended family lived there together,' said Michael. 'All the qualities she has as a person and an actress come from that close family background. I've always thought management ought to pay Judi an extra fee for being the teacher, the mother of the company. There's no one else who does that to the same degree.'

Back in rehearsal she said of performance: 'It should always be fluid. There can't be an absolute way of doing it.' Some days later there was an illustration of this when she replied to her former lover Frederik's invitation to meet his wife with, 'Dear Frederik. I'm longing to meet her. Some time.' She put that through several variations, emphasising different words, making different pauses, giving a different colour to each version, combining sharpness with sadness, a forgivingness of his crass proposal with a love of his crassness, tender and tart: apart from anything else it was a lesson in how malleable and capable of nuance the English language is.

One reason why she did nothing to prepare for *A Little Night Music* until the first day of rehearsal may have been that every evening she was starring in a magnificent revival of *Absolute Hell* by Roger Ackland. Judi played the eventually violent Christine Foskett, the drunken hostess of a London club after World War Two. It ends with Christine abandoned, alone in her bankrupt bar. She is overcome and the last words are 'Hell! Hell! Hell! Hell! Hell! Hell! Hell! Hell!' with varied emphases but constant intensity, unbearable.

'What drove that intensity? In her. In you? A terror of being alone?'

'My own fear, I expect. My own fear entirely. I have a thing that when I go into a rehearsal room I leave my bag nearest the door . . . I can't have it furthest away from the door. I don't know what they would say if I was on the couch. I have to have quietness inside myself somewhere otherwise I'll burn myself out.'

Back into the rehearsal room the morning after a performance of *Absolute Hell*, to sing 'Isn't it rich? Are we a pair? Me here at last on the ground. You in mid-air. Send in the clowns.' Tentatively she is beginning to dramatise the song and it is gaining both darkness and a helplessness at the futility of life; laughter in the dark.

'I'm an actor who can put over a song. I can't sing. But I can put over a song. I learned that in *Cabaret*.'

By the end of that run-through, in the bleak rehearsal hall, she is weeping, shaking, breaking down. The moment she finishes she says, 'I shan't be like that at all. A lot of that was locked up in Christine Foskett. Now Christine Foskett is dead.' (The run of the play has come to its end.) 'Desirée is taking over. I haven't made a coherent whole. I've made a bit of a mess of it.'

'I loved the breakdown,' Sean tells her. 'If she's lost him, the only life she has left is back on the road with many lovers.' She does not reply.

'Michael once said to me, "You can't ever be greater on stage than you are as a person." I said, "I don't believe that. I don't believe it. I absolutely don't believe it!" . . . I believe it now. Because the more you can push yourself, the more you can push the good parts wider, the better the game.'

She co-starred with Michael in *A Fine Romance*, a hit television comedy show. ('I like theatre best, then television, then films.') 'We played two people who couldn't really get it together,' said Michael. 'We'd got on together since 1971. We revel in each other's company. And that gave a second plot and a subtext to the awful inability of the two of them to express their affection for each other.'

'God gave her the most astounding voice,' said Peter Hall. 'In theatre the voice is nearly all. It allows humour, wit, sexuality. You listen to Judi Dench. You can't help it.'

'Her greatest strength,' said Sean Mathias, 'is her truth. Whatever she does you can't say to her – I don't believe that.'

'Do you always rely on the director?'

'Yes . . . Peter Hall said something very valuable to me when I played Cleopatra. He said – because I was very frightened – "Don't think you've got to come on in the first scene and play every facet of her. All you've got to do is show a little bit of her, then, gradually, as the scenes go through, you add a little bit more and then at the end you might have a whole person." '

Was she surprised to be asked to play Cleopatra?

Peter Hall recalls the moment he offered her the part: 'Judi said to me, "I do want you to know what you've let yourself in for. I'm not Cleopatra. You're starting your play with a menopausal dwarf." So I said, "Don't be quite so hard on yourself – let's *find* Cleopatra" – and she was magnificent. She went beyond herself.'

I saw the performance and she was indeed magnificent. 'She takes great risks,' said Hall. 'She makes it look easy; but it isn't.'

'Cleopatra's almost a myth,' I said to Judi. 'How do you begin?'

'Especially if you've met a lot of people saying, "*You're* going to play Cleopatra?" with undisguised incredulity!'

And she threw back her head and laughed loudly. This laughter of hers. It's a language. This laugh contained delight in the rudeness of those who had expressed 'undisguised incredulity'; delight in the knowledge now that she had 'shown them' what she could do; most of all, though, some sort of deeply amiable agreement with them!

'It put you on your toes?'

'That's what I like. I like that.'

'Was it much the same when you played Lady Macbeth?'

'It was. Coral Browne said, "*You* doing Lady Macbeth? The letter scene will become the postcard scene." ' This time her laughter was uncontrollable. Then, still glowing at the wit of Coral Browne, she said, 'It was something to get over.'

We cut into the film her delivery of the line: 'The smell of blood. All the perfumes of Arabia will not sweeten this little hand.'

This was followed by a cry which grew to a physical howl of pain: unbearable.

'We all went to Trevor's to see it.' Trevor Nunn had directed it. 'I was shocked by it. I was so disappointed. I was really shocked by it. I haven't watched any film I've ever done since.'

'What shocked you?'

'I thought I was doing something better than that.'

'Seen no films?'

'No . . . But I'm going to see *Goldeneye* though!' Her M is Triple A. The last rehearsal of *A Little Night Music* was now over.

She drove back home on the night before the opening. 'I do feel frightened. If you've done thirty-eight years in the theatre more is expected of you each time. And if we can get past that first night barrier, we'll be all right. I want Michael to like it as well.'

'She came back that night wiped out,' said Michael. 'We went to the local pub for a meal and she kept telling me she just couldn't do it. I told her of course she could. I'd no doubt she could do it. But she has terrible insecurities. Most of the best ones have.'

'I don't know any great actor who wasn't insecure,' says Peter Hall. 'Judi is more honest about confronting it. It psyches her up. It gives her something to surmount. I don't think you can have one without the other.'

'Why do you think you've been successful for so long?'

'I *like* it. I like it very much indeed. If you asked me what I'd play next week I wouldn't know. All I know is we don't retire. Actors are not young, middle-aged or old because they're so busy being other people. I'd like to die in my dressing room except I love my family so much I'd rather do it here.' In her home. 'I remember John Neville saying to me at the Vic, right at the beginning, "You must make up your mind why you want to act." ' She paused for a few moments. 'And I *did* make up my mind. I'm not going to tell you the reason. I suppose it's . . . it's a way . . . it's a way of communicating with people.'

Now fully plumed for the part of Desirée we filmed her as she trailed slowly from her dressing room up the steep stairs to the stage, head bowed, body heavy, emanating reluctance, sealed in apprehension. 'Break a leg, Judi . . .' 'Break a leg . . .'

It's the taking over another life that fascinates us. Most of us, or, surely, all of us want that. To *be* someone else. To have a different destiny. Or at least to have a taste of it. So we read stories from comics to Tolstoy or dream others into our lives in cinemas and theatres, on television, radio, at concerts. This one life is rarely enough, even more rarely good enough.

Actors do it. Great actors do it so that we believe it. For those few hours on the stage, Judi Dench *was* Desirée in some alchemical way. Out of long experience and habit and training, out of instinct and desire and imagination – all came together to lock her into another personality. She gave herself to it so fully, as the best do, that although we knew it was Judi Dench and saw Judi Dench, she was also Desirée, she became only Desirée and our imagination was ensnared. We suspended disbelief. Willingly we allowed ourselves to embrace what we might once have thought of as magic – one person turned into another. Perhaps something still rather beyond our grasp happens in Judi Dench's mind. Some sort of benign possession which can be renounced only after the last curtain call.

She was, Desirée was, a triumph. Sondheim's greatest song – taking in a life of lost opportunities and faded love – was heartbreaking. Spoken. In tune.

Jimmy McGovern

Some of the best contemporary British drama of the last fifty years has been on television and Jimmy McGovern has delivered two major pieces: *Cracker*, and *Hillsborough*.

Many of those I've interviewed have begun deep in the mire of a society which seemed to condemn them to cultural silence rather than encourage them to artistic achievement. Jimmy McGovern was born into a working-class Roman Catholic family in Liverpool, the fifth of nine children. In his childhood he was afflicted by a disabling stammer. He got his first real break on *Brookside*, a soap opera made in Liverpool for Channel 4, quickly recognised for the way it tackled politics, domestic sexuality and the inner city. I interviewed him just after he had finished writing *Hillsborough*.

Hillsborough is the name of the football ground where ninety-six people lost their lives, most of them crushed to death. All ninety-six came from Liverpool, a city whose fans are besotted with football, knowledgeable about football and aware of the depth of commitment such a passion can reach. They know that in football there can be discovered the excitement of drama rivalling theatre or circus or a rock concert; an elegance and strength and speed of movement which can be as aesthetically satisfying as dancing; and an association with the young contenders on the playing field which can convey some of the potency of comrades in arms. Add to this, in Liverpool, the need for pride in a city fallen from commercial and industrial greatness, its sea access to the USA no longer a resource, and there's little wonder that nowadays it sees itself, at its best, in the mirrors of music and theatre, comedy and football, and for many the greatest of these is football.

The Hillsborough Disaster was one of the biggest tragedies in football history. It was avoidable. The causes were common knowledge; the culprits were protected. It harmed the reputation of the police. It provoked radical changes in the layout of spectator facilities in football stadiums. But by the law of unexpected consequences, the new legal insistence on all-seating upped the prices and today fewer working men and boys can afford to go to the games. It revealed a scornful and brutal attitude towards the have-nots from the haves.

Jimmy McGovern, who had gone to watch Liverpool with his brothers since he was nine years old, was determined to write about it and to get at the truth. He used the drama-documentary form. That is, he researched the story and on that basis constructed a drama which was then acted out but held at all times to the real incidents, the verified comments, what had been documented.

Our programme covered much of Jimmy McGovern's work, but *Hillsborough* provided the substantial opening section and we began with the camera going the way the crowd had gone, the crowd that had been allowed to ignore safety guides and been allowed entrance by the police into a part of the ground which became a killing field. As the camera went towards the pitch a voice-over, from an eyewitness, said, 'As we got to the end of the tunnel we were *just sucked into the crowd*. We were three or four steps in and before we knew it there was an almighty surge and we were up against the crowd barriers.'

The barriers around the pitch looked like cages and functioned like cages as more and more supporters were irresistibly sucked into this small space. The result was crowd carnage . . .

I walked with Jimmy McGovern through a district called Kensington. 'A long time ago this was posh,' he said. It's just a few rows of small terraced houses now; a wasteland gap where children were playing football; the atmosphere, as in many working-class areas of former heavily industrial cities, of bewildered hopelessness.

'We used to come up and play in the reservoir over there. My family still live all around here. Every Friday night we go to the pub and play cards.'

The Liver Vaults stands smartly painted and inviting. It gives a focus to the area around it and inside it is warm, comfortably furnished, well-kept. 'A little bit of hush!' said the landlady's voice on the soundtrack as we went into the bar, lit up but only by our lights, full but only with our crew, and sat down at a polished table.

Hillsborough was the first call: when we talked he was still working on it.

'It's a story of massive incompetence and a death trap. We're going to explain exactly what went wrong and why it went wrong and the lengths the police went to afterwards to disguise the truth.'

In his report on the Hillsborough Disaster, Lord Justice Taylor said that although there were other causes, the main reason for the disaster was the failure of control by the South Yorkshire police. At the inquiry, the police case had been to blame the fans and the club. The judge concluded: 'such an unrealistic approach gave cause for anxiety over whether lessons had been learned.'

'Was *Hillsborough* something you *needed* to write?'

'The kind of thing I do is to find a good story with a good theme that makes me *angry*. Then I *have* to write it. It works fine for me then because the anger provides the energy and the drive and the feeling of outrage – that mattered particularly in *Hillsborough*.'

Throughout this part of the interview we showed extracts from the finished version of the play. The first portrayed crowds of young men pressing against closed gates, a policeman shouting into his walkie-talkie that the gates must be opened and the superintendent in a state of paralysis even though another police officer, sat beside him, urged him to 'open the gates!' Which, eventually, he did but by that time the crowd was densely and dangerously packed and with a force of its own, as of a force of nature, a high tide, an avalanche.

'Because it's a factual drama, everything in it had to be the truth.' I felt that this quest for truth was, in itself, a source of satisfaction to him. The roots of his life – the early intense Roman Catholicism, the later socialism, above all an ineradicable working-class decency – meant that for Jimmy McGovern truth is *the* grail. Drama-documentary is a form fashioned to bring together two truths: the documented facts and the emotional structure which only craft and fine imagination can weld together and bring to life. By the time he reached *Hillsborough*, McGovern's imaginative empathy had been clearly expressed in his play about a homosexual priest and his series *Cracker* which centres on a social wreck of a detective whose brilliance rests in *his* ability to imagine himself into the mind of the criminal.

'Every word said we had to stand up and say, for instance, "Yes, this is when that police officer said that." I just can't wait until they claim, "It's crazy, it just didn't happen that way." We'll be able to say, "There it is. In black and white. Every single word of this is truthful and *that* is the most appalling aspect of it." '

We cut to a young police officer walking out of a room with a woman who is stunned by what she has seen. This is immediately after she has identified the body of her son. He says, 'Where did your son stop off for a drink?' 'My son doesn't drink.' 'You'll be telling me he's a virgin next.' She turns on him in fury and grief. Another police officer asks an older man, 'Did Stephen have a drink before the game?' 'I hope so,' the man replies, in a low hoarse voice. 'I hope he was out of his mind. I hope he never felt a thing.'

The anger which these two short apparently simple scenes emanate is visceral. It is the force which goes through *Hillsborough* and makes it not only a great work of documentary-drama but a lasting X-ray of British society in that period.

'People had just come away from identifying bodies and the police were only asking two questions. Did he or she have tickets? And, crucially, did he or she have anything to drink? And the families have always maintained that was part of the plan. The police were going to portray them all as hooligans. And ever since then, there's been this myth that drunken Scousers arrived late without tickets and *they* caused it.'

McGovern saw this, rightly, as a police cover-up and a class libel on the Scousers. And the media added fuel. The *Sun* newspaper told its readers 'THE TRUTH' on its front page and asserted of Liverpool supporters that:

> Some fans picked pockets of victims
> Some fans urinated on brave cops
> Some fans beat up P.C. giving kiss of life

The words still have the power to initiate anger. There was no evidence for *any* of this. McGovern still has difficulty controlling his fury at the violence of these lies, added to the lies of the police.

'That story came from a press agency. It set up the myth.'

No matter it was denied, no matter the population of Liverpool ostracised the *Sun*: the Big Lie stuck. It is a naked exposure of the way the authorities and the media can attempt to twist the truth. British people thought such behaviour was not part of our life – in corrupt countries abroad, yes. And for many that was as much a shock as the incident itself. We never thought that a sort of bureaucratic fascism could happen here. Some had thought this about our society for years and there were previous examples but this was so blatant and cruel it broke what for many had been a tolerant contract between the police and the public and the media and the public.

Within twenty minutes of what it called 'the incident', while there were dead on the playing field and many actions were being taken by Liverpool supporters to save and protect their own, the BBC, the impartial voice of authority, shamefully blotted its record. 'There's no question now,' the commentator said, 'that the problem was caused by non-ticket holders forcing their way through a broken gate.' There was absolutely no evidence for this: it was fed to the BBC by the police. It was totally at odds with Justice Taylor's findings in his inquiry. But even so there was no closure for the Liverpool families. To many, it was yet another example of the Establishment closing ranks – as it had done so often when explaining away official incompetence or corruption which involved an injustice to ordinary people. There was contempt for Liverpool supporters.

Doreen Jones, whose son was killed there, said, 'Every major event has an accident and emergency plan. That was never put into practice in Hillsborough. I want to know why. I want to know why my son never got to hospital. Why only fourteen of the ninety-six got to hospital. I want to know who played God with his life.'

One of the stories in McGovern's docu-drama is of a man frenziedly searching for his daughter. He knows that one of his two daughters is dead. The other, he mistakenly believes, is still alive.

'In terms of drama it works wonderfully but you mustn't talk about drama in those terms. This really happened to people. This is a man with a desperate *need* to find out if his other girl is still alive and he's being treated in this way.' Fobbed off, pushed around, twice shown the dead body of the same daughter. 'It works as drama but, my God, when you realise it's real life, it's heartbreaking. It's frightening. This could be all of us.'

By 'all of us' McGovern means the powerless, the decent people.

'Was the connection between anger and writing in your work from the beginning?'

'Yes. It's always been there. Because there was a time when I could hardly talk. I stammered really badly and I found that if I made myself angry I could just storm through the words. They would be fuelled by pain and commitment – just to talk at all. A lot of people thought I was a bloody head case. But I *had* to have that passion just to get the words out. It's the same with the writing.'

'By the time the lawyers have been through your script, what chance have you got of saying what you want to say?'

'It's a nightmare. In the past, if you got a problem you could solve it with some kind of leap of the imagination but with this you cannot do that.'

'What did you find that surprised you?'

'I think the police had this mindset – all Liverpool supporters are scum. Quite a few of those lads who died were on the dole. This was 1989 in Liverpool. They were classed as worthless.'

McGovern almost chokes with bitterness. We see that in his face and hear it in his voice. The *New Yorker* film critic Pauline Kael said that 'Television is a lie detector.' It can also be a truth-teller. The un-stammered force of McGovern's work rages on the screen. It does not come over as propaganda. It is the penetrative power of television — which catches people in their own homes, in a familiar and safe place — that can make so many see and experience a wound in their society. Anger can be misused and even boring. Not here. Through the script and the casting, this event targeted shameful and ugly truths.

'We started off with a mess, trying to hit as many targets as possible. There were many targets to hit. It was horrendous the way people were treated. But there were too many targets. It was all over the place. So I honed it down and honed it down, making it clear, so the story in a way got smaller but became much more comprehensible. What I care most about is showing it to the families and as long as the families say "yes", we'll feel vindicated. We feel the truth has at last been told even if we haven't had justice. If they think it's good I'll be happy.'

Les James, the father of one of the victims, said, 'I thought that if anybody was going to tell the truth about Hillsborough it would be him. That's what we've been pursuing for seven years without success. He could perhaps redress the balance of the press coverage and by the media — by telling the truth. Because of his ability I thought he would make a job of it. So *I'm* quite happy he went ahead and did the film.'

It was a massive success. Perhaps it even changed our British mind a little. At the very least it showed us a true face. And the families knew that at last the truth was out there: a beginning had been made.

Because of his stammer and his poverty — he could not afford the uniform — Jimmy was 'given a dog's life' his brother Joey said, at the Roman Catholic grammar school to which he had won a scholarship. 'He had a really bad time there. He's not really what you would call a violent man. He kept it all in. The only way he can get it out is writing it.'

He got himself into the vivid and burgeoning fringe of Liverpool theatre life and had a play accepted. His mother, June, saw it.

'It broke my heart, that first play at the City Playhouse. It was called *City Echoes* and it was relating to our life and it was so good, it was really lovely. But it didn't suit. And I think that was the biggest disappointment of his life and I thought he'd give it all up then. He's a very sensitive man. He's too sensitive to be a man. Everything gets to him. I don't mean he isn't a man, but he's got so much feeling in him.'

'I couldn't understand the world of theatre,' he said. 'They have their own rules and they have their own language. I felt ostracised and alien.'

So thank God that television was there, that television drama was being written by the best dramatists of the day, that the level of production and acting was so high and the barriers that exist in British cultural life were dissolved by a democracy of talent which did not have to have inherited or learned 'their own rules . . . their own language'.

He began to work, still in Liverpool, on *Brookside*, which under Phil Redmond had produced, for Channel 4, a remarkable cross between a soap and a drama of contemporary conflicts.

'I just learned. I learned about TV. I learned to take criticism at *Brookside*. I learned to sit there and not throw a punch if somebody said my script was rubbish. I would never throw a punch. But you know that instant – "how dare you criticise my baby!" We thought we were providing an alternative agenda.'

Phil Redmond, key writer, begetter, executive producer of *Brookside*, said, 'Jimmy would always come in with a script and he would say, "This is shit." And the next week everybody would say, "It was a great episode last night, Jimmy," and he would say, "Yeah – it's still shit though."'

After what he describes as an 'apprenticeship . . . I knew the power of the camera, I knew film, I knew how to tell a story . . . but there weren't the resonances . . .' he moved on to do a film about a Catholic priest who hears in the confessional box from a young girl that her father is sexually abusing her. The father himself then comes to confession and taunts the priest. The young priest himself is fighting against his homosexuality which his faith abhors. His silence on the child abuse is discovered and vilified. His own sexual orientation is outed and in public one of his parishioners accuses him. 'It's in the Bible. Do you read the Bible, you pervert? "You shall not lie with the male as with a woman." *It is an abomination!'*

'I told a cracking story that made people think. It was at a time when the Catholic Church was in turmoil anyway. There's wonderful ideas like justice and truth and every society in the world builds an institution around those ideas "truth and justice" and then the institutions become more important than the principle itself. And that was happening in the Roman Catholic Church. They were trying to keep scandals secret.'

At the end, the destroyed priest looks at the image of Christ crucified on the cross and shouts, 'Do something! Light a candle, you smug idle bastard! Do *something*!'

It is, in the series *Cracker* that Jimmy McGovern gets closest to greatness as an imaginative writer. Played by Robbie Coltrane, whose size and intelligence seized the part, we had a maverick investigator whose character, attack and compound of self-loathing and intellectual clarity put him with the best in the genre. His impact on audiences was a double punch – to the solar plexus and to the intellect.

One of the triggers for the character was the American actor and avant-garde director John Cassavetes. 'In my mind he was an English John Cassavetes. I knew the drinking and the smoking and the gambling. I knew all that.'

'Had you been a serious gambler?'

'Yeah . . . yeah, but not with a huge amount of money because I was an ordinary working man. I lost more than I could afford to lose but I didn't *have* huge amounts of money. I know that complete addiction. I'm an addict. I drink, I smoke, I gamble – not heavily *now*, but I used to.'

When Robbie Coltrane, who plays Fitz, the chief and dominating character, got the script his reaction was that 'it worried me that the character was so unrelievedly awful. I thought, What a bastard. He lets down his wife. He's a terrible father. He drinks the whole time. He farts. He gambles all his family's money away. If he has any redeeming features, it's just th t he's so *smart* and so analytical and that probably precludes him from enjoying life. He's always distancing himself by saying – what does this mean?'

'He can get massively pissed,' said Jimmy, 'and start coming out with the most objectionable stuff but it's deeply truthful. There's a huge amount of self-loathing in Fitz especially when he's drunk. I just know him so well. All you needed then was a fascinating crime, a crime that comes out of rage and a feeling of injustice.'

'What struck me about the pilot script for *Cracker*,' says Coltrane, 'is that it was completely visceral . . . there was no . . . it's hard to describe because it's a unique view of things. He just gets straight into the heart of the matter.'

'I was a typical leftie,' says McGovern. 'I believed all the ideology. But – it was after Hillsborough – when you come up against the fact that people sporting the ideologies – Marxism or whatever – didn't actually care for you or your class anyway – that's the death of ideology. You've been lied to – and you've accepted the lies. There's an anger there – a feeling that nothing much matters except a sense of common decency. Like Orwell, despised by intellectuals but going on about that sense of common decency. I think that was *me* in '89, '91, '92. I think that's there in Fitz.'

The scholar John Carey in his eviscerating book *The Intellectuals and the Masses* examines most of the formative intellectuals of the late nineteenth and twentieth centuries and finds in almost all of them what McGovern discovered from his own experience: a disregard, more often a contempt for ordinary people and a conviction that because of their own privileged inheritance and education they could tell the world how to live. And expect to be thanked for it.

There's a short scene in one edition of *Cracker* where Fitz gives a lecture. He picks up one book after another. 'Spinoza,' he throws it away; 'Descartes,' he throws it away; 'Hobbes, Freud, Adler . . .' all thrown away, and then, 'End of lecture.' He walks off the stage.

'In *Cracker* we talked about racism and sexual violence and we made people *think*,' said Jimmy. '*Cracker* became a vehicle for all kinds of interesting arguments.'

Fitz's main instrument was his imaginative empathy, a quality of prime value to most creative writers. He will imagine his way into the mind of the criminal – the rapist, the racist – and present them with themselves, their own roots of thought.

McGovern can be contentious.

'All men are potential rapists. There is something sexually violent that we suppress. When you pull it out and examine it, it causes problems because we don't like to talk about it. It is wonderfully optimistic that the overwhelming majority of us resist these urges.'

We see a scene where a balaclava-hooded man attacks brutally and rapes a young woman in her flat. He pulls off the balaclava to reveal that he is black.

'I just want a black man and Fitz to talk about racism. One aspect of racism is the myth of the sexual prowess of the black man and it's nonsense. Intelligent black men despise that myth because it affects their lives.'

Coltrane seconded that Jimmy was 'fascinated by the subjects we think about and worry about the whole time – the fact that you're going to die one day, whether you're a good person or not, which, forgive me, you don't get on *Miss Marple*.'

There are times when McGovern's works knit into one. In a three-part *Cracker* there's a young tormented killer skinhead who is going out of his mind. He says to himself, 'Nobody gives a damn any more about white working-class males. We are now scum. No voice. No future. No connection save football.' This man's ancestors have fought in the army and died and endured the penalties of incompetent leadership all in the name of a Britain which he believes has now turned its back on them.

'It dawned on me,' Jimmy said, 'after Hillsborough, that if you said "working class" lots of people had this mental image of a football fan. They wouldn't confess to that but that was their mental image . . . wherever young men meet there can be violence but the overwhelming majority of football fans are ordinary, *decent* young men. Scorn was poured upon them. Alongside this was this increasingly well-paid police force. Thatcher really looked after them – and they, too, treated these football fans with total contempt.'

'The more successful you have become, does that make your access to that sense of injustice and anger more difficult?'

'Yes. The tragedy of writers in TV is that they expend so much energy to get to where they get to, to say, "I've got the clout to do this," that there's no energy left any more to write the things they really want to write. But if you choose your project wisely, the energy will come, the anger will come.'

There's something of the prophet in Jimmy McGovern, a man who finds himself in a wilderness of blighted hopes, false promises, casually crushed ambitions, old ways put on a bonfire. The man of whom his mother said, 'He's got so much feeling in him,' has been and still is tormented with what seems to me a mission to tell the truth through his great gifts as a dramatist. He's out there, self-exiled with the outcasts, looking for the truth about our condition, knowing it needs to be found and held on to. And put on television where millions can see it and believe their own eyes.

McGovern's strength is not so much in his characters, his stories, his dialogue or even his undoubted passion. All these are of a very high order and take him into the top handful of television dramatists. But he has something else. It comes with the background, the love and pity for those he knew so well and saw treated often so badly. It is his anger at what man has made of man and his great ability to make that anger universally felt.

Victoria Wood

We opened the first film (we made two) with Victoria Wood back-stage in what looked like an abandoned aircraft hangar. In the eerie ill-lit place a single figure strode about, punching the air, chopping and changing direction, alone in the shadowed space and apparently frantic, it seemed, to get out of it. Victoria Wood, in a comfortable suit, a shirt flopping over her trousers, was about to go on to the stage of the largest theatre in England – the Winter Gardens, Blackpool. Three thousand people were waiting for her one-woman show, Victoria Wood plus piano performing for about two and a half hours. Alone. 'I think about 3,000 people putting their coats on to see me. I've wanted to do this since I was five. Now, I'm here. The least I can do is enjoy it.'

A final flurry of punches, air-boxing, and then, 'I can't think of any reason not to start.' Her name is announced like that of a fighter about to enter a ring and on she goes and the wall of warmth hits her immediately. When we followed her on that tour, Victoria Wood was the biggest draw in the UK theatre circuit. 'I don't think I've seen a cleaner curtain,' she sings. 'He washes it more than his neck.' The stories and the gags drive the show like an engine. She is Britain's first woman stand-up comedian.

She's on a national tour for which she began to write in January, tried out in small clubs in March and April, took on the road in May and is now three weeks in, having sold out everywhere she's played.

'I'm not nervous now and I'm really glad I've got it all together. It's the first time without the children. It's much more fun if I

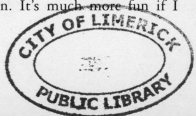

have them with me but it's better for them if they stay behind in London.'

She travels light. Her props and make-up are in one old suitcase. Her 'team' consists of stage manager and a sound engineer. The first thing she does in the rather gloomy dressing room is to stick family photos on the glamorously lit mirror. Her children figure in her act. 'One of them was really naughty this morning. I overreacted. I've had him adopted.'

'I used to think the real me was on the stage and the rest was fumbling to catch up. On stage I was talking honestly and communicating with people, which I'd trouble doing the rest of the time.'

We talked several times in Blackpool. Once after a lunch which involved her usual heap of chips, once after a performance in an empty hotel lounge while outside illuminated tram cars slid by somehow phantom even though embroidered with multicoloured bulbs. She was remarkably relaxed after the heavy evening stint, drinking, as usual, fruit juice – never alcohol and no cigarettes, that flawless complexion, monk-cut hair, poised.

'I'm very much in love with the simplicity of being a stand-up comedian. We have lights but we don't have a set. We just bring the audience in. It's a very simple experience.' When I talked to her a few years later she said, 'There's something very pure about it. There's nothing like hitting a gag and getting a laugh from 5,000 people' (which by that time she was doing, regularly, at the Albert Hall). 'There's nothing to beat that purity of entertainment. It's a very warm feeling. But it's very transient. The moment you're off the stage, it's gone. That's why so many of us turn to drink or drugs to try to keep the feeling going when you're not on stage.' Victoria turns to her family.

'How do you see the audience?'

She smiled and deliberately took the other meaning. My fault. I should have said, 'Who do you think your audiences are?' But *'see'*?

'I don't want to see them at all! I want to see a blank mass. I don't want particular people.'

She arrives at five o'clock for an eight o'clock show, to 'warm up my voice, such as it is. It can be quite lonely. I don't want to go on like the sad clown, but it *can* be quite lonely. There's nobody else to do it. I've got to do it. But I like being here on the stage in an empty theatre. I like being on stage. I'm stage-struck.'

She is open and organised about the story of her childhood. Being organised is an unmistakable characteristic. She was born near Bury in south Lancashire in 1953.

'I didn't have any friends. I didn't have anybody coming to the house or anything like that. They came for my sisters, mainly. My social life never did knock into gear. Then we left the terrace house and went to this big house on the hill, a mile and a half from school. I remember sitting in the garden wanting to be famous when I was five. I was the youngest of four and a bit anonymous. Maybe this was wanting to make my mark. I had to do something different. It was a big secret, a very solitary thing.'

'Did you want to be famous as a comedian?'

'I didn't know there was such a thing. Certainly I didn't know there were women. I saw Joyce Grenfell when I was six and that *certainly* planted a seed of a woman standing on stage alone.'

'Did you adhere to that?'

'When people complimented me at school about being funny, I went home and put it in my diary. I wasn't the class clown. Others were funnier than me. I used to tie people up and put them in cupboards. I wasn't exactly witty!'

Her mother decided to become a teacher when Victoria was eleven. Her father was an insurance salesman who played in a dance band.

'I used to play the piano with him. He was an entertainer. He would have loved to have done what I do. I couldn't cope with piano lessons. I got so nervous my hands sweated and slipped off the keys. So I stopped. I started playing on my own at home when my parents were out. For *years*. In private. For *years* – shut the piano lid when I heard the car. Then one day they said, "We know you play the piano." So I started having lessons. I was very good at sight reading and they put a piano in my bedroom.

'It was a strange life. Each of us had a separate room in this big house, big garden, on a windswept hill. I had a piano and a TV in mine and I played and watched and ate and read. I had a good vocabulary because I read all the time. I was left to my own devices . . . I don't know whether I was obsessive because I had nothing to do or just like that anyway. There was enjoyment in the sense that you could do what you wanted. I was shy until I went to the Youth Theatre and then the sun came out. My sister took me there and I thought, This is the thing I can do, having been told I was naughty and useless at school.'

I'm aware that often in these pieces I dwell on the beginnings. I do think our endings are there, as many others have observed. But also it seems to me that sometimes it's the most gripping part of the life of the artist. That journey out of dream to possibility, that complex negotiation to find an entry point in the real world for a private, often secret, what can appear to be a foolish obsession, that first leap on to the bottom rung. You could say that having built up her ability as a pianist, sated herself in television and literature, cultivated the loneliness of the long-distance writer and cannily absorbed the quiddities of south Lancashire life, the platform was in place.

Her favourite book as a child was *The Swish of the Curtain* by Pamela Brown and when she read from it, back in the lush sunlit garden of her childhood, the heroine's wonderful success on the stage, the triumph and the applause filled her face with delight. When she had finished reading from it, she was a girl again and clutched it to her, an unusual open passionate gesture. 'I *loved* that book. I still do.'

The applause is for her now – the length and breadth of the country – as they finally let her leave the stage and she is back in her dressing room. She takes off her make-up with dollops of cream rubbed into her skin very vigorously indeed – for two minutes. This exercise is undertaken two or three times a day. She glances at her watch as she is doing it.

'I've just realised I've come off and *nothing awful* happened. I can't deny that it's an effort to do. A series of little hills, that song that's so difficult to articulate; the first half hour . . .'

The phone rings and, as always when he's not in the audience, it's her husband. She speaks, reporting, quietly, proudly, a success. 'Yes. It went really well. It went really well. Don't speak up. I've got a camera crew with me. *Don't* speak up. And don't call me "touchy bottom". I've got to go and do the stage door thing.'

At the stage door are a number of women wearing simple bright yellow hats (more like custard coloured shower caps). It's part of the outfit of one of Victoria's characters – an old, rather gormless, immensely good-hearted woman who has a friend 'Kim-ber-ley'. Not, you would think, a role model. More anti-role model. But 'They look very nice,' says Victoria, and 'We had them specially made,' say the women, gratefully and enthusiastically, as they line up for photographs.

'People project on to any performer.'

'What do they project on to you?'

'That I'm nice. I'm *not*.' She smiles and smiles but clearly she means it. 'But that's what they think I am. Their best friend. I'm happy to be their best friend on stage.'

'What do you do for them?'

'I say "that's what life is" and make them laugh at it. Comedy's a really important part of people's lives.'

Later, in the empty Blackpool lounge (save, that is, for a film crew): 'Is there any way you can identify a good joke?'

'It's rhythm. It's unexpectedness. It's surprise. Having things coming off the off beat. It's a lot like music, really.'

To watch her on stage now, roving around, apparently mike-less, no notes or prompts of any sort, two hour long acts riding from ridge to ridge without a stumble, is to see the end product of an evolution which took many years.

'When I first did stand-up, I couldn't leave the security of the piano stool. Then I stood but in the crook of the piano so I had it all around me. Then I always had to have a stand mike between me and the audience. Then I was released into the freedom of not holding on to anything and I really enjoy it.'

After discovering the drama club she clung on at school and describes her 'good luck' in being able to stay on into the sixth form and then go to the University of Birmingham to study drama.

'What did you get from university?'

'I didn't participate. People said, "You can't act. Go and do stage management." They were very dismissive. So I just went off on my own and ate more – more eating, more singing and constantly being told I didn't look right, didn't sound right, the Noël Coward type songs I was doing were gone. So there was nowhere for me to work. Luckily I met Geoff – and that gave me a boost – but I remember saying to him, "I'm twenty-three and it's all over!" '

Geoffrey Durham, a professional entertainer, a magician, always helps her with her shows. 'I'm not a director. I just notice things when I'm in the audience. Who's laughing or not laughing and when. If she thinks they're right, she will take them into account.'

By the age of twenty-three 'I'd had four lucky breaks – including *New Faces* and *That's Life* [in 1976] which got audiences of 14 million and I still hadn't got an agent or got myself together.'

'But slowly her act stopped being a lot of songs strung together and started to be about *her* rather than a lot of songs,' said Geoff. 'When an entertainer starts to talk about themselves, *then* they're getting good because they have the nerve.'

'Nobody arrives on stage as a fully fledged comedian,' said Victoria. 'I'd had to go through some sort of tunnel.'

I remember seeing the early days of the tunnel. I saw her on *New Faces*. She was fresh, original and, already, in perhaps my rather rose-tinted retrospective view, the guarantee of what she became.

'It's easy to forget she was the first female stand-up comic,' said Geoffrey. 'There'd been Beryl Reid and Joyce Grenfell who did "character". But there was nobody, until Victoria did it, who stood behind a stand mike and told gags. It was a role she invented for herself.'

'When I first met Geoff he'd a job – end of the pier magician in Morecambe. We took a little flat in Morecambe and, apathy, we just stayed here. We pretended we liked it. We didn't really like it. We were lonely. It was a mad stupid decision. Eventually we bought a house in Silverdale' – a beautiful forested area in north Lancashire, near the sea but emphatically up-market from Morecambe. 'It wasn't a place for comedy. There's no comedy in scenery. You need people for comedy. I didn't have the *nerve* to move to London. I didn't want to compete.'

'I suspect that although you regret that time you get a lot of material out of it.'

'I just wish we'd had a bit more of a life, that's all. A great act, but no life . . . I was posed endlessly on piers. I was the "Northern Funny Girl".'

We then cut to her singing 'Pretend to be Northern', into which she crams every cliché that non-northerners consider the true characteristics of the north – whippets, hotpots . . . tripe . . .

'Yes. I had been fed in a way I was not even aware of. People came out of my pen that I'd not been aware of hearing . . . all these voices had sunk in . . .'

In what seems now to be rapid order she wrote a stage play, *Talent*, which was taken up by Peter Eckersley at Granada Television, who put it on, and then commissioned two further plays, and *then*, the real breakthrough, commissioned her to do her own series which she wrote for herself and Julie Walters. The two of them went on to seize the public's affection and the critics' respect for the next decade.

'I would set myself up as the victim. Julie was the cruel one. That was my own insecurity. About being fat, for instance. I worked through it in the sketches. In one of them she says, bluntly, "I feel quite bad about what I look like." And, in a boutique sketch, Julie Walters calls out to her assistant, "We've another fatso here." '

It was when she wrote *Victoria Wood As Seen On TV* 'I realised I had to write twice as much and throw half away. I'd written *Talent* once and never changed a word.'

'And Julie Walters?'

'I think she's admirable. She's so clever with her voice. And when she gets into the ring . . .'

'And eventually you moved south?'

'When I moved from the north, people said, "What will you write about?" I said I'd write about what *is*. What is now.'

'What finally made you take the giant leap 250 miles south to London?'

'We were still in Silverdale, up and down the motorway. I thought, We've got to have a normal life. A meeting that takes half an hour to travel to, not five hours. I was just trying to be a "normal person".'

'Do you think success helped you become a "normal person"?'

'No. Because I was successful in Silverdale and still barmy, so it wasn't that.'

'Barmy?'

'Yes. But not now.'

'Where did the barminess come from?'

'Partly from being very driven, very set on just one thing. To the exclusion of *everything* else. And also, I realise now, living in a world of books. I learned everything I knew from books, so life was a constant disappointment.'

'She's really changed,' said Julie Walters, 'she's become much happier and more confident, so she's able to give out.'

We cut to Victoria on stage in her act saying, 'You see I'm not a proper celebrity. They get drunk and dance naked on the table, which I just don't do . . . and tables in Pizza Huts are very wobbly . . .'

A play which moved her on in her career was *Pat and Margaret*. Two sisters who have been apart for many years are brought together on a television show. Patricia Bedford is 'one of the highest paid television actresses in America'. She is glamorous, cruel, swept up in her own image. 'When you think of me,' she tells her assistant, 'think *icon*.' Margaret is dumpy, hair frizzled, a bedsit lifer, the one who never flew.

'I wanted to show how people *perceive* themselves when they are famous.'

'They are both you?'

Her reply was both cheerful and chilling – and it hung in the air as had her previous emphatic remark that though people thought she was nice, she wasn't.

'Yes. They're both me. One who'll never get on, the impotent person, and one who's so determined there's no room for anything else.'

To play Margaret, Victoria made herself as unattractive, charmless and sexless as she possibly could. If she was the cruel Pat she was also cruel on herself as Margaret.

Because this, save for a redeeming postscript, was anything but the rediscovered love of long-lost sisters. The glamorous Pat, over in the UK for a book tour, saw this fright of a sister as nothing but an obstacle and an embarrassment and tried to get rid of her. She saw her sister Margaret as a blemish on her image.

'Some people behave as if what's written about them is true whereas we all know we're all frightened, vulnerable people. I was interested in somebody who just blocked off their past and acted as if they were *just* a famous person. Nobody's like that. Everybody has a history . . .'

In our film we returned to the end of another big night, this time in Manchester. She came out of the theatre to an empty street, the crowds long gone home. 'It's been really good,' she said, 'no complaints about it. But it's just lonely. It *is* lonely. It goes with the job.'

And she walked away quickly and then ran across the wide empty street, shining with rain and speckled with a few reflected street lights, hailing a taxi which did not seem to be on the horizon.

We filmed her again in 2007. In the meanwhile among a pantechnicon of work delivered, she had played the Albert Hall in London every night for three weeks and every night a sell-out. *She* had become a national icon – television shows and plays and documentaries – and she had given up stand-up.

'Do you miss it?'

'I don't crave it. I was always worried about being swept up in it so I stayed cool.'

'Was it an addiction?'

'Oh yes! But I've got so many others I can't be bothered with this one now.'

'You enjoyed it?'

'Oh yes! But it *was* quite lonely. I'm just not doing any at the moment. I've got nothing to say.'

And her marriage, which had lasted for twenty-two years, had broken up.

'At its most basic, it gives you more time. All I concern myself with is the two children. The rest of the time, it's *work*. That's all I do. So I suppose it has freed up a lot of my life.'

She had always wanted to write a sitcom. Victoria is a brilliant graduate of the university of British television. It has provided for many people the core of their real education. The quality of the best plays on television has been high and often higher than that in the theatre. Some of the finest writers, directors and actors have devoted their best energies to television. Its record in comedy has been dazzling; witty, memorable, an Ali Baba's cave. From her bedroom as a girl to her Morecambe flat as a young married woman, to Silverdale and then Highgate in London, Victoria has studied this medium and her instincts have taken her as often to the lighter frothier end of the spectrum as to that which featured writers she wanted to emulate.

The sitcom she wrote – *Dinnerladies* – was traditional. A studio audience so that the gags could get real-time laughs, and an ensemble of 'characters' prepared to stand and deliver.

'But when *The Royle Family* came on, suddenly we looked old-fashioned. We looked like the fifties. They were on film and naturalistic and they didn't need an audience because they didn't do gags. Gags need a laugh at the end. And then the American comedies came in, on film, and they looked so good, not just people standing in a line . . .' Despite the great success of the sixteen episodes she wrote and starred in (and did the warm-ups for before the recording), she did not pursue *Dinnerladies*.

She had changed her style since last we'd worked together. Then she had been short-haired, up for the job, glowing with the exhilaration of flying over the hurdles, her stage suit almost a combat outfit. Now her hair was longer, her appearance gentler, her compass pointed in a different direction, just a small shift perhaps but enough to take her towards a new goal and one which could not be pursued in the same way. She had, perhaps only for a while, left comedy and sketches and even the beloved gags and now sought to be much more completely immersed in a longer game.

Victoria had come across a book, *Housewife, 49*, the edited wartime diaries of a woman who came from the north-west, just a few score miles north of where Victoria had been brought up. The woman, Nella Last, had agreed to take part in a wartime exercise known as 'Mass Observation', in which 'ordinary people' – non-combatants – regularly recorded their experiences of the war. Hers were of outstanding quality, in the prose, in the observation and, perhaps for Victoria Wood most importantly of all, in what they revealed about the inner life and journey of an 'ordinary housewife' who, given the time of war and the act of writing, liberated herself.

Victoria saw it first as a 'wartime jolly – Spam, people painting their legs brown – but it became an emotional journey'.

For both of them. For the first time she was writing about relationships which could not be referred back to *her*. And because it was set in the war years, she had to find another idiom.

We filmed her researching the project in the town of Barrow-in-Furness, a shipbuilding town known now for its construction of nuclear submarines. She went to the house, to the charity shop Nella was encouraged to run, to the now abandoned carpentry works her husband used to work in. She discovered the woman's personal failures and her eventual achievements in re-forming her character.

Along the way, I think, Victoria re-found herself. She wrote the film – which won big audiences and many awards – and starred in it and appointed herself executive producer.

'I wanted to have a say. To talk to the Art Director and say, "I've been to the house." I just wanted to keep my vision right to the end.' She was on the way to taking as much control of a whole production as she had of her one-woman show.

When she took the musical version of her television hit show *Acorn Antiques* on a countrywide tour, she co-directed it.

'Is this now a bid for total world domination?'

'It's simplicity. You're not having to go through other people, that's all.'

The stand-up fame has given her the satisfaction of becoming who she wanted to be as a child, as an adolescent, as a young and shy woman and as a competitor in the crowded bazaar of British comedy. The money was now there to fund a life lived without noticeable material excess. It is the next move on to which her obsession has now latched – taking all the resources of film and theatre and making them work to her purpose, to get *there*, wherever she is driven.

I still worry about the 'not as nice as you think' and 'cruel'. Perhaps it is the knowledge that people's remarks overheard are cruelly exploited to comic advantage and perhaps thereby the people somehow diminished? But that is contradicted by a song like 'A Better Day' which, rattling through as it does, tells the story of a young seventeen-year-old member of the 'underclass' who has thrown up her dire job and has now a bleak 'life' in a new consumer society to look forward to. The hope she hangs on to is very touching. It is an insight into what Victoria herself is, emphatic to damn the damage done by the Thatcher years and yet with the hope of a better day.

'You're full of self-doubt.'

'I know I can always make something better. The only way is to spend more time on it, to look at every angle, to see every detail. It's not an arrogant thing. I think lots of people could do what I do if they spent that much time doing it.'

Having achieved everything she dreamed of aged five, now, it seems, she is out to achieve everything she was told she was unfit for at drama college: but not alone this time. In good company. Watching her go will be one of the guaranteed pleasures to come.

Beryl Bainbridge

Beryl Bainbridge's reputation as a novelist was fixed early and high. *The Bottle Factory Outing* brought her into the literary light, and what Laurence Olivier called 'the right kind of light'. She received the admiration of her peers, the appreciation of what has become a growing and faithful corps of readers and instant take-off into the metropolitan literary circuit – which she both teased and entertained. Like many people, I guess, but certainly like many I know of great talent, she can appear to be several different characters – dedicated writer, ribald company, austere critic, unbuttoned imbiber of the grapes of life, devoted friend, often appearing faux-naïf, and funny, very.

It is not that she deliberately puts on a face to greet the faces that she meets: it is, I think, the jostling of contending personalities, the irresistible urge to slip from one to the other for the hell of it, perhaps the delight in not being bound in a single predictable role. And she did start out as an actress, in Liverpool.

I've known her over many years. We were part of a group of writers – Iris Murdoch, Bernice Rubens, William Trevor, Fay Weldon, John Willis, John Bayley – who toured Israel in the late seventies. On the first morning we got in a small bus and set out for Jericho. Beryl decided to keep a diary. The first entry read: 'Missed seeing camels.' It was a wonderful trip – argumentative, warm, thoughtful, exhilaratingly exhausting.

Iris Murdoch, talking about Plato to me, said, 'He provokes love.' John Bayley collected boiled eggs at breakfast, pocketed them and offered them around like sweets as the day went on. John Willis electrified the British Embassy at a party they gave for us by the ferocity of his attack on what he saw as their snobbish shortcomings. There were visits, via Amos Oz, to Arab writers, readings with Israeli writers, attempts to understand the Palestine-Israeli runes – so much, and Beryl hammering out questions: 'But what I don't understand is why . . .' 'But I still can't quite get it . . .' She read from her novels with enviable panache. On the last evening she decided that the best way to slip me a message across a very big table at a late official dinner in Tel Aviv was to crawl under the table, deliver it from the depths of the tablecloth and crawl back. A friendship was born.

There is no one I respect who does not both admire her work and get pleasure from her striking views and often idiosyncratic arguments.

You edge your way through the hall in her terraced house in north London. You have to edge. The stuffed buffalo takes up most of the space. The house is a cluster of artefacts whose centre of gravity lies somewhere between an extravagantly decorated Romany caravan and a collector's item museum of curios and works of art. The Catholicism of her background is there as is the evidence of her talent as a painter. It must have been an Ali Baba's cave for her children. Her study, where I did the interview, though not unadorned, gives much more of a clue to the core of Beryl Bainbridge: the writer. And yet even the study is not at the still centre. Beryl has a den – I've never been there – which I gather is bare, stripped for work. Her life is built around her writing and when the enforced ban on her smoking coincided with or led to a writer's block she was in a bad way. She has since resumed.

I interviewed her on the publication of her third historical novel. The first had taken the subject of Captain Scott's expedition to the South Pole; the second, the *Titanic*; this one took her to the Crimean War. None of them subjects for the faint-hearted. All of them well covered in previous books, research-heavy, and so tough to find an original point of entry.

Why, though, firstly had she switched from contemporary to historical fiction?

'There's a perfectly valid reason. The only reason I began to write at all was to write about my childhood. There was no point in fiction. Life itself was more interesting. But I thought I needed to put in a plot. There's nothing as strange as what happens to you in childhood. There was such violence in my family – not physical; verbal violence. It wrecked me for years. By the third book, all that nervousness about childhood flew out of the window. After twelve or thirteen novels I had used up all the material and I was not the same person.'

We talked about *The Birthday Boys*, her novel about Captain Scott's fateful attempt to be the first man to get to the South Pole. Our conversation was intercut with remarkable film shot at the time of that brave, rather eccentric group, sadly under-equipped, struggling mightily against conditions that were to beat them and then kill them. These often well-off, well-educated men acted, literally, like dogs, like the huskies their rival Amundsen had shrewdly commanded. Scott's men put on harnesses and dragged a caravan of heavy sledges through what was to them a hitherto unimaginable climate. There's pluck and camaraderie galore. The old black and white footage could be an epitaph for what was best in the boyish aspect of Imperial Britain.

An early insight came from an unexpected source.

'I found that one of Captain Scott's best friends was Barrie. I wondered what that fey little man and his Peter Pan character had in common with this explorer and man of action. Then I saw they were tailor-made for each other. Scott goes off to a Never Never Land, they become the Lost Boys, they never wanted to grow up and it was a Great Adventure. Just like Peter Pan.'

Beryl had acted in *Peter Pan*.

She decided to tell the story through the accounts of five men: Scott himself; Captain Oates, who had been at Eton; Bowers and Wilson the doctor, both of whom, like Scott, were educated middle-class men, and Taff Evans, 'a normal working man', said Beryl. 'I knew I had to begin with Taff and what he thought about the others. Then I felt at home.'

'What about the language of the period?'

'My father was born in 1889. Same year as Hitler. The language of the north didn't change much, not even after the First World War, not really until Hollywood. He spoke in very archaic language. The danger is that you parody it.'

'Scott?'

'I wouldn't have liked him twenty years ago. Now I'm slightly right wing in me old age. I like good manners, that sort of thing. He must have been special because Kathleen Scott chose him. She was an out-and-out bohemian, so he's OK. Oates at first thought that Scott was a bumbler and a blubber and he got in a paddy about nothing. In the end he came to admire him. 'He spared no one, not even himself,' Oates wrote. 'He drove us on by sheer force of his will.' He said he was like Napoleon who when he was told he couldn't cross the Alps said, 'There shall be no Alps.''

'You had to keep in your head the pulse of five men moving towards ice, snow, temperatures below sixty degrees. A goal fixed in front of you. Their feet were rotting.'

When they got there they saw the Norwegian flag. Amundsen had beaten them to it. 'They felt cheated. Scott knew that even if he did get back, he'd lose both feet.'

Oates's last words leave his spirit alive as he left the tent, not to be a burden, and walked to his certain death on those wastes of snow. He had been afraid to remove his socks because he knew that his toes would come off and create 'an awful stink'. 'I may be gone some time,' he said. Like the dying Sir Philip Sidney's offer of his water bottle to a wounded soldier with the words 'thy need is greater than mine', they represent an apotheosis of English gentlemanly Christian-framed gallantry: with style.

When the four others were finally discovered dead in their frozen tent, of Scott it was said that from his expression – compared to the tranquillity or resignation of the others – he looked to be in agony. 'He had obviously suffered dreadfully.'

'And they're still there,' said Beryl. 'Still there, those boys, eighty years on. Deep down that's what I'm interested in. As if you and I, here now, here for the next hundred years. Everything that happens to one still going on.'

It was a strange thought, resonant, elliptically explained as is her way, mystical, well removed from her adhesion to factuality.

'Do you have a responsibility to the history as much as to the fiction?'

'You have to be spot-on accurate. I left school at fourteen. Had no exams. To look up things, to go to the London Library. It's a very heady feeling.' (She acted out the last half dozen words.) 'I loved it.'

We cut to Beryl on a night train to Odessa researching for her historical novel set in the time of the Crimean War. She had gone from snow to snow. Interviewed in the train she said, 'They were deep into winter. It was bitterly cold when they were waiting to lay siege to Sebastopol. People froze.'

She had copies of official records with her and read out: 'Our casualties were: deaths from all causes came to about 21,000; 2,755 were killed in action; 1,761 died of wounds; 16,297 died of cholera, typhoid or scurvy – over 80 per cent.'

I came back to an earlier point. Her emphatic move to historical fiction and the primacy of 'facts' took up John Ruskin's idea that painting should always be based on *fact*; that a painting of a lake should have water and something like a lake in it. His first great apologia for Turner's paintings, which he championed so successfully, was based on his own extensive knowledge of meteorology. The accuracy in cloud painting that he found in Turner's skies, dismissed by other critics as too muddled, was, Ruskin argued, his strength. Ruskin correctly and in detail pointed out that Turner's knowledge of cloud formation outstripped that of 'any meteorologist in Europe'.

In a related way, Beryl seems to be saying the same things. Just as the accurate observation of nature by Turner outdid any 'made up by originality', so Beryl says, 'I don't see the point of making something up. Reality is so much more.'

'But you are using your imagination to create historical fiction.'

'You only embellish. From your imagination that's filled up with your memories and experiences. It gets filled up like a bucket.'

There's disagreement here. I think that imagination is a realm associated with but distinct from memory. It is capable of leaps of empathy, of travelling great distances in a split second, of discovering what was not there before, of absorbing whole new worlds – in novels, for instance – from the lightest nuance. Imagination is the most distinctive and the least known faculty we have, the prime differentiating faculty and maybe we will never get a purchase on it, only know that we rely on it, profoundly. When he was asked what was the most important factor which enabled him to do his work, Einstein said, 'Imagination, above all, imagination.'

The Siege of Sebastopol has been visited by many writers. Tolstoy fought there and wrote his first book after the experience. Dramatically, for our country, William Howard Russell, the journalist for *The Times*, reported back in terms which changed politics, the place of the public in the information chain, and journalism itself.

Beryl pointed out her territory to the camera. 'This is Sebastopol. That's the Black Sea. That's the entrance to the Mediterranean. We wanted to get it off the Russians. When our army came it could have taken Sebastopol. But they dithered about with France. They waited for months. And lost thousands of men. Finally they laid siege and smashed it to pieces.'

'How did you find the subject?'

'I read an article that after years Sebastopol was now open to the public. I had an image of it being built on a vast graveyard. Built on bones. A morbid interest. I wanted to go there.

'There are six sections or parts of this novel. The titles are taken from photographic plates by Roger Fenton, the first war photographer. These photographs accompanied Russell's reports. They are all posed but I wondered what had happened to the people in the photographs and what had happened to the people outside them.'

'Where did the idea of writing about this as a historical novel come from?'

'The London Library. There was this report of an Oxford don found dead on the job, as it were, in a brothel. It was a great scandal. The idea of starting with this brothel death and his son who left the country to be a soldier.'

'Balaclava is what Crimea is most remembered for now.'

'It was a dreadful mistake. They rode straight into the Russian guns. I didn't write about the Charge of the Light Brigade. It's been done. Probably better.'

She did write about the Battle of Inkerman.

'This was a soldiers' battle. Not organised. Not regiments. Forty thousand Russians made a surprise attack at 5 a.m. The idea of people fighting in fog appealed to me. You don't know where the enemy is coming from until the moment he arrives. Dreadful things happened. Men bayoneted each other and were locked together. It might have been a dream but for the bodies lying around.'

She went to Odessa for the Crimea novel. For the *Titanic*, one thing she did was to study a model.

'I like to see what I'm writing about. I didn't know port from starboard until I saw this. There's four funnels but painters who show all four belching out smoke are wrong. One of them was a ventilation shaft.'

She began on the *Titanic* after the book on Scott.

'I thought I knew what wealthy people thought like by then. Oates was upper class.'

Her comments are so unselfserving they can sometimes seem slight. As here for instance. But she had absorbed herself in Oates's thinking, his manners, comments on others, everything she could find out, and adopted, even perhaps acted out, the role of Oates. Once in it she had gone through a door into another room, unknown or barred to her before then.

The *Titanic*. 'The Ultimate in Floating Opulence. Unsinkable.'

'Why did you tell the story through a wealthy young American?'

'I needed him not to be in steerage. He wouldn't have known what was going on anywhere else.'

'There are strong class conflicts.'

'Class is a jolly good thing for a novelist. It's a quick way to establish things. There was Guggenheim on board. He changed out of his pyjamas into full evening dress and he made his valet do the same. Then he stood on deck smoking a cigar and shouted, "Tell my wife I died like a gentleman." He'd brought a mistress on board but she was on a lifeboat.'

'You set this young American idealist against a Machiavellian "every man for himself", Scurra.'

'I like Scurra. At times I thought he'd been on board that ship again and again. That's why nobody knows where his cabin was.'

'The *Titanic* became a symbol, a metaphor . . .'

'It was only at the end that I realised that two years later World War One started. That first iceberg promised the second.'

Rather out of the blue, she said, 'It's all to do with childhood. At the end of the Second World War we were marched off to the cinema to see Belsen.'

'In all three novels, people are tested in the face of death.'

'I think about it a lot. Probably you'd handle it better if you were just on your own. I couldn't cope with the death of my family. As you get older you are more aware of the horrors in front of us. We know too much about what can go wrong.

'The world is changing because I'm changing or have changed. The struggle's over. The money struggle is sort of over. One's clinging to the edge of a cliff. Now I prefer the books which kept you in check in the past. I don't think I would set a book in the here and now. I don't know enough about the here and now.'

Said without a hint of self-pity or self-importance. Melancholy, true to herself, as ever. So the interview ended.

We went downstairs for a drink. For both of us, the first of the day. And suddenly, as they wrote in the old days, 'the house was full of laughter'.

I see Beryl often but never often enough. The last time was a few months ago when her publishers gave her a birthday party. She was wearing a light velvet coat, which made her seem to flow rather than walk across the room full of her children and grandchildren as well as some of her friends. She made a short, even a brisk speech, thanking those who had helped her publish the books and make a career, as well as a vocation out of being a writer. And most of all, after illness and other difficulties, she was writing again.

As she stood there with the rest of us crowded around her and talked so gracefully, so sensibly, I thought how indomitable she looked, spare in herself, unsparing. Her private complexity alchemised into the clarity of her books.

Tracey Emin

Tracey Emin came to the stage of the Savoy Ballroom at the South Bank Show Awards in 2000. She was already known as the wild woman, the 'bad girl' of the Young British Artists. She wore pigtails and said, 'I have an ulterior motive for coming here today. When I was a child about ten years old, when most of the other kids were playing I confess I would sit in front of the mirror and imagine I was being interviewed by Melvyn Bragg.' She looked across at me. I was confused by the unexpected compliment. 'This is as near as I will ever get.'

Afterwards, in good company, she got drunk in the American Bar and was asked to leave. A little earlier on a television discussion show she had asked, 'How many artists are here? I'm here. I'm drunk. I'm leaving now. I'm going to see my friends.' Which she did.

'I don't set out to be controversial. I do what I want to do.'

She wears gorgeous dresses, she is aware of the splendour of what she calls 'my tits' and often displays them with bold old-Hollywood brio, and after a tortuous route through alcoholism she has emerged as a brand artist of her generation.

There is her extreme self-awareness and interest in the media. There's the total obliviousness to the decorous codes of serious television discussion programmes (the *disapproval* on the faces of her fellow guests). Then the early and inflexible rule 'I do what I want to do' and the use of her body and her life as the very raw material for her art. This goes some way to describing her. But there is the essential alchemy. She can look like a fairground fortune-teller but the future she tells is always her own and it is what she has made us want to see. She has something of Carmen about her and something of a free radical. How unfashionable to write this but – there's the gypsy in her and in her soul.

I see Tracey now and then in London haunts and always with pleasure. She's feisty, fun and success has settled her a little. But when we did the film, I knew her only slightly.

We met for the first filming in the Colony Room, of which she is a member, as are most of her Britart pals and as – significantly for all of them – was Francis Bacon, the *genius loci*. We met in the early morning, when it was empty, and each of us clutched a large glass of still water as we sat awkwardly at the bar. Tracey was dressed to impress with a wide-collared maroon leather bodice or basque, wide-parted and deeply cleaved. The challenge to the audience was to get over that and pay attention. The display was part of her right to be a voluptuous celebrity and to be a serious artist, both.

'Some people think that if you're a celebrity you can't be taken seriously,' I said.

'Middle England people don't want to move the goalposts. I am moving them. It's true they're not going to find my work as serious because of the celebrity thing.'

'That's going to change, isn't it?'

' 'Course it is. A lot of museums have my work. But I want to have a good time while I'm here. What's the point of being an artist if you don't enjoy yourself? I can be a celebrity as well as being taken . . . *moderately* seriously!'

The last words are said roguishly, mockingly, a smile that gently puts what she sees as the whole nonsense in its place.

It is odd that people think celebrity is new. The National Portrait Gallery is dedicated to the display of celebrated people. Fashion has swept up military men and orators, sportsmen and actors, and artists of all varieties again and again, lionised them, indulged them, spoiled them then embarrassed them and often ruined them. It's the way of the world. It is, I think, the modern popular media which have whipped it up to a frenzy. And the scale of modern rewards and of course in the case of avant-garde artists like Tracey Emin and a few others, the maddening fact that they seem to get away with murder in crazy work which seems so easy but coins millions. Unfortunately, many people and some critics, but especially young people, love it which is even more maddening. Tracey and Co might be the future.

We went to her studio, a large converted clothing warehouse just off Brick Lane in the once down-at-heel East End of London which for a few decades at the end of the twentieth century became the nesting place for thousands of artists. She wanted a bottle of red wine on the table, in a tribute to Francis Bacon, and once again she arrived dressed to kill. For a morning interview. I emphasise this because she was very aware of her appearance and therefore so was I and so were the viewers.

I wanted to talk about *Everyone I Have Ever Slept With 1963–1995*. This was a tent inscribed in capital letters of various colours and sizes with all the people Tracey had slept with between 1963 and 1995. It was shown at the Royal Academy and lit the blue touch paper.

'Most people didn't see *The Tent*. They just thought it was about the people I'd had sex with. The people who did see it were pleasantly surprised to see that it was about intimacy, about being close, all inside the metaphor and idea of sleep. It was my brother, we're twins, I slept in the womb with him. And my grandmother. She couldn't walk so I lay in bed with her and held her hand. I would like it if more people could go inside *The Tent* but they can't because it would be destroyed.'

We went in, with good lighting and a good cameraman.

The bright colours give it the vigour and gaiety of a Romany caravan. It glows. And the names are vivid but also intriguing. So many. BARBEE (on mauve). LUCEY BAXTER (on pink). ALLIE SMITH (on black). JOHN SETTERFIELD (on blue). BILLY CHILDISH . . . on and on they ran around the tent, inside and out, the letters themselves varying in colour and size and thickness, a work that makes you smile and stop and think. A work, in my view, that earned its place in that Royal Academy exhibition.

'The biggest problem I had with *The Tent* was the illicit' (under age) 'sex thing. People were saying, "Why have you put my name on your tent? You shouldn't have done that." I said, "You shouldn't have fucked me, then, should you?" I was on the moral high ground.'

My Bed provoked an even louder reaction. It is a spectacularly unmade bed, a blitzed island in its own little sea of the desperate evidence of loneliness. 'There's many artists who've used the symbol of a bed but they haven't actually shown the bed. When you go to the Munch Museum in Norway you see his bed and you think, Oh! He slept there. And it becomes a portrait. More important than his work.'

'Why?'

'It's like a transmission of substance. Something happens. Maybe it doesn't happen with everyone. It's the real thing.

'*My Bed*'s the best thing I've done in my life and I still think it is even after six months being slagged off by the press. "An unmade bed. The bad girl of Art." "Mistress of the Mattress." "As seen drunk on TV . . . the bad girl of art is in frame for the £20,000 Turner Award. She's a Prize Troublemaker." ' Charles Saatchi bought it for £150,000.

'It wasn't a joke for me. I was pretty low. I hadn't got out of bed for four days. I hadn't eaten properly for weeks. Drinking like a fish. Couldn't sleep. Then got totally paralytic. Came back, couldn't get out of bed and I thought, If I don't drink water I'll die. So I crawled to the kitchen and crawled back and thought, It's disgusting! It's vile! It's incredibly ugly! Then I looked again. I saw all these things out of that room in a different place in my head and I thought, It's great! It's finished! It's my deathbed. Then it became something beautiful.'

And the critics. 'It was odd. The *Mirror* and the *Sun* – they were great. They showed photographs of their daughters' bedrooms and asked, "Is it Art?" That's great. That's what I want. I want connection. Their daughters loved it. But what annoys me is the so-called liberal intellectual broadsheets. I'm sick of journalists paying off their mortgages and their bills by writing bad pieces about me. Why not champion some people? Why slag me off? I'm not slagging them off. It's a waste of time and space.'

Tracey Emin was brought up in Margate, in its day a bold bright popular seaside resort, rich in entertainments and attracting visitors from T.S. Eliot to the pleasure-hunting crowds from the East End of London.

'I dream sometimes of Margate. It's a real Margate. I think about it when I was eight or nine, the smell of the sea, the fish and chips, the neon – its heyday. Now it's derelict. A place for refugees.'

Margate made her. But only after it had all but unmade her. She hated school and played heavy truant from the age of thirteen – coffee bars, 'exploring Margate's Golden Mile', the lunchtime discos, the cider on the beach, the sex.

'It was something you could do and it was for free. You'd go to a pub, you'd walk home, you'd have fish and chips, then sex, on a beach, down an alley, on the green, in the street. It didn't matter I was young, thirteen, fourteen. It didn't matter they were men of twenty, twenty-five, twenty-six. It never occurred to me to ask them what the attraction was. I knew. Sex was what it was. I can't say it was my fault but I really did enjoy egging those men on. I chased them. I was thirteen. I must take that responsibility. But at the end of the day a twenty-five-year-old man should really know better than to sleep with a thirteen-year-old girl. It was a good education. When I was fourteen I said why go to another country when you can sleep with someone? It's a completely different experience. Your mind goes to a completely different place. But by the time I was fifteen, I'd given up shagging. I thought sex was boring. I got my real kicks on the dance floor. I felt I could defy gravity.'

You could slap 'Dickensian' on it, see it as an illustration of the unbridled voracity of the poor, as an immorality tale, the story of a victim, an abused, an oversexed child; or an adventuress already set on her course – to let her body and her views take her where they would and let go, go, go.

She often mentions Edvard Munch. He was an adolescent idol and still is. His paintings are obsessed with Edvard Munch. When I saw a big exhibition of his work at the Royal Academy, I could scarcely believe the extent of his self-preoccupation. Yet it worked. Like Rembrandt's many self-portraits, more than fifty of them, they work because they are works not of vanity but of art. Munch seems to have alerted Tracey

Emin to the possibility of herself being the essential subject and focus of her art. And I think that what she said next in the interview, which is largely true, was *the moment* when she made the first decisive move in a direction which eventually led her towards unconfined autobiographical artworks.

It seems she was an exceptionally good dancer. She was a hot favourite in a competition which if she'd won it, could have taken her 'really up there. To the Empire Leicester Square Ballroom. Dancing on TV: 1978 The British Disco Dance Championships.'

In her autobiography *Strangleland* she describes the final scene. She danced wonderfully. 'I thought I could defy gravity. As though my soul were flying free.' People started to clap. 'I was going to win! Nothing could stop me.' And then the men who had slept with her and others who wished they had congregated and started to chant, 'Slag! Slag! Slag!' 'A gang of them: "Slag! Slag! Slag!" I couldn't hear the music any more or the clapping. My head was spinning. I'd lost it. I ran off the dance floor, down the steps to the sea and I thought, I'm leaving this place. I'm better than all of them.' In our film she danced again and as she danced she chanted, 'Shane, Eddie, Tony, Doug, Richard . . . this one's for you!'

She lit yet another fag. 'I don't see why I was such a slag. All I did was sleep with a few people. It's not a crime.'

But 'Slag' got her out of Margate and she was on her way.

She had no O-levels, scant schooling, no knowledge of the labyrinths and ladders of the education system. But she had nous, talent and the desperate drive to 'leave this place'. It's another film, but she managed to get a foundation course in art, applied to various colleges, including St Martin's. ('It was awful. I came out thinking, I don't want to go there anyway. Shithole! I hated it.') 'I got into Maidstone but they said I had to have two A-levels in English and History which was impossible. I couldn't do them. I went every night. I couldn't do them. 'Cos I can't spell. So it didn't matter what I wrote.'

The kindness of strangers and the fact that in her art classes she was getting grade ones fiddled her into Maidstone 'from 1987 to 1990 – the happiest years of my life'. She left with First-Class Honours. 'It was brilliant. We were an art school but we were totally aware of what was happening in the country all the time. But my work was shit. It was just like a copy of every German Experiment you've ever imagined.'

She reached what is thought to be the pinnacle of achievement for an art student – she got into the Royal College of Art. 'Amazing. After all I'd been through I'd still say those were the worst two years of my life. The best thing about the RCA is that letter saying you've got in. After that it goes downhill.

'At the RCA I learned something fantastic. I learned – if this is art I don't want to know about it. If this is being an artist it doesn't interest me. I'm leaving this place.'

She got a studio and decided she wasn't a good painter. Got depressed, got pregnant, had an abortion. 'After the abortion, the idea of painting, creativity, made no sense whatsoever. Flapping a bit of oil paint on a canvas, making a picture, that's not art. There's hundreds of people can paint a picture of the New Forest but they'll never be artists. It's something about the essence and integrity with which people do things. There was no point in making art that somebody had made 1,000 years before or 600 years before. I had to create something totally new or not at all.'

And then there arrived what has been ever since and ever more deeply her guiding idea. An idea she has lived by, worked by, been praised for, been criticised for, but held to.

'I realised that *I* was much better than anything I'd ever made.'

'Drinking and sex are important in your work.'

'Sex is really important. I like sexy things. There's sex and there's making love to someone. Nothing in the whole world can beat that. Such an obvious thing. It pushes the world round.'

There are many frontal nude drawings by Tracey of Tracey, legs apart, head thrown back. Recently she had an exhibition which featured a film of her masturbating.

'Most time when I've made work about sex I haven't had sex. I've gone for two years without sex and of course you're frustrated. Men think about sex every two seconds, whatever it is, but I think I'm up there with any man, totally. And to not have sex for two years – you don't even masturbate – people think you wank all the time if you don't have sex but what happens is you haven't had sex and you know you're not going to get sex, it's the last thing you do is have a wank. So you put that energy into other things and be creative.'

Thus spake Tracey, thus to the British television public one Sunday evening on *The South Bank Show*. The interview itself had become part of her method of ceaselessly embellishing the art object called Tracey Emin. She does what she is and vice versa.

We went to her gallery, the White Cube in Hoxton, area of the Young Brit coven, fashion hot spot, money-spinner extraordinaire. She originally called the exhibition 'UPGRADE', to indicate how much better her life had become. The central feature was a child's playground-sized wooden 'Hellter-skelter'. Hellter? A witty play on words? 'It's because I can't spell. The idea of the helter-skelter is such a good metaphor. You climb up all those stairs and you have a hell of a good time coming down.' There's a wall-hanging/blanket, one of a series over the years, which are decorative, memorable and covered in cloth cut-out prints, Tracey's noticeboard to the world. 'TOTAL PARANOIA', and again the happy trick of the mis-spelling, 'I AM DISGUSTED BY YOUR ENVEY' and 'EVERYTHING YOU STEEL WILL TURN TO ASH'.

Still searching for a title, Tracey said, 'I thought, You forgot to know my soul inside a neon heart. My boyfriend said, "At least put a spin on it – you forgot to kiss my Big Dick." '

As part of the programme, Tracey wanted to be filmed having tea with her mother, a handsome woman, as well dressed as Tracey, and though conservative, still that dash, her daughter's mother.

Tracey: 'Do you think you've been a good mother?'
Pam: 'Yes I have.'
Tracey: 'What about the vast amount of freedom Paul [her twin] and I had when we were young compared to other children?'
Pam: 'Maybe. But remember me telling you and I'm always your friend and if you get pregnant tell me . . .'

Pam and Tracey (chorus):   'in time to get an abortion.'

Tracey: 'When Dad went to Turkey you had an affair with someone half your age, didn't you?'

Pam (embarrassed, playing with her napkin):   'Stop telling your
mother's secrets, Tracey.'

Tracey: 'You set up all those rules for me based on yourself, ever
since I was young.'

Pam (interrupts, calm again):   'I just couldn't imagine you, as
you were, having a child or two children, that couldn't be your
way of life.'

Had she ever asked her mother those questions before? 'No . . .'

'I don't know what to say. You chose to ask her on television?'

'I was always brought up, the honesty thing, it didn't matter what
I did as long as I told them what I was doing. Now with my parents I
want the answers from *them*. I want the straight answers.'

Her parents never married. Her father, a Turkish-Cypriot, already
had a family when Tracey and Paul were born. He admits to twenty-
three children. He figured a little in her early life and then drifted away,
became estranged. A gift of gold and dynamite for Freudians: a sad
inheritance that Tracey not only survived but made rich.

These days they are close, she said, and touchingly she cherishes a short
length of home-movie footage which is a back shot of a bronzed plump
middle-aged man in big white swimming trunks tentatively advancing
into a poster blue Mediterranean. She has written: 'we are joined together
by blood, the stars, the sun and the moon. I love you, daddy . . .'

A last lap at the bar in the Colony Room, back on water. She talked
warmly about the 'gang' of her contemporary artists, her family. 'We
never share ideas. We've got the same ideas. We slag each other off
as well.' She smiled, happy in the closeness of that state. 'When I'm
doing a show I bat it about with Sarah, Carl, Matt, Guy, everyone, to
get their opinions. The same with Jay Jopling.' (Owner of the White
Cube Gallery.) 'I ask his opinion. He's got to feel good about where I'm
coming from. He has to sell it.'

Straight out. She takes and makes the world as it is. Yet that is belied in her constantly changing expressions in the interview, from earnest to flirtatious in a flash, from rather naïve cunning to anger, from certainty to a look of helplessness. Her expressions, rather like but more frequently and fluidly than those of Pavarotti, catch and match the moods behind the words.

She has made enough money 'to find a place', the studio in which we did the interview, 'to do it properly, to organise it', as I saw, meticulously. 'That's brilliant. Artists in attics in the freezing cold, that's a hundred years ago. To be a good artist now you have to understand commerce, finance and the media. If you don't want to take them on, don't be an artist, do something else.'

No quarter, no argument, the credo of a street fighter. In some measure she is. But also a romantic, a wild card, most of all a dedicated artist who is unafraid to make every aspect of her own reality her subject.

Did posterity interest her?

'Not at all. If it did I'd make my work out of different materials. Some people have children but I'll have press cuttings. I've said this on a blanket I've made.

'I see myself as an old woman living in a hotel somewhere and the walls are covered by my press clippings.' (She is happy at the contentment in prospect.) 'Maybe the odd person does some research and comes to visit me. I'm not such a bad old woman, a bit nutty and quite together, except I am surrounded by myself . . .'

We ended the interview and acknowledged each other. 'Thanks . . . thanks.' Then Tracey turned to the camera, looked down the lens and smiled directly at her public.

It is not difficult to dismiss Tracey Emin's work. *My Bed* could have been made to be dumped on. The masturbating artist would once and quite recently have been called pornography. *Everyone I Have Ever Slept With 1963–1995* a naïve cross between clever exhibitionism and folk art. It is easy to be disparaging about Tracey's work.

But it stays in the mind, I think. So far? Yes, but so far, so good. One day at a time. More than that.

I think she has hit a nerve of the time which is neither common nor simple. That some of her work appears common and simple is part of the plot. Appearances in her work are and are not deceptive. *The Tent* embraces, in its cosy womb, many verities of love – for the most tenderly familial to the most transiently sexual. It's the story of a life. The life the viewer can fit in and flit out of along the way.

She has taken herself as the subject to a degree which reminds many people that they have a self worth art. She has probed it dangerously because she wants to test the nerve as many of us do or would like to do. Tracey's out there and who knows? Her own elegiac picture of her lonely future could be mistaken.

To meet and spend time with her is to be with someone almost imploding with the energy she brings to bear on being a walking talking living doll of contemporary art. But a doll that wakes up at night to wake up the rest of us to what is in us out there.

Ian McEwan

On Saturday, 15 February 2003, at the lowest estimate 1 million people marched, peacefully, through London to demonstrate their opposition to war on Iraq. It was the biggest protest for peace in British history. Ian McEwan chose that day on which to set his novel *Saturday*. His story on that day centred on the life of a successful neurosurgeon, Henry Perowne.

McEwan's first book of short stories in 1976 won the Somerset Maugham Award and established him as a writer to be watched and admired. Subsequent stories and novels increased his reputation and, as his sales grew, he became a writer critically valued and widely read, his novels filmed, his talents called on for an oratorio, a television play and as an intellectual commentator, particularly, recently, on science.

He was part of a group loosely corralled by the editor of the *New Review*, the late Ian Hamilton. Ian's magazine was run from a tumble-down office in Greek Street and from the pub next door, the Pillars of Hercules, where we drank often and too much. In the beginning, Clive James, Russell Davies, myself and other friends were asked to pitch in. We did so as much for Ian Hamilton as for the magazine. The magazine became influential and, together with Ian's wit, critical ferocity and poetic charisma, it attracted a group of writers a few years younger than us – notably Ian McEwan, Martin Amis and Julian Barnes. It was probably in the Pillars, then, that I first met Ian McEwan, bumped into him from time to time over the years, asked him on to *The South Bank*

Show in the seventies, made a short film at the beginning of the eighties and then a fuller portrait at the time of *Saturday*.

We talked in Fitzrovia, in his London house, which is the model for the house of his protagonist, Henry Perowne.

'Why that day?'

'I felt some responsibility to the present. Like a lot of people after 9/11 I did no writing for six months. I became a complete news junkie, out of that sense of wanting to be part of those anxieties, that the world had changed but you didn't know *how*. That's what I wanted to catch. When I started writing and got to about 20,000 words, I saw that a "day" would be a very useful structure. It's a road that many writers have gone down before.'

'Did you go on the march?'

'I was around it, not on it. I was rather like my hero. I had contradictory feelings. I had quite a lot of contact with Iraqi exiles, some of whom were longing for the country to be invaded. I was a little perplexed by the joy on the streets.'

Over some of this we showed aerial archive footage of the rally, a rich flood, a river of people wall to wall in the streets flowing orderly towards Westminster and Parliament. There were close-ups of placards – 'Not In My Name', 'Freedom For Palestinians' and, mostly, 'Don't Attack Iraq' – close-ups too of people, their tolerant expressions making the strident placards the more telling.

'It's a "state of the world" novel. How did it change after 9/11?'

'I think *we* changed. Time will tell. Maybe it's just a local eruption with a bigger swell behind it. Climate change, for instance. But I've always been interested in how large-scale events and private lives interact. I did give Perowne a fair bit of the white noise of my own thoughts.'

'Such as?'

'Certainly one of the thoughts about the march on the day. And he goes to buy fresh fish. The sea's emptying of fish yet he can't stop buying it and eating it and enjoying it. How much our sympathies have expanded – they now include foxes and we've just discovered that fish feel pain.'

We film a dramatisation of some excerpts from the novel. In one of them, Perowne drives around his part of London, McEwan's part of London, in his car. 'Shamelessly, he always enjoys the city from inside his car where the air is filtered and his hi-fi music confers pathos on the humblest details.' He toys with the notion that these prosperous streets might be seen as unsure in a world of terrorism but concludes: 'It isn't rationalism that will overcome the religious zealots but ordinary shopping, and all that it entails – jobs for a start, and peace, and some commitment to realistic pleasures, the promise of appetites sated in this world, not the next.

McEwan's enthusiastic descriptions of London reflect the pleasure of his return, after sixteen years in Oxford. 'I wanted to do London again.'

His hero is almost perilously well off.

'He is a man deeply in love with his wife, not troubled by the state of his children, passionately involved in his work' – he may also have added, very comfortably off – 'in other words, life was fine, let's get that out of the way and see what there is to worry about – and it's the world itself. It's odd that we can compartmentalise our lives: we are deeply worried about Iraq and yet friends are coming to dinner and we'll have a wonderful time.'

To research the novel, McEwan spent time with an eminent neurosurgeon and there are descriptive passages of operations on the brain which come directly from that research and conversations.

There's also a lengthy description of a game of squash. 'I wanted to capture some of the furious competitiveness and aggression in a game of squash, that dissipates the moment it's over.' He then spoke of the emotions involved, 'the humiliation, the torture . . . his character was exposed, it's an extended metaphor . . .' He describes it in terms of war.

'You were brought up in a military family. What did that bring you?'

'My father's background was Glasgow, working class. He was quite a disciplinarian, a regimental sergeant major, feared by the men, hated too.'

'Do you find any influence on your writing from your parents?'

'He found it hard to be openly affectionate. Fathers never fare as well as mothers do in my fiction. My mother was very warm, close, intimate, slightly neurotic, tense. At the age of eight or nine when my father was away I used to sleep in my mother's big bed and I'm sure Freud would have had a lot to say about that – being physically close to her. Being sent off to boarding school was a real wrench. I don't think I wept like a lot of boys, I just sort of shut down for years. Until I was sixteen or seventeen when I woke up, reading poetry, listening to music, thinking about girls.'

Ian was the first student to go on Malcolm Bradbury's creative writing course at the University of East Anglia.

'Going to UEA for a year was a fantastic stroke of luck for me. I was the only student on the course. It consisted of seeing Malcolm or trying to see him in the term in which he was meant to be teaching. I saw him on three occasions for twenty minutes. Usually in the pub. I'd give him a story. He'd say, "I like it a lot. What are you doing now?" I'd say, "Well, I'm thinking about writing a story about a boy who rapes his sister," and he'd say, "Oh fine – when can I have it?" And that would be it. There was no "course". But he was the Superstar Professor. He was my readership. It meant I wrote with a purpose. I must have written twenty-five or thirty short stories in that year.'

In a brief interview years previously I had put to him remarks from critics that his subjects could be called distasteful, even disgusting.

The young McEwan, too shy then to look straight at the interviewer or the camera, said, firmly, 'I'm taking it for granted that the unconscious exists and that things go on in our minds that we are not aware of in the day-to-day reflections of our conscious minds.'

'They also earned a reputation for being shocking and even perverted. They dwelt in dark crevices neatly stepped over by generations of novelists. Were you aiming to do that?'

Back in the 'present', the *Saturday* interview.

'I used to *deny* that, but I think I did want something rather bold and bright. I think I ended up by writing myself into a corner.'

'But looking at the violence in those early stories. Does it have any connection with being brought up in an army camp? Those people are training for war. It must have come from somewhere.'

'There was what you've described there plus a fantastic degree of repression, a very polite lower middle-class world in which however terrible things were no one ever said, "I am unhappy." Life must go on. It was held down, locked in, and I think this was what I was writing in my late teens and early twenties. I felt tremendous liberation. It's rather like a shy person who's had three glasses of wine at dinner and decides he wants to be bold like everyone else and goes too far. I blurted out those stories.'

We talked about *The Comfort of Strangers*.

'It came out of a depression. It's certainly the darkest thing I ever wrote. I thought I was coming to the end of all I could do in fiction. I thought that by the time I finished this short novel I'd never write again or I'd have to do something entirely different. I can't really think where it came from. I'd spent a rather awkward week with a close friend in Venice. It seemed a very good setting for a couple who were lost.'

A young, hapless English couple are stalked and preyed on by a rich Venetian who eventually kills the young Englishman.

'I was never fully satisfied with the novel. I was writing myself into silence with this fantastically destructive, bleak, murderous story of one couple's psycho-sexual drama spilling out over this vulnerable English couple who seemed incapable of defending themselves. There was a fantastic disjunction between what I talked about with friends and what I wrote about. I felt as if I was only writing out of a tiny corner of my mind. Two things happened. One was that I worked with Michael Berkeley on an oratorio around the nuclear issue – *Or Shall We Die?* The other was that I wrote a film, *The Ploughman's Lunch*, with Richard Eyre. These two projects were getting away from myself, from the solitude of writing. I'd started writing in 1970. That was 1986 – sixteen years later I finally thought, Now I can start to write properly.'

He began to 'bring' science into his work.

'I'd always read a great deal about science. It wasn't just an interest for me. It was like a sort of metaphysics. By the time I wrote *Enduring*

Love it was the way I wanted to try and understand the world. A lot of writers *use* science. I wanted to go one step further and see if I could write a character who had so absorbed science that that was how he saw the world. The great opportunity was in evolutionary physiology. The biological sciences bring us an account of the world which showed us that science could start to invade the patch we thought was ours. So you could actually read scientists not only on revenge as a human emotion but the organs of love or social accounting or how we return favours. I think Frankenstein started the idea that to think rationally is to think coldly. I think this is a terrible misconception. You don't have to be a cold-hearted psychopath to think that rationality will get you out of a situation and sometimes instinct doesn't get you to the right place.'

We brought in *Saturday* to extend the discussion about the novel's 'patch'.

'When Henry Perowne hears the "Goldberg Variations", he thinks, Genius. When he reads *Anna Karenina* he thinks, Well, anyone with a notebook could have accumulated all that detail. It doesn't give him that breathless sense of sheer inhuman quality of perfection he hears in Bach.'

'So are you saying that Perowne is lacking something by not fully understanding fiction?'

'I know, as you must, people who have never read a novel or a poem and they're completely sentient conscious people whose mental lives are as rich as anyone else's. It's one of the arrogances of the literary culture to think that only by reading literary novels can you be a fully qualified human being. It's nonsense.'

'That's true. But is that how it affects you?'

'I can't live without literature. But I meet many people who do not read books and I used to think, when I was an arrogant nineteen-, twenty-year-old, that they were asleep. I thought my parents were asleep because they didn't love literature. But it's nonsense. We have to be very careful in the literary culture not to believe we hold the key to all mythologies in this.'

'I agree. But looking at other ways of arriving at the truth about the human condition, do you think that scientists, for example, are finding out things that are more worth knowing about than you find in *Anna Karenina?*'

'I think we have probably not yet bettered a device than the novel for looking at what it's like to be someone else. Movies are fantastically crude in this respect. They can't do consciousness. They can't give you the life lived on the inside. Even poetry can never quite give you what it's like to be an individual moving through a long period of time in a society.'

'I think the phrase of Henry James's calling the novel "a loose and baggy monster" is relevant,' I said. 'It can incorporate particle physics and buying fish at the market.'

'I agree completely.'

'You've written about terrorism as a failure of the imagination.'

'If you really want to drive a planeload of people towards a building you have to close down an instinctual part of yourself. In other words you withdraw that sense of what it is to be someone else and so I say that cruelty, of which terrorism is one branch, is a failure of the imagination.'

'One strand in *Saturday* is about consciousness and how matter becomes consciousness. Your neurosurgeon hero deals with the brain in a practical way and in an intellectual way. He's convinced our behaviour is determined by chemical events and codes in the brain and one day all these will be revealed to us. Do you think that?'

'I think they *will* be revealed to us but I'm not sure quite what we will know that we don't already know about how to behave, how to live. You could crack the neural code but will it tell you how to behave? But Perowne has a faith that in the philosophy of the natural view of life there is a beauty and a grandeur. I did want to give him my sense of the natural world – rich, warm, human, not cold and abstract.'

There was an early television play, *The Imitation Game*, which we discussed in an earlier interview. It was set in Bletchley, in World War Two, where a group, overwhelmingly male, cracked German codes which, it is reliably said, brought victory a year earlier than otherwise. Ian's central concern, though, was to do with his feminism and his main character was a woman. She was on the outside, as by far the majority of the women in Bletchley were, serving the men but excluded from what was going on. A young 'insider' had a brief affair with her. His impotence led to an anger which led to her imprisonment for reading the classified documents he had let her read.

'Why Bletchley?'

'It's almost the too perfect model for feminism. I wanted a story about a woman who goes from the outer edge to the middle where she will be destroyed. My men were accused of being stereotyped, half-drawn. A lot of people thought I'd loaded the odds and this is true, but that's your privilege as a writer.'

His heroine, broken, eventually realises her thoughts and says, 'As long as we stay on the inside and don't kill . . . women make war just possible. Something men can feel tough about.' And she realises too that her would-be lover's impotence is part of the same straitjacket of thought.

Ian explains his novels in terms which are theoretical. He makes them seem embodied ideas. First the context, then the characters. This, though, is rather belied by a closer look at how he actually works.

'I work very slowly. In longhand usually, trying out sentences on a piece of paper until I'm satisfied with them.' (We filmed several sheets crammed with his neat handwriting, sometimes diagonally across the pages, sometimes notes underneath the notes.) 'Sometimes I'm writing one scene and I see my way through to three chapters ahead to another scene that has some relationship to it. So instantly I'll sketch that out . . . it advances the book, it has a certain shape. I wouldn't dare spell it out to myself. To put it into words would break the very fragile sense of urgency. In many ways it's a laborious technique. The reason I've liked it so far is that it does guarantee a colossal concentration on the language itself even though there's the inevitable drudgery that attends the writing of any novel. At certain times I feel delirious with the discovery of what's on the way though. It does seem to me that the *real* life of the novel is not the characters but the actual language itself. The surprises it springs on you.'

'Lawrence again. He said he didn't know what he was going to say until he read what he'd written.'

'Absolutely! I also find it not only in terms of any particular project. I can see now how the short stories led to *The Cement Garden* and *The Imitation Game* but at the time one is just groping. It's almost like a diary of one's thinking, and internal life.'

Ian has achieved double top: reviews from the finest critics and a vast readership. So it would seem odd to write about him without referring to *Atonement*, his best-reviewed and most globally successful novel.

Atonement took McEwan a league up in the writing rating stakes. He is now regarded in the USA as *the* leading voice of contemporary British fiction. The film of the book took its elegant storytelling and searing subject matter into world cinemas.

He seems unfazed by all this. As it happens because of a recently arrived neighbourliness, we see a bit more of each other than before. He sparkles with his enthusiasms, his wit has sharpened, he is still recognisably the writer on the campus, and after many a summer, has settled with his wife Annalena, herself a writer, into a very modern literary life.

Iggy Pop

I arrived in Miami in the late afternoon into a swamp sun from spring showers London. As usual after the transatlantic haul I woke up at about three in the morning; too much wine and coffee on the plane; too much buzzing in my head in the quiet darkness after hours of non-stop listening to the tapes. Instead of the usual book, night-time television (I once discovered Alan Bennett in Chicago at 4 a.m. – *Bed Among the Lentils*), I put in the earplugs and listened again non-stop for the next four hours to Iggy Pop – 'I am a passenger. And I ride and I ride and I ride . . .' I think that stint finally dug it in for me. And when I turned up at his modest one-bedroomed, one-storeyed, neat, glowingly white-painted clapboard house in the suburbs, I could have sung along. I was up for it.

So was he. You do not anticipate from the ancient, gnarled, furiously talented wild man of rock, the enthusiasm of an ingénue and even less the manners and courtesy of a southern gentleman. But there he was, deeply polite, nothing faked, long lank dyed blond hair falling on his shoulders in cavalier fashion, shoulders not bare as is the whole upper body in those performance-art concerts but covered in a dazzling white shirt, three buttons opened, showing a rather scrawny neck and a leather-hide tan.

His voice is deep and gravelly, the words measured, neither glib nor with any taint of seeking to ingratiate. Sentences picked out with a simplicity you feel he's worked on. His gaunt cratered face – bearing traces of so many nights of excess but now relieved of their burden – is never long without a smile, used to reinforce the point, as if to say 'I mean that'.

We were in the small sitting room. Because it was out of the sun we needed heavy lights. There was no air conditioning. You could feel the heat of the Everglades sweeping in.

Iggy Pop and the Stooges came out of Detroit at the end of the sixties. As well as making his music, though partly because of his music, he has managed to remain the *enfant terrible* for forty years. His emergence coincided with that emergence of flower power, hippy happiness, peace and love. Iggy foretold punk. He has been a serious drug addict of many varieties, suffered a mental breakdown and until recently been either broke or bankrupt.

We began with a clip of 'I Wanna Be Your Dog' with Iggy punching the air, pummelling imaginary opponents, his scraggy upper body muscled and glistening with sweat, his jeans slipping way down his bum and at the front somehow not riding down over the crotch. He makes a mad dervish look like ballroom dancing.

'Why do you push yourself so hard on stage?'

'It's just something in the way the music's going to get performed. And if it's going to get physical then it's going to get physical. I think it was Elvis that said [good imitation] "Aah jus can't help maself." There's a lot of that.'

Then we see his dive into the crowd. It's a racing dive. Full stretch and sudden, relying utterly on the welcoming sea of hands to bear him up. He drowns in their arms and then emerges, is hoisted up and surveys the cheering audience like a conqueror, and they pass him back to the stage as if delivering him carefully to an altar: the band has not paused for breath.

'Your performances, it seems to me, are either highly calculated or in some way possessed. You talk of a feeling hitting you on the back of the neck, exploding in your head – there's the sense that you have to unleash this on the audience. Did you feel that?'

'I hope so. It comes from a lot of different places. It comes from the nature of amplified music. There's a resonance. It wasn't there before

275

things were plugged in . . . And then some of it comes, I suppose from (he gurgles the next phrase) "deep childhood problems" . . . that sort of thing. Things you've gotta work out for yourself, anger, fear . . . then some of it's good old theatre.'

'You were brought up in a trailer park just out of Detroit?'

The trailer-park, trailer-trash image was part of his early allure and difference. But it was not, not *quite*, so.

'My parents were lower middle class. They were both educated. My dad was teaching high school, not making a great deal of money and my mother was a private secretary.'

'What did you get out of the trailer park?'

'I began to get a sense of rock 'n' roll as working people's music. It triggered something.'

'What?'

'That these people . . . are nicer . . .' – he nodded emphatically and threw up his arms – smiled broadly '. . . than the more accomplished members of our society . . . you can take what that infers from there . . . Triggered a respect for simplicity . . . How about *that*?'

'When did you start playing music?'

'I was thirteen . . . I started going to school in the comfortable town of Ann Arbor. I started meeting kids who had guitars, amplifiers, Ray Charles albums . . . wooo!! . . . whole albums of Duane Eddy and Elvis. I got seriously corrupted.'

He became the drummer in the band The Iguanas – hence Iggy. He was born Jim Osterberg. The Iguanas, a high school band, photographed in smart matching uniformed outfits, short hair, not unlike the early Beatles. They hit high school fame with a cover of a Bo Diddley hit.

'There was a huge response in the school. People knew me! Hey! I'm popular. It began to dawn on me that any serious career in the real world that I chose was going to be a continuation of what I was experiencing at high school. I was going to sit in the same oppressive room all day and listen to someone talk about something sequentially logical that would just degenerate into some kind of buzzing in my head. I was gonna *feel* bad and I thought, I can't do it . . . I can't *do* it . . . and it occurred to me music might be an escape.'

He became increasingly interested in the Blues and went to Chicago and proved sufficiently talented and persistent to play the drums for bluesmen Big Walter Horton and Johnny Young in the black clubs.

'I was pretty impressed by the atmosphere when you go into those bars. It wasn't so much the playing. It was the audience. They were *rowdy*. And I'd never *seen* women with such big bottoms. And I'd never seen bottoms *move* like that! It was the *shit*, man. It was the shit. I wanted to be like that.'

'But you quit because you said that black people should play the Blues.'

'I wasn't gonna master that particular form. There were people who could imitate that better'n I was gonna. But I had a brainstorm. I smoked my first joint down by the Chicago river and sat there and I thought I could take these same themes, these same attitudes, and I could make "white suburban delinquent music". I had two pretty tough years trying to do this with some vigour.'

The clarity and dedication of the teenage Iggy Pop are striking. There's the touch of Huck Finn, down by the Chicago river, the honesty about his ambition, the easy slide into black Chicago, the rigorous self-assessment, and then the all-American setting out on his own independent path. Although Iggy Pop did not altogether come from the condemned trailer trash, he was close enough to adopt it with conviction. But alongside that was a thoughtful calculation of the music he wanted to make and the niche of originality he could perhaps discover. He has pursued that goal, that idea, despite a life lived more often than not in a state of wreckage. His self-belief has never wavered, nor has his dedication to this pursuit.

'You'd learned a lot from the Blues and you wanted to transfer that to describing your own life?'

'Yes. And to try to create a new musical form. And to do that it was going to be necessary to have people who knew even less than I did.'

It's a remark that from a lesser source could seem little more than a pose. Iggy meant it. He wanted a clean slate and the lucky pair chosen to be his core workers were the Asheton brothers, Scott and Ron (drums and guitar). Scott says, 'Jim called and said, "I'm in Chicago – let's start up a band. I'm creating new music. I want to teach you guys how to play." We created our own instruments. We'd start off a set with just some water in it. We'd have a mike on top and have that play and play before we came out.'

They called themselves The Stooges.

'It was the perfect time.' (End of the sixties.) 'Rock 'n' roll was changing. People were looking for a new thing. We were definitely a new thing.'

The Stooges were not technically proficient players but that was not what they were trying to be. Scott: 'Simple and powerful stuff was what Jim liked and it catapulted him into his stage frenzy. He had a way of moving to the music that was compelling.'

When you look at film of the early performances of 'No Fun' he is like a wolf, on all fours, the upper body now naked, feral.

'We had two songs. "No Fun" and "I Wanna Be Your Dog". Nobody had come up with something . . . [here he pauses and delicately emphasises the next phrase by moving both his arms in stages over to his left] . . . quite . . . like . . . that. And it was close enough to the vanguard. I thought, Well, there must be 50,000 people in America who could hear this.'

In 1969, they came out with their first album.

'It went down *really well* and made a very strong impression on a certain minority. It upset the shit out of the New Age Corporation-structure-to-be, all of whom had beards and long hair. They hated us. A whole new set of people were going to come in and beautify America' – even now he finds the notion hilarious – 'you know, in a peaceful and psychedelic way and take over and it was all complete lies. We were messin' up the programme. The common quote was "These guys can't play." We couldn't play "Johnny Be Good" . . . but we could play something else.'

'Your own performances . . . the diving . . . people said, "He's frightening." '

'I just thought one thing you don't want to do is get up on that stage and leave not having engaged . . . I wonder if it's the soul of some half-drunk blues man.'

By 1970 they were into their second album, John Coltrane, Los Angeles and drugs.

'Marijuana was first. Then the psychedelics – something you did on Sunday. By the end of the recording in Big Bad Los Angeles, cocaine had entered the vocabulary. After that heroin was around.

'It escalated from snorting to shooting up. Drugs became your life. It's a shame. It wrecked my health mentally and physically and eventually wrecked the band.'

The manager, Danny Fields, watched them go down. 'One time I went to get Iggy. He had a needle in his arm and blood was coming out. I sprinkled toilet water on him. I thought, This is no good. I said, "I can't do this." '

There is sad footage of the band slumped on stage, legless; they were sad but there is also the feeling that some might see them as a public poster of the ravaging effects of that music, an exhibition of the consequences of excess. That, too, like his route to new music could seem to some to be a true depiction of one key aspect of the music of the time.

In 1970 he met David Bowie in a bar in New York. Bowie was on the way up. He became Iggy's friend, benefactor and champion. They appeared together on a television chat show.

'I'd never seen Jimmy,' said Bowie, elegant, styled, cool, unlikely coupled with the open oblivious Iggy swaying on the TV sofa beside him, 'but I'd heard his albums. It sounded like nihilistic rock. It was the nihilism which fascinated me. I *love* nihilism.'

Tony Zanetta said that Bowie 'responded to the most dynamic thing that was happening in American rock 'n' roll'.

Iggy went over to London to do what proved to be The Stooges' third and final album. One number was 'Search and Destroy'.

'I saw that in *Time* magazine about Vietnam: Search and Destroy. I thought, Let's take it and use it in another way. I thought, Ain't I somebody who's very destructive in personal relationships for the sake of artistic endeavour? Yeeeaah!'

In 1972, The Stooges gave their only concert in the UK, in King's Cross. John (Rotten) Lydon was there and punk came across the Atlantic. The idea of punk, a critic said, was 'Fuck you. We don't care if you don't buy our records.' Later that year, David Bowie went on the phenomenally successful Ziggy Stardust tour of America based not a little on Iggy Pop. The Stooges followed him and all seemed to be set for blast-off, but 'I became unsound,' said Iggy.

The luxury mansion in LA; drugs; demands for more and more money from the Bowie coffers. Iggy went into a tailspin. A lot of nights he was found lying in the gutter on Sunset Boulevard with cuts on his arms and chest. His show became more and more self-destructive, culminating in a very bloody night in 1973 when someone threw a champagne glass on to the stage. It broke. He picked it up and 'went at it with his chest'. The photographs run with blood. 'I was on a mission to destroy the world and that made it hard to communicate with management, who were less likely to throw their weight behind the scheme of a dying madman than a going concern. By the time the album was out I had no relationship with management any more.'

The photos are sick and sad. Iggy bloody or zonked or both, wide vacant-eyed, out of it.

'I quit The Stooges. I'd shot my shot. I had to do something else.'

He admitted himself to a psychiatric hospital. David Bowie was his only visitor.

'He was jolly. But never disagreeable. He always exhibited pretty good spirits and I saw him 24/7 for many days at a time. He was together. He was together. But, you know, there was stuff going on.'

They ended up together in Berlin where they tried to rebuild their lives. They shared an apartment there for about a year and an half.

Our idea of a pioneer, an innovator, the artist who cuts through the present to find a new path is not generally associated with someone like Iggy Pop. But he's there.

'Were you still on track to do something with your music that no one had done?'

'Oh yes. Oh yes. And I had found my boy! Here was somebody very, very talented. He wanted other outlets: there were certain things he wanted to do with me that he chose not to do under his own flag. We went for it. I tended to egg him on in that way and he was only too willing to go further and further.'

Bowie was astounded by Iggy's spontaneity. 'He would make up lyrics on the spot. I've never seen anybody about to make up lyrics that fast.'

'He picked up a ukulele one afternoon,' said Iggy, 'and started at it. He said, "Call it *Lust for Life*." He'd probably got it from the movie of the book of the painter with Kirk Douglas, van Gogh, doing self-torture which fit the artist he was recording. The song says people with real enthusiasms are vulnerable to getting really fucked up, really screwed. Here was a loony. I didn't have any money. I wasn't think-ing about money. I wasn't thinking about *succeeding* and once you drop *success* it's amazing what can happen.'

Bowie said, 'The collaboration was because I was intoxicated with what I thought Jimmy stood for — I would never ever want it to be thought I was some sort of Svengali behind what he was doing.'

'The Passenger' ('I am the passenger and I ride and I ride through the city's backsides I ride') came out as a B side in 1977 and never made the charts. Now it's thought to be one of the best songs of its time.

'It's from a poem by Jim Morrison. You can't get out unless you change cars. But you can't really get out of the bloody car.'

He moved to New York.

He toured hard in the decades following Berlin: small venues and many of them. He needed to. A friend said, 'It's hard, sustaining a career. That's the hard part.' Other early songs began to creep back into fashion. He played the old repertoire.

In the late nineties, 'I became disillusioned with life in Manhattan. Inner voices saying, "You can't ever leave New York. If you do you won't know anybody. You won't know what's going on." A lot of people are trapped there. I never want to feel that about a *place*. So I left.'

In Florida he drives around in an old, gleaming open-topped Rolls-Royce. That is his sole conspicuous extravagance. Financial life is steadier now. His music is used for advertisements and films, there are the tours and the royalties.

'People expect stars to be loaded. But you were old-fashioned broke.'

'Yes. Until my middle age. It's a wonderful middle age. That's to do with solvency.'

'And you're reunited with The Stooges?'

'Good things are happening for me and for us. There's recognition. We've gained fans. Maybe they've just heard about *one* of the songs. I'll do a show and feel in a great mood. Damn! There's nobody to be angry at today. It becomes a problem! I have a fixed address. Things like that. I own a shirt. It's got to be cleaned. Gentility.'

The room was sappingly hot. We were at the end of the interview.

We'd filmed a concert and cut to the last number. The jeans were still at half mast. The bared torso was jaunty and lean, the arms still muscled, punching the air.

He was all but lifted off the stage. A security guard supported him and more or less carried him down the ill-lit passage to his bleak dressing room. He was limping badly. He sat down, sipped water, a towel was put around his neck, a fighter at the end of another tough bout . . .

In his house we knocked off the heavy lights and opened the door and the windows.

'I enjoyed that,' I said. 'Really enjoyed it.'

'Me too.'

'You look exhausted now.'

'Yeah . . .' He walked slowly towards his bedroom.

Afterwards we had a fruit juice in the small back garden, cool under trees and the little breeze from the stream. The shirt was off.

P.D. James

P.D. James, the Baroness James of Holland Park, London, has, all her thinking life, been much preoccupied by death. And fascinated by violent murder. Her manner, appearance and way of life could be the perfect disguise. I have known her only over the last quarter of a century (she is now steaming towards ninety) and it seems to me she has never changed. She is a purposefully busy, alert woman, attractive, acutely intelligent an often disconcertingly observant companion.

To be with Phyllis James is to be in the best company, under wide skies, apparently unshadowed. Yet inside that lightness there are demons and horrors and inside her study she draws them up from a deep well without particularly wanting to examine them. Which is one of the reasons why meeting her for the purpose of interview rather than lunch, or at a literary festival, or just around town, could have been a trial. Save that her open friendliness was unalloyed. Yet I knew that I would be asking some questions she would not much want to answer. Why not? Because the roots of her work and the roots of her conversation can seem poles apart. To talk about her work entails pushing against the stockade she has built around her for most of her lifetime.

There can scarcely be a more appreciated, even loved, figure in London literary life, in national literary life, than P.D. James. Together with a handful of others, Beryl Bainbridge, Seamus Heaney, Alan Bennett, Judi Dench, she is someone people are glad to see and for good reasons. Her work, of course, but it is also the quality of honesty, of fun and of engagement with whomever she encounters. Mention of her brings a smile to the face of everyone who knows her. It is, I think, a compound of moral qualities and talent and an unaffectable pleasant manner.

We prepared the interview. She decided not to do it in her home in Holland Park, a house which she painted green – 'so that taxi drivers can recognise it easily'. We met rather formally one morning in handsome, richly furnished rooms in Holland Park itself. She was dressed for a companionable dinner party – elegant, not too smart, comfortable, up for the interview. She plunged in immediately.

'Murder,' she began, 'is tied up with our fascination with death. Whatever reasons we use to explain it, it's still a great mystery.'

The urgency of her expression and the intensity of her delivery need to be noted. She was indifferent to the camera: the words were the total event.

'Earliest man when he murdered someone, he would say, "I have power to do this." A mixture of awe and horror. I think that mixture of awe and horror remains with us. People who don't murder and people who do are interested in it.' Her head leaning, almost jutted forward. She smiles often and laughs often when she talks but when you slow the image down or freeze the frame it is striking how full of pain and distress the eyes are: if they are the windows to the soul then P.D. James is a soul – in which she believes – sometimes in torment, and yet, manners, training, discipline and love of life will always be there to mask it and I hope transform it.

'I've always been interested in death – always have been.' She is apologetic. 'When we discussed in the family where we would go for the summer holidays, I would think, If we're still *here*. It's odd for a child. I don't dread it. I don't sit down and think about it. It's just always *there*.'

We intercut this part of the interview with Phyllis being escorted around a forensic field course by a senior police officer. It was used to test the observational powers of young detectives. She studied the evidence as if she too were about to sit the examination. They were looking at a 'dead body' at this point. 'How did he die?' She took her time. 'There are no obvious clues . . . None that one can *see*.' The officer nodded approvingly.

'I've learned something surprising about murder,' she said, back in the warm brown glows and glints of the interview room. 'It's after the first strike that the adrenalin surges, the lust for violence takes over. It's after we strike that first blow . . . In fictional murder we are using a popular form to distance this atavistic fear of death – as an affirmation of our belief that we have a controllable universe.'

The details of death fascinate her. In the novel *A Taste for Death*, she writes: 'the blood was everywhere. It seemed to her [the person who discovered the body] that she herself was drowning in blood. Blood drummed in her ears. Blood gurgled like vomit in her throat. Blood splashed in bright globules against the retinas of her closed eyes . . .'

'It is always a crucial moment in your books when the body is discovered: that's not unusual. But for you, who discovers it and how the discoverer describes it . . .'

'. . . is of *huge* importance. I always describe it through the eyes of the character who does the finding. It's a moment of great horror and I want the horror to be conveyed to the reader. This is what the book is about. The book is about somebody brutally done to death.'

'You've said you "make sure you get that right". How?'

'Well!' Laughter. I'll stop writing this. Again and again Phyllis as it were takes the top off her answer by beginning with laughter – sometimes pensive, sometimes gleeful and in many shades between the two. 'Not by going to the actual scenes, thank God! I just get it from books by doctors and pathologists . . . pretty lurid pictures and one can use some kind of imagination to an extent. But you must use what the pathologist actually finds.'

Adam Dalgliesh appeared in her first published novel. That novel is rather more like Agatha Christie crossed with Dorothy L. Sayers than P.D. James when she hit her stride.

'You've said of Dalgliesh, "We'll go together." '

'I don't think I'll kill him off.'

'How did you arrive at him?'

'I wanted someone basically believable who could develop. I gave him the qualities I myself admired – courage, but not foolhardiness, compassion, but absolutely no sentimentality. And I gave him *reserve*.'

We filmed Phyllis with Andy Baker, the Head of Homicide at Scotland Yard. She said, 'Thank you for helping me with my novel. I wasn't sure about some things. Like the "murder bag". Now I know it was *not right*.'

'It's much more of a team effort today,' said Andy Baker. 'We follow up in the community. We record everything because of the requirements of Human Rights and European law, and so on . . .'

'You admire the police?' I said.

Her reply was emphatic.

'Most of them are a great deal more intelligent than the public thinks.'

She has moved Adam Dalgliesh into an increasingly starring role over the years. He now has his own special squad which enables the author to take him into politics and High Matters. 'He's a bit of a maverick really . . . A few years ago the Head of the Murder Squad told me that he thought Dalgliesh was "a good cop". I was very pleased!'

'The people's estimation of the police is lower than it used to be, isn't it?'

'I think that's part of a wider thing. Society has changed *tremendously* since I was a child and that attitude reflects those changes. After the war, society was held together by a very strong web of interconnecting communities and common beliefs. For one thing it could still be called a Christian country. It wasn't necessarily better but there was a belief in things that were strong pillars of society – the Church, monarchy, the law, Parliament. Now people believe what they would like to believe . . . in certain ways and areas people live together in a very tenuous and fragile peace. The police have to cope with that . . .

'When I was a child my parents said, "If you're ever in trouble find a policeman." In some city areas I can't see those words being said now. We had policing by consent. Is it consent now? Now it's an almost impossible job, requiring huge qualities of leadership, politically, understanding humanity *and* more and more laws, increasing the burden on them.'

This, a larger argument about the police, is part of a larger argument about society which Phyllis returns to, like many of the rest of us, with a mixture of nostalgia, common sense and a fear that the change we are experiencing will have unexpected consequences for our children and our children's children and of a negative kind.

It is surely permissible to suggest, as I did to Phyllis, that even in my own past many local societies, which can be called communities, in cities, towns and villages policed themselves. It seemed you were always in earshot and eyesight, at one or two removes from your family.

'That's changed. It's now a restless society. But I don't think one can go back. People of my generation have to be very careful. All was *not* well in our world. It was *certainly* not well. Nevertheless it was an extremely peaceful society. We're not going to get back to that. The police are now questioned. All certainty is questioned.'

Back on the forensic test trail, Phyllis was shown a handbag lying in some damp ground. That took no time at all. 'It's been there quite a while,' she said. 'It's one of your red herrings.'

P.D. James was brought up in East Anglia and she has a house in Southwold, a picture-postcard fashionable seaside town, bracing, high class, exceptionally pleasant.

'You had a difficult but, you always add, a satisfactory childhood?'

'My parents' marriage was not exactly happy. In those days people put up with that. Divorce never occurred to them. Such a disgrace! I value them for what I inherited from them. My father was very intelligent. He had little education. He became a tax official, which didn't use his ability. My mother was *not* so bright but very loving, kind, rather sentimental. She would have done very well married to a country clergyman and had a big family. My father was a very authoritarian figure.'

'Did he frighten you?'

'Oh yes! He frightened my friends too! And my boyfriends! Everybody. People came to our house in trepidation. He wasn't sadistic but he was frightening. But now, in old age, I very much value his qualities – such as the fortitude – he was in the First World War – he was a brave man, a dutiful man.'

'Your mother had mental health problems.'

'Yes. She was in the local mental hospital for some time. That happened when I was about fourteen. She disappeared. So my father and I ran the family between us.'

'Fourteen's a sensitive age. It must have been hard.'

'And in those days there was something rather disgraceful about it. You kept quiet about it.'

When I was re-viewing the film as part of the research for this, I used the pause button frequently to have the time to make notes. In this sequence, the still frames, as it were the still photographs, of P.D. James, show the distress only just held at bay by the fortitude of the face she wore to meet parts of the interview.

'Today she would have been treated with drugs. It would not have been necessary to put her into a mental hospital. Things to that extent have improved greatly. I can remember we three children crying. We'd get up and get our breakfast. It was odd but it was all right. My father took me to visit her with him and I remember the *smell* – there was a drug they used to use with a very strong smell. It was rather a grim place.'

'How upset were you? Can you remember?'

'Not as upset as now I imagine I would have been. So it may be I was greatly upset and put it at the back of my mind and did not acknowledge how upset I was. It was something not talked about at school. There's such a gap there. I have repressed some of the feelings I had at that time . . . I would go with my father every Saturday; my brother and sister were left in the house. I recall, on the bus-ride, a miscellaneous group of passengers making this same journey for the same purpose. The small ward. My mother clutched the sheets with restless fingers, looking at us imploringly, constantly reiterating her wish to come home . . .'

P.D. James went to Cambridge High School as a paying pupil – £2.50 a term; she had failed to get a scholarship. She left at sixteen when she was capable of earning a wage. 'I had the very good and liberal education that the old grammar schools provided. I had studied more

Shakespeare than most of the young people who go to university to study English these days. But I am not highly educated.'

'You've fooled a lot of people, Phyllis!'

'My doctorates have been unearned!'

'And you looked for a job?'

The civil service. She Began by helping to issue ration books in wartime Cambridge. Then she moved to London. 'I rather wish I'd gone into the services, because as a novelist it would have been extremely useful. But I was vaguely a pacifist. In London we were bombed at the time. When my second daughter was born that was one of the first weeks of the V1s. So I have plenty of experience of warfare.'

'Your husband was in the army in India. He came back very disturbed by that and never really recovered.'

'When he came back he was mentally ill. But he didn't get a pension because it was never accepted it was anything to do with war service. I had two small daughters and I needed a safe job. I lived with my parents-in-law so the children had a very stable home with a great deal of love and care. I went off to work first for the Health Service, then, after exams, for the Home Office.'

'Testing.'

'It was tough. I think in some ways I am tough. It was certainly survivable. I wasn't having to come home and collect the children from care and make a meal. To some extent I was rather privileged.'

In her *Time to be in Earnest, a Fragment of Autobiography* she writes: 'There is much that I remember that is painful to dwell upon. I see no need to write about those things. They are over and must be accepted, made sense of and forgiven and afforded no more than their proper place. I have always known that happiness is a gift and not a right . . . I have no intention of lying on the psychiatrist's couch . . . But then I am a writer. We fortunate ones seldom have need for such an expedient.'

There was a time, a couple of years ago, when she invited me for tea in Holland Park. On this occasion it was rather formal and so it proved. But it was not awkward. She wanted to talk about my novel *Remember Me* and what I had said about it in an interview with a mutual friend of ours, the critic Peter Kemp. Which was that the experience of writing an autobiographically based work of fiction, based on my first marriage and the suicide of my wife, had not allayed (nor was it intended to) any guilt and shame, but rather intensified them. Out of her own experience she wanted to talk about this and had invited me to her house for that reason. I found it difficult but quite exceptionally helpful. I'd guess that I am far from being alone: others too will have benefited from her wisdom born from difficult times and the thoughtfulness in the bone of her character.

It is good to know, despite the common 'feet of clay' belief, despite the prevalence of 'negative copy' about the famous, that some, certainly P.D. James, are even better than you think.

The effect of her experience with her mother and then her husband was 'never wanting to read books about mental illness, never wanting really to cope with it any more, never really wanting to write about it in any serious way . . . and there is a great deal of anger about some of the things that have happened in psychiatry in my lifetime . . . especially psychiatrists saying that the patient was normal and the family were responsible for the illness – that was cruel in the extreme.'

'What drove you to write? Nobody asked you or commissioned you. You certainly had enough to do. What drove you?'

'The absolute *necessity* to do it. The psychological *need* to do it. I suspect it's the same with you. You don't say to yourself, "I was born to write," but you do *feel* – this is what I was meant to do, this is what I *need* to do! I must do!'

It was an explosion of words. With the more impact because it came from such an apparently unshakeable, composed, distinguished woman.

'I was working in the Health Service and going to the City of London College in the evenings to get a certificate for Administration so I could get a better job, when one day it dawned on me. Rather like a thunderclap. There's never going to be a convenient moment to write this first novel. Here you are, in your mid-thirties, if you don't get started, one day you'll be saying to your grandchildren, "All I ever wanted to be was a writer." And I knew if I had to speak those words my life would have been a failure. So I somehow made time to do it. It was a psychological necessity.'

'You kept your job going until you were six months short of sixty. A demanding job. Short holidays.'

'I never had the courage to put my talent absolutely on the line economically. Partly because in the 1920s I saw mass unemployment and I can remember the sign "No Hands Wanted". I had two children. I wanted a cheque at the end of the month and so I kept going until I qualified for the pension. Also I found the job fascinating. Most of my books have grown out of work experience.'

'Why the detective novel?'

'I love the sonnet form in poetry and the detective novel has its own *structure*. I like a beginning, a middle, an end, the *shaping* of it. That and the fact that we are dealing with life and death.'

In a way, I felt that was what she had come to the interview to say.

She remains a Christian.

'My religion is based on a very primitive belief in God and a primitive belief in the love of God and that it is possible to be in touch with Him and that He actually cares. As regards theology and dogma, I believe what I want to believe and what I can't believe I leave. What I can believe seems to be sufficient for me. My loyalty to the Church of England is very traditional. I was christened into it, it is the Church of my forebears, I love its liturgy and its prayers.'

'But what do you feel about the ousting of the King James Bible and the Book of Common Prayer?'

'A great grief.'

'What do you think has been lost?'

'A *huge* amount. Those of us brought up with it were so fortunate. Not only in church. The day began in every school, from Eton to the simplest village school, with an act of Christian worship in which you heard the King James Bible read, you said the Lord's Prayer, you were exposed to this extraordinary language and source of all sorts of common expressions.'

'A country is held together by language,' I said. 'The bible language was old, but we liked it old. Do you fear that if it is not held within hard covers it will flutter away?'

'It will. There's an extraordinary ignorance about the Bible and Christianity. After all, we're part of Western Christendom. How can people appreciate art and a great deal of music without some knowledge? It used to be part of our blood and bone.'

We filmed P.D. James in the chapel of Oriel College in Oxford. It was evensong and the young boy choristers sang as boy choristers had sung evensong for centuries, their faces sculpted and shadowed by the candlelight which cast an ancient glow over the sacred sounds. P.D. James was there with a few others. All over the United Kingdom, in the cathedrals and in some of the colleges of the older universities, this beautiful service is performed. It is not unusual that the choir outnumbers the congregation.

But as Phyllis sat there, securing herself in the faith of her 'forebears' and in a culture of religion in which she found so many entrances to peace and enlightenment, I found it impossible not to see it as also an act of gallantry. This may be approaching the last call for what is best in a Church, the Anglican Church, which, like all other Churches and all other institutions which have wielded power, has acted badly and worse. But at its best the Anglican Church can still be tolerant, calm, capable of provoking thoughts of beauty and intimations of a fundamental mystery which can be felt if not seen or understood. For many this is not the case: some see it as nonsense, others find it pernicious. It does however embrace and is embraced by P.D. James and others, now and in the past. Their conviction is not, I think, simply to be dismissed. Certainly on that evening in Oriel College Chapel, she appeared to be concentrated in a state of peace.

On she went in the crime museum with the curator, debating the question of whether the noose is more barbaric than a lethal injection. In the House of Lords she speaks up for the personal liberty and the power of the state being cut down, she debates the Animal Rights Movement 'because I'm interested in them; when you cease to be interested in such things you may as well be dead.' Answering, at her local literary festival in Southwold, a questioner who asks how she can get the terrible scenes she describes out of her head, because she, the questioner, can't! Phyllis takes time before she replies 'There *are* things I *don*'t write about because I would *not* be able to get them out of my mind – torture, the torture of children . . .' The questioner nods his approval.

Garlanded, applauded, celebrated wherever she goes and, praise be, delighting in her great success.

Acknowledgements

All of these programmes were made by teams. None could have been made without the contributions of several people. Those mentioned here are just a few of the many directors, film crews, editing crews, researchers, production controllers and PAs from over the years.

1. *Paul McCartney (1978)*
   Research: Simon Cochrane
   Producer/Director: John Carlaw
2. *Harold Pinter (1978)*
   Research: Jamie Muir
   Producer/Director: Andrew Snell
3. *Ingmar Bergman (1978)*
   Research: Nick Young
   Producer/Director: Andrew Snell
4. *Andrew Lloyd Webber (1978)*
   Research: Mark Holloway
   Producer/Director: Alan Benson/Daniel Wiles
5. *Francis Ford Coppola (1979)*
   Research: Nick Young
   Producer/Director: Alan Benson
6. *Toni Morrison (1981)*
   Research: Steve Jenkins
   Producer/Director: Alan Benson

7. *Alan Bennett (1984)*
   Associate Producer: Claire Holland
   Producer/Director: Archie Powell
8. *Francis Bacon (1985)*
   Research: Tony Knox
   Producer/Director: David Hinton
9. *David Lean (1985)*
   Research: Steve Jenkins
   Producer: Nick Evans Director: Nigel Wattis
10. *Eric Clapton (1987)*
    Research: Frances Dickinson
    Producer/Director: Chris Hunt/Jonathan Levi
11. *David Puttnam (1988)*
    Research: Frances Dickinson
    Producer: David Thomas, Director: Daniel Wiles
12. *David Hockney (1988)*
    Associate Producer: Mark Holloway
    Producer/Director: Alan Benson
13. *Martin Amis (1989)*
    Research: Christopher Walker
    Producer/Director: David Thomas
14. *Dame Edna/Barry Humphries (1989)*
    Research: Melissa Raimes
    Producer/Director: Nigel Wattis
15. *Seamus Heaney (1991)*
    Associate Producer: Rosie Alison
    Producer/Director: Tony Knox
16. *Rudolf Nureyev (1991)*
    Research: Tristram Holland/Madonna Benjamin
    Producer/Director: Patricia Foy
17. *Luciano Pavarotti (1995)*
    Research: Chris Walker
    Producer/Director: Nigel Wattis

18. *Judi Dench (1995)*
    Research: Leo Burley
    Producer/Director: Nigel Wattis
19. *Jimmy McGovern (1996)*
    Associate Producer: Leo Burley
    Producer/Director: Susan Shaw

20. *Victoria Wood (1996)*
    Associate Producer: Simon Cherry
    Producer/Director: Nigel Wattis
21. *Beryl Bainbridge (1998)*
    Research: Archie Powell
    Producer/Director: Christopher Walker
22. *Tracey Emin (2001)*
    Research: Lucy Allen
    Producer/Director: Aurora Gunn
23. *Ian McEwan (2003)*
    Research: Antonia Bolingbroke-Kent
    Producer/Director: David Thomas
24. *Iggy Pop (2004)*
    Research: Claire Holland
    Producer/Director: Leo Burley
25. *P.D. James (2006)*
    Research: Claire Holland
    Producer/Director: Gillian Greenwood

It was John (now Lord) Birt's idea to ask me to edit and present *The South Bank Show* for London Weekend Television (LWT) in 1977. His colleague, Nick Elliott talked me into it, served for a while as executive producer, and became and remains a close friend.

Poems by Seamus Heaney are from *Opened Ground Poems 1966–1996* © Seamus Heaney, 1998, reproduced by permission of Faber & Faber Ltd.
9/11 2001 attacks 266

Index

297

Don Carlos (Verdi) 208
Don Quixote (ballet) 198
Douglas, Kirk 281
Dr Barnardo's 50
Drake, Sir Francis 65, 201
Dublin 2, 101, 105
Dudinskaya, Natalia 193
Durham, Geoffrey 238
Duvall, Robert 63, 65
Dyer, George 103–4

East End, London 18, 19, 20, 99, 100,
    124–5, 256, 258
Eastwood, Clint 65
Easy Rider (film) 123
Eckersley, Peter 239
Eddy, Duane 276
Edwards, John 99, 100, 104, 107, 110
Egyptian art 97, 104
Einstein, Albert 250
'Eleanor Rigby' (song) 13–14
Eliot, T.S. 54, 85, 258
Elizabeth II, Queen 91
Ellison, Ralph 70
Emin, Paul 262
Emin, Tracey 4, 254–64
    My Bed 257, 263
    The Tent (Everyone I Have Ever Slept
        With 1963–1995) 256–7, 263,
        264
Enigma 142
Epstein, Brian 13
Establishment Club, Soho 175
Evans, Edgar 247
Evans, Dame Edith 215
Evans, Taff 247
Everly Brothers 48, 58
Evita (Lloyd Webber) 52–3, 55, 59
Eyre, Richard 269

Faber & Faber 54
Fauves 98
Fellini, Federico 36
Fenton, James 156
Fenton, Roger 250
Fields, Danny 279

Fine Romance, A (television comedy
    show) 217
Finian's Rainbow (film) 62
Fonda, Jane 142
Fonteyn, Dame Margot 195, 196
Forster, E.M. 83, 84
Forsyth, Bill 139
Fowlie, Eddie 118
Fraser, Lady Antonia 7, 19, 20, 33, 157
Frayn, Michael 86
Frazer, Sir James; *The Golden Bough* 67

Gable, Clark 116
Garbo, Greta 136, 137–8
Garland, Judy 53
Garland, Nicholas 175
Garland, Patrick 84
Garner, Margaret 74–5, 76, 81
Garnett, David: *Aspects of Love* 57
George III, King 91
Gerry and the Pacemakers 12
Gilmore, Jim 179–80
Giselle (ballet) 196, 198
Gloucester Crescent, Primrose Hill,
    London 86
Glyndebourne 152
Godfather, The (film) 3, 61, 64–7
Godfather, The film series 63, 68–9,
    136
Godfather: Part II, The (film) 3, 61, 66
Goldeneye (film) 219
Golding, William 161
    Lord of the Flies 24
Gothic Revival 55
Goya, Francisco de 98
Grade, Lew 51
Granada Television 239
Graves, Robert 152
Great Expectations (film) 111, 116, 121
Greene, Graham 85
Greenville, Alabama 72
Grenfell, Joyce 235, 238
Grosvenor Hotel, London 120
Groucho Club, London 99
Guggenheim, Benjamin 251–2
Guillem, Sylvie 198